"For far too long, the Great Revolt has been overlooked in the grand sweep of history. Stephen Dando-Collins finally gives this epochal event the focus it deserves, and in the way that only he can. Full of tragedy and triumph, heartbreak and heroism, *Conquering Jerusalem* deftly balances masterful storytelling with exquisite attention to detail. This book is a must read to understand this conflict, which still reverberates to this day."

—PHILLIP BARLAG, author of *Evil Roman Emperors, The History of Rome in 12 Buildings,* and *The Leadership Genius of Julius Caesar*

"The first Jewish-Roman War of 66–73 CE was a struggle that had enormous consequences, not only for Jews, but for Western Civilization as a whole. Before the war, Jews belonged to many sects: there were Pharisees, Sadducees, Essenes, Zealots, along with smaller groups like the monastics of Qumran and the followers of Jesus of Nazareth. Like a meteor, the war extinguished everything except the Pharisees, ancestors of rabbinic Judaism, and the Christians of the Greek and Latin speaking provinces touched by Saint Paul. The war itself was a complex event: the struggle between the various factions among the Jews made it almost as much a civil war as a war against Rome. Meanwhile the Roman Empire was in a state of civil war itself in 69 CE when, at the death of the emperor Nero, military leaders from all parts of the Empire sought, and briefly succeeded, in establishing themselves in the center of political power. It was Vespasian, the general sent by Nero to put down the Jewish revolt, who re-established stability in Rome and founded the new Flavian dynasty of emperors, while his son Titus, at the head of his father's legions, brought the struggle to its fiery conclusion. Stephen Dando-Collins tells this story in *Conquering Jerusalem* as a rip-roaring yarn that clarifies both the complexities of combat and the political maneuvers that influenced the outcome of the military struggle."

—DAVID RICHTER, professor emeritus at the Graduate Center of the City University of New York

"A gripping and pacy account of the Great Jewish Revolt against the might of Rome from its chaotic inception to the final destruction and levelling of Jerusalem in AD 70. Stephen Dando Collins narrates his well-researched account of the complex and often harrowing events with a punchy clarity. One can't help thinking that the revolt might have succeeded were it not for the extreme level of factionalism and infighting that beset the Jewish cause from beginning to end."

—PAUL N. PEARSON, author of *Maximinus Thr--- From Common Soldier to E---*

CONQUERING
JERUSALEM

CONQUERING JERUSALEM

THE AD 66–73 ROMAN CAMPAIGN TO CRUSH THE JEWISH REVOLT

STEPHEN DANDO-COLLINS

TURNER
PUBLISHING COMPANY

TURNER PUBLISHING COMPANY
Nashville, Tennessee

www.turnerpublishing.com

Conquering Jerusalem

Library of Congress Control Number: 2021937173

Cover design: Rebecca Lown
Book design: Erin Seaward-Hiatt

9781684425471   Paperback
9781684425488   Hardback
9781684425495   Ebook

Printed in the United States of America

With warm gratitude to my longtime New York literary agent and good friend, Richard Curtis; to my supportive publisher, Stephanie Beard, and editor, Heather Howell; and my fellow soldier in the battle against the vicissitudes of life, my dearest wife, Louise.

TABLE OF CONTENTS

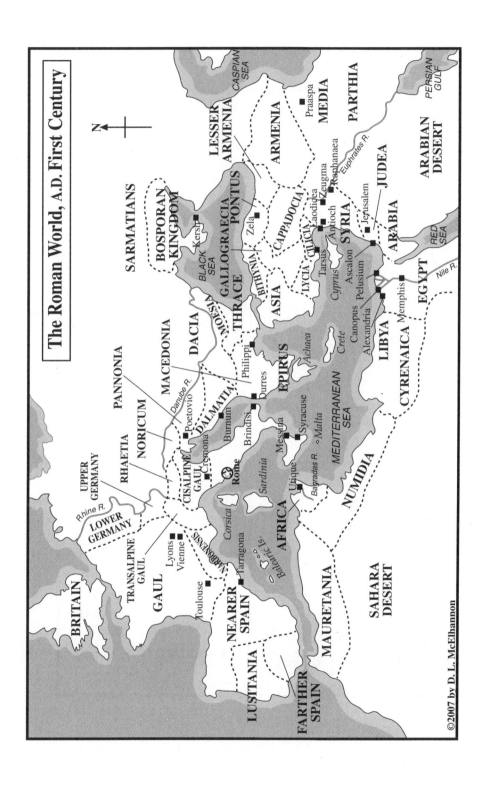

The Roman World, A.D. First Century

©2007 by D. L. McElhannon

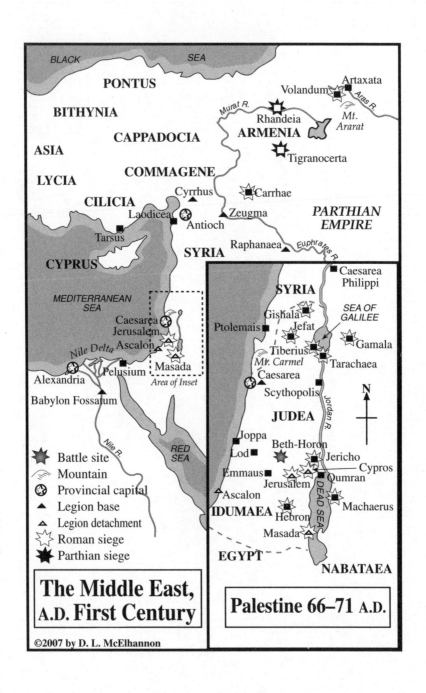

BLACK   SEA

PONTUS

BITHYNIA

CAPPADOCIA

ASIA

LYCIA

COMMAGENE

CILICIA

Cyrrhus ▲

Laodicea

Tarsus

Antioch

SYRIA

CYPRUS

Volandum ■ Artaxata
Murat R.

Rhandeia
ARMENIA
Mt. Ararat

Tigranocerta

Carrhae ■

Zeugma

PARTHIAN EMPIRE

Raphanaea ▲   Euphrates R.

MEDITERRANEAN SEA

Caesarea
Jerusalem
Ascalon

Masada

Area of Inset

Alexandria

Babylon Fossatum

Pelusium

Nile Delta

Nile R.

RED SEA

Caesarea Philippi ■

SYRIA

Gishala
Ptolemais   Jefat

SEA OF GALILEE

Tiberius   Gamala
Mt. Carmel   Tarachaea

Caesarea ▲

Scythopolis

JUDEA

Jordan R.

Joppa
Lod   Beth-Horon
        Jericho
        Cypros
Emmaus   Jerusalem   Qumran
Ascalon   *DEAD SEA*
IDUMAEA   Hebron   Machaerus

Masada

EGYPT

NABATAEA

N

✦ Battle site
⌒ Mountain
✪ Provincial capital
▲ Legion base
△ Legion detachment
✦ Roman siege
✶ Parthian siege

The Middle East, A.D. First Century

Palestine 66–71 A.D.

Vespasian, commander of the second Roman campaign to terminate the Jewish Revolt, during which he became emperor of Rome. Bridgeman Images.

Titus, who took over the Judean campaign from his father and completed the conquest of Jerusalem in AD 70. Bridgeman Images.

Masada today. Here, the Jewish Revolt began and ended.
© Copyright, Dana Friedlander. Courtesy Israeli Ministry of Tourism.

The theater at Caesarea, Roman capital of Judea, once frequented by Rome's legionaries, is still used today, by Jewish audiences.
© Copyright, Noam Chen. Courtesy Israeli Ministry of Tourism.

Roman theater, Beit Shean, Israel. The theater at Scythopolis, Judea, a city that remained loyal to Rome throughout the Jewish Revolt. © Copyright, Noam Chen. Courtesy Israeli Ministry of Tourism.

Model of Jerusalem. Jerusalem, AD 66–70, with the Antonia Fortress, with its four towers, and the Second Temple, center. Bridgeman Images.

Jerusalem's Temple Mount today, showing the Western Wall, or Wailing Wall. In AD 70, this was the site of desperate fighting.
© Copyright, Noam Chen. Courtesy Israeli Ministry of Tourism.

Mount of Olives, Jerusalem, today. Site of the Garden of Gethsemane, and of the camp of the 10th Fretensis Legion during Titus's siege of Jerusalem.
© Copyright, Noam Chen. Courtesy Israeli Ministry of Tourism.

A tunnel beneath Jerusalem's Temple Mount remains as it was in AD 70, when Jewish rebels hid here following the fall of the Temple.
© Copyright, Noam Chen. Courtesy Israeli Tourism Ministry.

On the Arch of Titus, a scene from the dual Triumph of Vespasian and Titus, Roman soldiers carry a Menorah taken from the Jerusalem Temple.
© Copyright, Louise Dando-Collins.

The author at the Arch of
Titus, Rome, which celebrates
the conquest of Jerusalem.
© Copyright, Louise Dando-
Collins.

COIN STRUCK BY THE EMPEROR VESPASIAN, COMMEMORATING THE CONQUEST
OF JUDEA.

Bridgeman Images.

PREFACE

For decades, I researched the legions of Rome before, starting in 2002, publishing a series of books about individual legions and key moments in the history of ancient Rome. In some of those books, I included chapters on the First Jewish Revolt—the Great Revolt as the Jews still call it, the Judean War as the Romans called it. Only now, in *Conquering Jerusalem*, have I devoted a single book to the revolt. This gave me scope to go into much more detail about the background, people, and events of the revolt, and enabled me to draw upon numerous archeological and forensic discoveries made since 2002, discoveries that have often shone fascinating new light on those people and events.

Neither side comes out well in this story. Both were at times equally heroic and often equally brutal and barbaric. In the end, the Jewish freedom fighters lost their war and lost their holy city, which had been the focus of the revolt and of the Roman military campaigns to end that revolt. Yet, today, Jerusalem is once more the heart of the Jewish faith, while, thanks to Christianity, an offshoot of Judaism, the Roman Empire and its gods have long gone. It just goes to show that, sometimes, faith can have its rewards, and the tables can be turned, if you wait long enough.

I

MENAHEM'S SURPRISE
ATTACK AT MASADA

In the middle of a hot day in the late spring of AD 66, death rode on the backs of mules to Masada, a massive rock horst rising on the eastern edge of the Judean Desert. On the eastern, Dead Sea side, 1,300 feet below, lay the Dead Sea Basin. There was a plateau atop the rock, 1,800 feet long and 900 feet wide. And on that plateau in the first century BC, Herod the Great, king of Judea, built two palaces, protecting them with a wall thirteen feet high running around the plateau's edge and reinforced by scores of guard towers.

This Masada fortress was the first fortified structure that Herod developed outside Jerusalem once he became king in 37 BC, and inside it he established a large cache of weapons and an extensive food supply, in case internal enemies or the army of his foe Queen Cleopatra of Egypt forced him to take refuge here. Following Herod's death in 4 BC, Judea became a sub-province of the Roman province of Syria, and apart from the brief period between AD 41 and 44 when Herod's grandson Herod Agrippa I ruled as king of Judea, Roman troops had garrisoned Masada.

On this day in AD 66—according to some interpretations of the Jewish calendar, it was June 1—bored Roman sentries on guard in the gate towers on the eastern side of the plateau watched as a supply train of mules slowly wound its way up a narrow path to the fortress. This was called the Snake Path, both because it was long and thin and because it snaked its way up the cliff face. The watching sentries were men of the 3rd Gallica Legion. As its name implies, this legion had been founded in Gaul. In the 30s BC, when it had marched for Mark Antony in the Roman East, the unit's recruitment grounds had been relocated to Syria. To distinguish it from Rome's two other 3rd legions, the 3rd Augusta and the 3rd Cyrenaica, the unit's Gallica title was retained and its battle honors remembered.

The last time the 3rd Gallica Legion had seen full-scale military action had been eight years back, in Roman general Domitius Corbulo's AD 58 campaign in Armenia. Ever since, the 3rd Gallica had been Judea's resident legion, and one of the unit's ten cohorts, or battalions, had always been stationed here at Masada. It was a lonely posting. During this era, Roman legionaries were not permitted to marry until their twenty-year enlistments expired. Rome's first emperor, Augustus, had seen this as wedding his troops to their legions, but Roman administrators had come to realize that many legionaries took de facto wives and fathered illegitimate children, and it was better for army morale for troops to have their loved ones close. As a consequence it had become the custom for legionaries' family members to live outside their bases. But here at remote Masada, that was not possible.

Some legion bases around the empire were established in strategic locations where there was no existing town. In these cases, a town, called a *vicus*, rapidly grew outside the camp walls as legionaries' family members, who usually followed the legions across the empire to their new postings, set up home, and traders quickly joined them. In Britain, for example, this was the case with the present-day English cities of Gloucester, Wroxeter, and Chester, all of which began life as legion bases in frontier areas.

In Judea, some men of the 3rd Gallica Legion had family members living right on their doorsteps. Five of the legion's ten cohorts were stationed in the sub-province's Roman capital, Caesarea Maritima, on the Mediterranean coast. These cohorts included the legion's most senior, the 1st cohort. A so-called double strength cohort, it contained eight hundred men, always remained with the legion commander, and was charged with guarding the legion's golden eagle standard. Flourishing Caesarea had a population of 125,000, which would have included many legion families, and, in Caesarea, off-duty legionaries could take their loved ones to the circus to watch chariot races and to the drama theater overlooking the sea, which is still in use today.

The five remaining cohorts of the legion were stationed at five outposts spread around the region. Down the coast at the port of Ascalon (today's Ashkelon), a little to the north of Gaza, the resident cohort's loved ones lived in the bustling city that housed their fortress. Legionaries at the inland hilltop fortress of Cypros at the entrance to Wadi Qelt, overlooking the oasis city of Jericho seventeen miles east of Jerusalem, had only to go down to Jericho to see their loved ones. Families of the cohort stationed at the rocky hilltop fortress of Machaerus, in a desolate landscape east of the Dead Sea in today's Jordan, would have lived down the hill in Machaerus's Lower Town. Perhaps only the 3rd Gallica cohort recently transferred to Jerusalem from Caesarea were in a more lonely location than the men at Masada. Spread between Jerusalem's Antonia Fortress and Herod's Palace, those troops were forbidden from going out into the exclusively Jewish city unless on policing duties; their families would have remained back at Caesarea.

As for the legionaries at Masada, the nearest settlement capable of housing their families was the ancient oasis town of Ein Gedi, which features in the Old Testament. Fourteen miles due north of Masada, close to the Dead Sea, Ein Gedi was the capital of one of the thirteen toparchies—counties, or administrative districts—that then made up Judea. The springs of Ein Gedi produced water aplenty to feed the town's lush vineyards and palm groves. In all of Judea, only the gardens of Jerusalem were more productive than those of Ein Gedi. As later events make clear, seven hundred women and children, the family members of the 480 legionaries of the 3rd Gallica based up on Masada, lived among the thousands of Jews who then populated Ein Gedi.

It was from Ein Gedi that the mule train to Masada traveled. Departing at the crack of dawn to beat the baking heat of the afternoon—as all who venture to Masada in summer do to this day—the train carried the food supplies that were regularly brought to the Masada garrison. The fortress had vast underground water storage capacity and produced a small quantity of fruit and vegetables in its gardens—the soil on the Masada plateau was quite fertile. Pigs were known to be present, and possibly other livestock, which the legionaries slaughtered as required. For emergencies, Herod's Masada storehouses were filled with dried fruit, beans, and seeds, as had been the case for a century. But a legionary's diet was based on bread and olive oil, and the nearest cornfields and olive groves were many miles away. Of equal importance, there was no firewood for cooking and heating at or near Masada.

These requirements necessitated the supply trains that the Masada garrison depended on, and the plodding mules that were now slowly ascending the Snake Path to the fortress were weighed down with baskets of wheat, amphorae of olive oil, lamp oil, and wine, and fagots of firewood. Arriving below Masada at around 11:00 a.m., the mules and their Jewish muleteers had commenced the ninety-minute trudge up the Snake Path.

As set down in legion camp regulations, ten legionaries from the duty century of eighty men were on guard in the stone towers flanking Masada's closed Snake Path Gate, wearing jockey-style helmets on their heads and segmented armor over their red tunics. They were "fully armed" as the Romans described it, with sword and dagger on their belts and upright *pilum*, or javelin, in their right hand. Their curved wooden shields bearing the 3rd Gallica's emblems of three bulls and the ram of the unit's birth sign, Capricorn, leaned against the wall close at hand.

A picket of half a dozen sentries lounged outside the gate, cursing the heat. Inside the fortress, another three sentries stood duty outside the praetorium, the fortress's administration center, and eight were outside the camp commandant's quarters, both of which were located at the front of the Northern Palace, the larger of the two palaces built by Herod. The commandant was almost certainly the camp prefect of the 3rd Gallica Legion, the equivalent of a modern major and a Roman legion's third most senior officer.

Camp prefect was the highest rank to which an enlisted man could ordinarily aspire. Next in rank below the camp prefect were the legion's centurions, the equivalent of lieutenants and captains in today's military, several of whom served under the camp prefect here at Masada. While the 3rd Gallica's legionaries were mostly Syrian-born conscripts aged between eighteen and forty-six, with an average age at enlistment of twenty-four, their camp prefect and centurions came from all corners of the Roman world. Promotion to a higher grade—there were ten grades of centurion—often entailed transfer across the empire from legion to legion and from legion to auxiliary cohorts.[1]

We don't know the name or nationality of the camp prefect in charge at

Masada in AD 66. He may have been a Gaul, a Spaniard, a native of Asia Minor, Northern Italy, or North Africa. He would have been of mature age, in his forties or fifties. And he would have been tough. Roman centurions and camp prefects maintained discipline with a vine stick, precursor of the swagger stick of British Army officers, which left welts on the backs of their men from frequent lashing. In the worst cases, camp prefects and centurions could have their men executed for infractions of Roman military law, which was more severe than civil law.

In larger Roman military camps, the commandants, who were legates of the Senatorial Order or senior tribunes of the Equestrian Order, were permitted to have their wives and children live on the base with them. Even though the camp prefect in charge at Masada, being an enlisted man, was not permitted to marry, we know from archaeological evidence that his eighteen-year-old de facto wife was living in his quarters at this time, possibly without the formal permission of his legion's commanding officer back in Caesarea, but more likely with a dispensation because of the remoteness of the posting and the seniority of the camp prefect's rank.

We don't know the young woman's nationality, but we do know that her hair featured two long, beaded braids that hung down either side of her head. Braided hair was common to both Roman and Jewish married women at the time. Neither do we know how long the couple had been together, but it may have been for several years, because women in this era could legally become engaged at age twelve and marry at thirteen.

It was just another day for the men of the garrison. With the camp prefect attending to duties in Masada's praetorium, most of his centurions were off duty, as were at least four hundred of the legionaries at the camp. Men who had stood night guard duty were asleep in their barrack rooms. In other rooms, men were washing and repairing clothes. Others were shaving with razors—all Roman citizens of this era were clean-shaven. One-time cobblers who were now soldiers were repairing military sandals. Armorers were making arrows for the cohorts' artillery, sharpening swords, and repairing shields. Several sick men probably lay in the Masada barrack's small hospital.

At the fortress's tanning yard, legionaries were laying out leather in the sun to be later used on shields and to make belts. At the mosaic workshop, men who had been stonecutters in civilian life were cutting floor tiles for a building extension. Some men were working in the gardens, others tending livestock. Legionaries assigned to cooking duty for the day were grinding corn for the regular legionary light lunch of a piece of bread smothered with olive oil. Smoke was already spiraling up from bread ovens. In addition, not a few men were probably sitting on steps in the sun playing dice or board games such as Roman chess.

The administration of the guard century fell to its *optio*, the equivalent of a sergeant major today. The optio of the guard would have reported to the commandant that the mules of the regular supply train had been spotted making their way up the Snake Path. How regularly the supply train came to Masada we don't know; perhaps monthly. Three times a year, a train carrying the cohort's pay came up this path, its mules laden with coins minted specifically for the 3rd Gallica Legion at the official mint at Emesa in Syria, home to the Temple of Elagabalus, the Syrian sun god worshipped by men of the legion. That pay train would have come escorted by the legion's cavalry squadron. This train, carrying only supplies, was accompanied by its civilian contractors, with a muleteer leading each mule. If there were a hundred mules, there were a hundred grimy, bearded local muleteers, all perspiring hard as they made the climb.

Returning to the gate, the optio summoned off-duty men to unload the mule train once it was inside the camp and then to carry the supplies to several of the fortress's twenty-nine storerooms. As the lead mules arrived outside the double wooden gates, the men on picket duty greeted the muleteers with smiles, and the gates swung open from within. If any muleteers were riding, they dismounted, for no one, neither a general nor a king, was permitted to ride inside a Roman military camp. The 3rd Gallica sentries gave each muleteer a perfunctory body search to check for weapons as they passed, with the civilians lifting their cloaks to show they were unarmed. Then, once all the mules and their drivers were inside, the men of the picket followed them in, eager for mail being carried by the train. The gates closed.

The commandant would have come out onto the praetorium steps as the train arrived. He would have been expecting official correspondence—a response from the legion's commander to his last report; tidings of promotions and new postings; copies of the *Acta Diurna*, the neatly handwritten official daily newspaper from Rome that came filled with news of the deaths of leading citizens, of house fires in the capital, of military successes in far corners of the empire, and chariot racing results, all to be posted on the camp notice board once the commandant had read them. The commandant was probably also expecting a few tasty delicacies such as fresh Ein Gedi dates and imported Italian fish paste among the supplies, for his wife and himself to enjoy at dinner.

As legionaries, most of them unarmed, crowded around the mules, the leader of the muleteers, a middle-aged man, reached into a mule's load and surreptitiously removed a dagger from where it had been hidden. This man, a Jew and a native of the city of Gamala in the Golan Heights, was Menahem ben Judah. His grandfather Hezekiah had opposed the pro-Roman rule of King Herod the Great. His father, Judah the Galilean, had founded the Zealot movement, a religious group that advocated Jewish nationalism in the face of Roman control of Judea. Tracked down and arrested, Judah had been executed by the Romans. If that wasn't enough to engender hate of the occupying Romans in Menahem, he had also seen his brothers Simon and Jacob executed two decades back for seditious activity.

For years, Menahem had been leading a covert band of Jewish nationalists, which Romans called the Sicarii, or "daggermen." Under Menahem's leadership, the Sicarii had assassinated Jewish officials and Roman collaborators by sidling up to them in crowds, drawing a dagger from beneath their cloaks, then stabbing their victims before melting back into the crowd. The Sicarii were the original "cloak and dagger" operatives. In more recent months, anti-Roman fervor had grown in Jerusalem in response to the oppressive rule of Caesarea-based Roman procurator Gessius Florus, a Greek from Ionia. This growing revolutionary spirit had given Menahem an idea.

Unimpressed with the current Jewish leadership, the ambitious Menahem had seen a way to grab the reins and head a Jewish uprising against Roman occupation. He had gained intelligence about the supply trains to the Masada garrison and about the internal layout of the Masada fortress. Perhaps he had coerced the usual supply contractor to help him. But Menahem—described as "a cunning deceiver" by Flavius Josephus, the Romano-Jewish historian who is our principal source for these events—had come up with a "treacherous" scheme to get his men and himself inside the Masada fortress without raising the suspicions of the Roman guard cohort.

Josephus doesn't give us details about the ruse employed by Menahem, but everything points to the supply train as the tool of his surprise attack. We do know that Menahem's plan was to overwhelm Masada's Roman guard via trickery and then loot the fortress of its arms cache, which he and his men would take to Jerusalem to arm his intended Judea-wide uprising.[2]

On the command from Menahem, his men also drew daggers from hiding places on mules. The optio was probably the first to feel Jewish steel slice his throat. Others sentries quickly died in the same way as Menahem's men attacked the nearest armed Romans. The unarmed off-duty men were the next to die amid cries of shock and alarm. This all took place before the eyes of the fortress's unarmed commandant. Turning, he dashed back inside to his quarters to grab his sword. His wife was there, along with two of the camp prefect's personal servants. One servant was a freedman in his early twenties. Freedmen were former slaves, and all centurions and camp prefects had freedmen working for them to handle their personal needs as a mixture of butlers and business managers. The other servant was a boy of only eleven or twelve, probably the body slave of the centurion's wife.

"Take her to the bathhouse and keep her safe!" the camp prefect commanded the freedman.

The bathhouse was part of the Northern Palace, which Herod had built in 25 BC. This palace, larger and newer than the Western Palace, spread over three levels on a spur at the very edge of Masada's northern cliff. Across the palace's rich mosaic floors ran the frightened young woman with the freedman and the slave boy close behind, their sandals echoing loudly on the stone. They scampered down steps to the middle level, where there was a reception room with a semicircular portico that looked across the barren yellow hills toward Jerusalem sixty miles to the northwest. The terrified trio continued down to the lower level, occupied by the royal bathhouse, which also had a portico that looked out over the spectacular view. Below the bathhouse was a sheer drop; there was no escape from here. Closing the bathhouse door, the trio barricaded themselves inside.

When the commandant reemerged into the sunlight with his sword, Menahem's Sicarii were already battling the sentries outside the praetorium and commandant's quarters. Outnumbered and unprepared, the Romans soon fell victim to their Jewish attackers despite their armor. Those attackers were equipped with the swords and spears of the now eliminated gate sentries. Clad in just his tunic, the commandant joined his men in taking on the insurgents. He may have taken a few of his assailants with him, but the camp prefect was to die with his troops.

Meanwhile, led by Menahem's chief lieutenant Apsalom, more Sicarii surged into the cohort's barrack block, which stood like an island in the center north of the plateau, fifty yards from the Snake Path Gate. Inside, the Jews slaughtered every surprised legionary they found, including men in their beds. It's possible that the camp gates were opened and more Sicarii who had secreted themselves behind rocks along the Snake Path under the cover of darkness the previous night now gained admittance to the fortress and joined the massacre of the Roman garrison.

As Menahem's men went throughout the fortress, dealing with Roman sentries who had locked themselves in the towers of the Western Gate by burning them out, and searching for unarmed legionaries in hiding, Menahem was more interested in liberating the keys to the fortress armories. His eyes would have widened with delight when he unlocked the doors to reveal Herod's vast collection of swords, shields, and spears and the supplies of cast iron, brass, and tin that had been stockpiled to make weapons and ammunition.

At this point Menahem was summoned to the Northern Palace and Herod's bathhouse, possibly by his nephew Eleazar ben Ya'ir, one of his lieutenants. His men had found the bathhouse door closed. After battering it down, they'd discovered the young woman, the freedman, and the boy cringing inside. By the time that Menahem reached the bathhouse, the freedman and the boy were lying dead on the floor in their own blood, their throats slit by Menahem's men. The camp prefect's wife was on her knees, begging for her life.

Menahem questioned the young woman. Perhaps she was Syrian, perhaps she came from the large Greek population of Galilee and Samaria. Deuteronomy, the fifth book of the Jewish Torah and the Christian Old Testament, sets out rules for the handling of female captives in war. According to these, Menahem was entitled to make the girl one of his wives: "Suppose you see among the captives a beautiful woman whom you desire and want to marry, and you bring her to your house; she shall shave her head, pare her nails."[3]

But if he determined that she was Jewish and "lay with" with a Roman officer, Menahem could show her no mercy—Deuteronomy also states, "There shall be no whore of the daughters of Israel."[4] From what followed, it may well be that the camp prefect's young wife was indeed Jewish. Perhaps telling her that he was going to shave her head and make her his wife,

Menahem drew the dagger from his belt and grasped her by the hair. But Menahem proceeded to scalp the girl, brutally slicing her hair away from her skull, scalp and all, as she screamed in pain.

What happened next is open to speculation, but the likely explanation of the girl's fate is this: Menahem, still holding the girl's now detached hair, ordered her taken out onto the bathhouse portico. One daggerman took her arms, another took her legs, and, her head bathed in blood, she was roughly carried out. Menahem followed.

"Throw her over!"

Screaming, the camp prefect's wife struggled for her life. But she was weak, and Menahem's men were strong. Lifting her over the stone balustrade, they let go of her, and she fell hundreds of feet to her death. Looking down, Menahem saw one of the young woman's sandals on the floor, dislodged as she struggled to escape her fate. Reaching down, Menahem picked it up. Ordering his men to stuff the bloody corpses of the Roman freedman and the boy slave into the hypocaust beneath the floor of the bathhouse, to befoul and defile it, Menahem climbed the steps back up to the plateau with the girl's hair and sandal in his hands.

Seeing that Apsalom and his men had dragged the stripped bodies of legionaries out into the open, Menahem ordered a massive fire lit in the main street of the camp, using the Romans' wooden shields for firewood. The standards of the cohort kept at the camp altar were also brought out. The legionaries of the 3rd Gallica had sworn to defend these standards with their lives. Two standards took the form of a pair of silver raised hands on poles. These had belonged to the two 240-man maniples, or companies, into which the cohort was divided. Below the silver hand were round silver images of the emperor Nero Caesar and his new wife Messalina.

Legion cohorts normally didn't have their own standards, but as this cohort was serving separately as a vexillation, or detachment, of the main legion, it marched under a square crimson cloth banner called a vexillum, which hung from a wooden pole and crosspiece that formed a cross shape. This banner bore the embroidered image of three bulls and the inscription "LEGIIIGAL," identifying the 3rd Gallica Legion, plus the cohort's number—"COHVI," for example, if it was the sixth cohort. Menahem ordered all three standards thrown onto the fire, along with the bodies of the Roman dead.

All this was prescribed by Deuteronomy: "And you will gather all the spoil of it into the midst of the street thereof, and will burn with fire the city, and all the spoil thereof every piece." Not even the standards could be spared, despite their value. "The graven images of their gods you will burn with fire; you will not desire the silver or gold that is on them or take it for yourself."[5]

The Jews considered all Roman standards showing animals or humans to be graven images, and to mollify them, for years Roman standards had been covered when being carried through the streets of Jerusalem. Not even coins bearing the images of Roman emperors were supposed to circulate in Jerusalem. Based on Deuteronomy, too, it seems that Menahem ordered that Herod's palaces at Masada be put to the torch. But he left the storerooms and legionary barrack intact, for he intended to occupy Masada, and while he himself would soon depart, he would be leaving a Sicarii garrison here.

Archaeologists have determined from the ruins that a number of buildings at Masada were put to the torch during the Jewish Revolt. For many years, scholars thought these fires related to the later Masada events of AD 73, which will be related in Chapter XIX. However, bearing in mind Deuteronomy's strict instructions to Jews in times of war about destroying captured cities and spoils by fire, it is highly unlikely that Menahem and his Sicarii followers, who strictly observed Jewish law, would have left Herod's luxurious, hedonistic, and (to them) sacrilegious palaces intact for seven years after capturing Masada. It is far more likely they fired the palaces as soon as Masada fell to them. From the archeological evidence, we know the Sicarii left storehouses intact, and for several reasons we also can deduce that until AD 73 the Sicarii garrison used the Masada barrack that had housed the Roman cohort. For one thing, a stash of Jewish coins minted later in the revolt was found under the barrack floor by archaeologists.

As the fire in the center of the fortress grew more fierce, Menahem, still carrying the now dead girl's hair and sandal, walked to a storeroom directly across the fortress courtyard from the Snake Path Gate, a pillared room built against the northern section of the western wall. Menahem ordered this room cleared and turned into a synagogue, and here he deposited the hair and sandal of the wife of the Roman commandant as an offering to Yahweh, God of the Jews. We know this because, between 1962 and 1965, Israeli archaeologists working at Masada dug up the remains of this synagogue, and in its ruins they discovered the girl's braided hair and sandal, still intact.

Those archaeologists also unearthed the bones of the man and boy who had been interred in Herod's bathhouse. At the time, Israeli authorities, assuming that these were the remains of Jews who had perished here during the events of AD 73, gave the remains full Jewish rites. But then in 2007, anthropologist Dr. Joe Zias and forensic scientist Azriel Gorski published the results of forensic tests they'd conducted on the remains. From the teeth in the bathhouse they determined that the man was aged twenty-two to twenty-four and the boy eleven to twelve. They also established that the hair had been cut intact from the head of the woman, using a sharp instrument, while she remained alive. The findings of Zias and Gorski overturned the earlier assumptions that the woman, man, and boy had been Jewish patriots. The experts felt the trio had in fact been Romans, or at the very least affiliated with Masada's Roman garrison, and had died at the hands of Jews—Menahem and his Sicarii.[6]

As the flames destroyed the remains of the butchered Syrians of the 3rd Gallica Legion, their camp prefect and centurions, along with their standards and shields, Menahem opened the doors to the military storehouses. His men subsequently unloaded the mule train's supplies and replaced them with weapons and ammunition. Then, leaving part of his rebel group holding Masada, Menahem took the majority of his men, including nephew Eleazar and deputy Apsalom, and set off down the Snake Path with the mules.

Menahem's destination was Jerusalem. Along the way, he would attract hundreds more Sicarii to his band. Now, he had the arms as well as the incentive to lead a broad Jewish uprising, plus the credit for taking Masada. Roman blood had been spilt. Hundreds of Rome's best fighting men had been annihilated. Rome would not take kindly to that. For Menahem, there was no turning back. A monumental, history-changing event had begun. The Romans were to call it the Judean War; the Jews, the Great Revolt; historians, the Jewish Revolt. Ahead lay seven bloody years of war.

II

MAYHEM IN JERUSALEM

E ven before Menahem reached Jerusalem with his men, arms, and plans
to seize control from the Roman occupiers, Roman blood had been
spilt in the city. Events had snowballed in Jerusalem after a protest against
the harsh, arbitrary, and sometimes illegal rule of Roman procurator Florus had been initiated by an official at the Jewish Temple, Eleazar ben
Ananias. A leader of the radical Zealot movement and "a very bold youth"
in the words of Josephus, who knew him well, this Eleazar had convinced
priests in charge of sacrifices at Jerusalem's six-hundred-year-old Second
Temple to ban the offering of sacrifices made in the name of foreigners.
This effectively prevented the habitual offerings to the Roman emperor
Nero and was deliberately designed to incense the Roman administration.
"This was the true beginning of our war with the Romans," historian Jose-
phus was to declare.[7]

Josephus calls Eleazar a Temple governor or superintendent. Modern
authors have styled Eleazar the Temple captain, with some stating he
commanded the Temple guard; there is no evidence of this, and there
certainly was no single Temple captain at this time. The Temple was
administered by fifteen superintendents of roughly equal rank. All had
different duties, from supervising the opening and closing of the inner
Temple doors to caring for the robes of the Temple priests. Thirteen of
these superintendents were appointed by the seventy-one-member Great

Sanhedrin, Jerusalem's supreme council of elders, while two superintendents were popularly elected. Both elected officials were entrusted with power over Temple finances.

One of this latter pair was the Superintendent of the Curtains, who had charge of the making of and caring for the massive curtain made of expensive purple cloth that separated the Temple's holiest room from the rest of the Temple, and a spare curtain of similar manufacture. In the view of some scholars, the Superintendent of the Curtains traditionally bore the name Eleazar, and if this is the case, Eleazar ben Ananias may have held this post in AD 66 when the popular uprising was sparked in Jerusalem. Another priest, Jesus ben Thebuthus, would surrender the curtains to the Romans during the siege of Jerusalem—shortly before the AD 70 fall of the city and following the death of Eleazar.[8]

Eleazar's father Ananias (also written Hananiah), a wealthy Jewish priest of the Sadducee sect, had in AD 48 been appointed high priest at Jerusalem by King Herod Agrippa II—known as Agrippa, he was the son of the original Herod Agrippa. The high priest was the most senior member of the Great Sanhedrin and chief Jewish judge in Judea. In AD 52, Ananias had been sent to Rome by the then Roman governor of Syria, charged with ill-treating the people of Samaria, the Samaritans. Ananias had been tried before the emperor Claudius, who had acquitted him, after which Ananias returned to Jerusalem, retaining great respect among the Jewish people.

At the time of the outbreak of the revolt at Jerusalem, the high priest was Matthias ben Theophilus, who had been appointed by Agrippa in AD 65. Matthias quickly disappears from the record, and from the outset of the revolt until the following year the post of high priest stood vacant. There is no reference to Matthias being killed in the uprising, which is extremely well documented by Josephus, who was in Jerusalem at this time. Josephus, then a thirty-year-old Jewish priest by the name of Yosef ben Matthias, the son of an influential and wealthy priest of the Pharisee sect and a descendant both of a high priest and of Jewish royalty, would only later take the Roman name Titus Flavius Josephus once he was granted Roman citizenship, after AD 70.

High Priest Matthias seems to have died in office in AD 66 of natural causes. Into this vacuum, with the leadership of the Sanhedrin vacant, stepped young Eleazar the Zealot and his father, Ananias, the former high priest. Once Eleazar had initiated the banning of offerings in the name of foreigners, a group of elders led by Eleazar's father had been elected as a provisional Jewish government of Jerusalem. As their first act, the provisional government had refused to send the usual annual tax payment due Caesar to Procurator Florus at Caesarea, hoping that this would prompt Florus's immediate superior, Cestius Gallus, proconsul of Syria, to remove him and install a new, more reasonable procurator over the sub-province of Judea.

Procurator Florus had come to Jerusalem at the time of the Passover in March or April and had let loose the 3rd Gallica cohort and cavalry then stationed in Jerusalem, armed with wooden clubs. Josephus claimed two thousand civilians died at the hands of these troops, while leading Jews with Roman citizenship were arrested and illegally crucified as agitators—by law Roman citizens could only be executed by decapitation. But when many of the million residents and pilgrims then in the city angrily filled the streets in protest against this brutal treatment, Florus had lost his nerve.

Agreeing to replace the offending 3rd Gallica cohort with another from Caesarea, Florus had scuttled back to his palace on the coast. A replacement cohort had duly marched into Jerusalem, and the original cohort of the city's garrison withdrew. The replacement 3rd Gallica cohort that took up the Jerusalem station was, we know, led by a Centurion Metilius, while the five-hundred-man cavalry unit now stationed at Jerusalem was provided by Roman ally King Herod Agrippa II.

The thirty-nine-year-old king, clean shaven in the Roman fashion, handsome as a youth but now considerably overweight and with a receding hairline, ruled over various cities and territories in and around Judea and appointed the high priests at Jerusalem. Some seven years before this, together with his sister Berenice, a noted beauty who was just a year younger than him and bore the honorary title of queen, Agrippa had interviewed the arrested Christian apostle Paul. Subsequently exercising his right as a Roman citizen to have his appeal heard at Rome by the emperor, Paul had been escorted to Rome by a Centurion Julius and a detachment of legionaries from the 3rd Gallica Legion's Caesarea garrison.[9]

More recently, Agrippa and Berenice had unsuccessfully tried to convince the warmongers among Jerusalem's Jews not to antagonize Rome. Driven out of the city by their own people, they had lately withdrawn to the safety of Berytus, today's Beirut in Lebanon, which was then a coastal city in the southwest of Syria province. It was then that the king had sent five hundred of his personal cavalry to Jerusalem to support the 3rd Gallica cohort now based there.

King Herod Agrippa II's cavalrymen were descended from Jewish refugees who had come from Babylon the previous century and settled in cities including Batanaea in southern Syria. Calling themselves Babylonian Jews, they had traditionally provided the core troops of the Herodian family's armies. The cavalry *ala*, or wing, sent by Agrippa to Jerusalem was led by an experienced Jewish general, Philip bar Jacimus. It had been Philip's grandfather who had led the Jews from Babylon and personally trained the cavalrymen. Up until his Jerusalem posting, Philip had been governing the Jewish city of Gamala in the Golan Heights on his king's behalf.

It hadn't taken long for massive crowds to rise up and attack the new garrison in Jerusalem, this time armed not only with clenched fists and invective but with clubs, stones, and rudimentary spears. The rebels' initial focus was the Antonia Fortress in the northwest of the city. This stood beside the Temple Mount at the western end of Jerusalem's Second Wall. At the same time that Herod the Great strengthened the Masada and Machaerus fortresses in 37–35 BC, he had created the Antonia from the ruins of an earlier fortress, naming it after his close friend and Roman patron Mark Antony. This was partly through genuine friendship but also aimed to ensure that Antony, then Roman commander-in-chief in the East, continued to grant the concessions Julius Caesar had made to the Jews after Herod's father Antipater had led Jewish troops to the rescue of Caesar when he was besieged in Egypt in 47 BC.

Among those concessions, Jewish men were excused from service in the Roman army, an obligation imposed upon the young men of every other Roman province, including Britannia. Caesar's other concessions included the banning of Roman coins bearing the images of people or animals from circulation in the holy city of Jerusalem and the prohibition of the display of Roman standards in Jerusalem. Antony had confirmed these concessions, as had all the emperors of Rome.

The Antonia, this fortress named for Antony, was a handsome rectangular building with walls eighty feet high, which surrounded a central courtyard. Large stone towers stood at each of the four corners. Public entry to the Antonia was up a long, narrow flight of stone steps, from which the Apostle Paul had attempted to address an angry Jewish crowd that accused him of taking a Gentile, or non-Jew, Trophimus of Ephesus, into the Temple.

Linking the Antonia to the Temple Mount, which it was intended to guard, were a secret underground tunnel and a pair of overhead bridges. Early in the uprising the Jewish mob had broken down the overhead bridges. This allowed the rebels to now surround the Antonia, cutting it off from the rest of the city, and lay siege to the fortress. Centurion Metilius was under orders from Procurator Florus to protect both the Antonia and the larger Palace of Herod in the Upper City, which sat on the slopes of the hill at the southwestern end of the city, known today as Mount Zion. The palace was where the Roman procurator, the proconsul of Syria, King Herod Agrippa II, and other official guests stayed when visiting Jerusalem, and it was fabulously furnished and decorated. With only 480 legionaries, Metilius left one of his 240-man maniples stationed at the Antonia while he held the larger Palace of Herod with the second maniple and Philip's five hundred dismounted cavalry.

The surrounded legionaries defending the Antonia were hugely outnumbered by tens of thousands of excited rebels and too stretched to defend every foot of wall. After a two-day struggle, these defenders were overwhelmed by Jews who broke into the fortress. All 240 legionaries in the Antonia were killed, after which the rebels looted the fortress of its weapons and ammunition and then set fire to its buildings. Once rafters and floorboards burned, floors and roofs collapsed, leaving the once beautiful Antonia a hollow, blackened shell. Three of the Antonia's four towers were destroyed in this rampage, leaving just one tower, on the western side, intact and usable.

The elated rebels flooded across town to the Upper City, where Centurion Metilius and the remaining 240 men of his 3rd Gallica cohort were bottled up with King Herod Agrippa II's cavalry behind the walls of the sprawling Palace of Herod. By this point, the small Roman force at the palace had been joined by one of the leaders of the Jewish provisional government, Ananias, the former high priest. Pro-Roman at heart, Ananias had never intended that Roman troops be killed in the uprising. He had only wanted to send a message to Proconsul Cestius Gallus in Antioch. Now, Ananias was scrambling to save his own neck. With civil disobedience turning to the slaughter of occupying troops, Ananias pictured with dread the sight of Roman legions descending on Jerusalem en masse to enact revenge upon those responsible.

Arguing with his Zealot son Eleazar, who believed that Jewish numbers and dedication would outweigh the training and experience of any Roman army, and who was prepared to confront the legions when they came, Ananias had fled with his brother Hezekiah to the Palace of Herod in the night. There, they sought and were granted sanctuary with Centurion Metilius and his Roman troops, believing they could hold out until a Roman relief force arrived from Caesarea.

This was the situation that Menahem found when he arrived at Jerusalem from Masada with his men and weapons—some estimates put his band now at ten thousand armed men plus another thirty thousand camp followers. By force of arms and personality, Menahem took charge of the revolt in Jerusalem, lording it over Eleazar and his Zealots with his well-equipped fighters and the trophy of Masada to his credit. Combining his force with Eleazar's partisans, Menahem immediately commenced to attack the Herodian palace.

Seeing that the defenders were vastly outnumbered, Philip, commander of Agrippa's cavalry, wasted no time in commencing negotiations with Menahem. As a result, the rebel leader agreed to allow the cavalrymen to leave the palace and withdraw from Jerusalem with their arms. This would reduce the palace's defenders by two thirds. Besides, Menahem was particularly interested in getting his hands on Philip, whom he considered a traitor to the Jews for fighting alongside the Romans.

Philip in turn didn't trust Menahem. Suspecting that he would be murdered if he left the city as his cavalrymen rode out, Philip sought refuge with Babylonian Jewish relatives from Batanaea who were residing in the city at the time. With these relatives standing surety for him, he was allowed by Menahem to stay with them in Jerusalem. Still, knowing that Menahem would use any pretext to kill him, after four days Philip escaped from Jerusalem using a disguise that included a wig—which suggests he was bald or had a shaved head. He then made his way back to his home at Gamala, where he had left two daughters in the care of servants of King Herod Agrippa II.

The following day, former High Priest Ananias and his brother Hezekiah were found by Menahem. These two leading Roman sympathizers were hiding in the tunnel of an aqueduct leading to the palace. To demonstrate the fate awaiting all Jewish traitors, Menahem executed Ananias and Hezekiah on the spot and subsequently boasted about it.

Meanwhile, the Roman commander at the surrounded palace, Centurion Metilius, sought to also negotiate a withdrawal from Jerusalem for his surviving men and himself. Refusing to discuss terms with Romans, Menahem pressed on with the assault.

By sheer weight of numbers the rebels broke into the palace interior, driving the legionaries from its walls and isolating them in the palace's three immense towers—the Phasael, the Hippicus, and the Mariamne. The tallest of these, the Phasael Tower, was 145 feet high. Low on food, water, and ammunition, a centurion and roughly eighty legionaries holed up in each of the three towers.

With the Roman troops cut off in the towers, Menahem called a break in hostilities and took his Sicarii commanders to the Temple to pray, with Menahem wearing royal robes and his captains wearing captured Roman armor. As they entered the Temple, they were ambushed by Eleazar and hundreds of his Zealots, who had been waiting in hiding for them. It had been naïve of Menahem to think that Eleazar had forgiven him for the murder of his father and uncle. Eleazar may have disagreed with his father but not to the point of countenancing his execution. Able to convince the people that Menahem was acting as oppressively as Procurator Florus had done, Eleazar had set a trap for Menahem. As Zealots killed Menahem's men all around him—including his deputy, Apsalom—Menahem himself fled into the Temple and disappeared.

Some of Menahem's Sicarii succeeded in escaping the city, among them Menahem's nephew Eleazar ben Ya'ir, who would reach Masada and take command of the Sicarii holding the fortress. Menahem himself was soon found and hauled from where he was hiding in the eastern cloisters of the Temple. Eleazar had him horribly tortured for killing his father Ananias, before eventually killing him. Eleazar now assumed charge of all partisan forces in Jerusalem, and the Zealots once more became the controlling party.

Taking refuge in the inner court of the Temple during this bloody struggle between Menahem and his Sicarii and Eleazar and his Zealots was Josephus, the future historian. After Menahem was killed by Eleazar, Josephus emerged from the Temple. He was to claim that he now joined the "peace party," made up of elders of the Sanhedrin and leaders of the Pharisee sect who were opposed to rebelling against Rome. In the face of the armed Zealots this group pretended to support them while urging them to let the remaining Romans of the 3rd Gallica cohort depart the city unharmed. With Josephus soon to accept the appointment from Eleazar as a general of Jewish partisan forces in Galilee, a role which he would zealously carry out for several years, it's to be wondered if he was as opposed to the armed insurrection at this time as he made out in later writings.

Eleazar was no less bloodthirsty than Menahem. Determined to eliminate the last Roman occupying forces in Jerusalem and ignoring the peace party, he quickly resumed the assault on the 3rd Gallica men in the palace towers. Once again, Centurion Metilius sought terms, and on a Saturday, during the Jewish Sabbath, Eleazar sent three priests to represent him at a truce parley. This trio shook Metilius's right hand and gave their sacred oaths that if he and his men came out and disarmed they would be allowed to depart the city.

The Roman troops duly came down from their towers and lay down their swords and shields. Eleazar's men stood back with smiles on their faces. As soon as the legionaries were separated from their weapons and had formed up and marched from the palace, Eleazar and his men drew their swords and surrounded them.

"The oaths! The oaths!" the Syrian legionaries protested. But it was to no avail. Eleazar and his men cut their throats. The legionaries were so shocked by the betrayal they died without offering resistance.[10]

Only one Roman was spared. This was their leader, Centurion Metilius, who swore to become circumcised and convert to Judaism if he was permitted to retain his life. We never hear of him again, which suggests that Metilius soon perished at the hands of his Zealot captors; perhaps as soon as the act of circumcision, with a priest slicing off more than the man's foreskin. So it was that, again via treachery, yet another cohort of the 3rd Gallica Legion had been wiped out. No foreign troops remained in Jerusalem, and for the first time since the reign of Herod the Great, the city was fully in Jewish hands. In a matter of days, Eleazar and his Zealots had conquered Jerusalem from the inside. All they had to do now was keep it.

III

REVOLT ACROSS THE MIDDLE EAST

As news spread across Judea and beyond that Jewish rebels had taken Jerusalem and Masada, killing hundreds of Roman troops, rebellion and counter-rebellion spread throughout the region.

Northeast of Jerusalem, at the fortress of Cypros on a barren hill overlooking the city of Jericho in the Jordan Valley, another cohort of the 3rd Gallica Legion was serving garrison duty, oblivious to the fate of their comrades at Jerusalem and Masada. Jericho had a pleasant climate in winter, which had led to Herod the Great using it as a winter resort, building three palaces there. The Roman garrison's job was to ensure the security of those palaces and to watch over the road to Jerusalem. Local Jewish rebels surprised this cohort via a similar ruse to that which Menahem had used to infiltrate Masada. And this cohort, too, was wiped out to a man by insurgents in quest of weapons, who surprised and cut the throats of the Syrian legionary garrison.

East of the Dead Sea, yet another 3rd Gallica cohort was based at yet another outstation, the fortress of Machaerus. Like Masada, this fortress had been rebuilt by Herod from an earlier fort as both a defensive post and a holiday resort, creating one of his favorite retreats. It had been at Machaerus that John the Baptist had first been imprisoned and then beheaded in AD 28/29 at the behest of Salome, stepdaughter of King Herod Antipas, son of Herod. Machaerus had been part of Herod's early warning system. On a clear day it was possible to see Machaerus's fortress from Masada, and in Herod's time it was possible for a pall of smoke from a fire beacon lit in a Machaerus fortress tower, warning of a foreign army invading from the east, to be seen at Masada. A beacon then lit at Masada could, weather permitting, be seen from the Phasael, the highest guard tower at Herod's Palace in Jerusalem to the north, giving the king time to prepare Jerusalem's defenses.

The Machaerus fortress also now came under surprise attack as the Jewish rebellion spread with the speed of a wildfire. This garrison, however, was alerted to the insurgents' intent and managed to close their gates and keep out the rebels. The centurion in charge of this cohort subsequently negotiated his unit's withdrawal. In his case, the centurion was wise enough to have the rebels to agree to let the legionaries depart *with their weapons.* Subsequent events tell us that this cohort succeeded in making a difficult passage through now chaotic Galilee to the provincial capital Caesarea on the coast, to rejoin the five cohorts of the 3rd Gallica stationed there along with the five auxiliary light infantry cohorts and a wing of auxiliary cavalry also based at the capital.

How pleased Procurator Florus and the commander of the 3rd Gallica Legion—likely to have been a Tribune Nicanor, as will later be explained—were to see the cohort commander and his men march into the Caesarea legion headquarters after abandoning Machaerus can only be imagined. The Machaerus fortress contained a cache of weapons sufficient to arm seventy thousand men, a cache now in rebel hands. The cohort's commanding centurion was likely punished rather than praised, but the 480 men of his cohort would be needed in the tough days, weeks, and months ahead.

The majority of Caesarea's residents were of Greek origin—Josephus calls them Syrians, in part because they included retired Syrian legion veterans and the descendants of Syrian legionaries. On the news of what had taken place at Jerusalem, Masada, and Cypros, many of these descendants of legionaries in Caesarea turned in fury on the city's Jewish residents, massacring twenty thousand of them in a single bloody day to avenge the loss of close to fifteen hundred Roman citizen soldiers of the 3rd Gallica. Those Caesarean Jewish men who weren't massacred in this counter-rising were taken prisoner by Procurator Florus's troops as they attempted to flee the city. Florus consigned the surviving male Jews to the oars of the fleet of galleys that had been established at Caesarea by Herod the Great as a means of punishment of Jewish malefactors. Not a single Jew was left in Caesarea.

Across the region, the Jewish and non-Jewish residents of scores of villages and a dozen cities fought each other, some for revenge, others for control. The Jews took the initiative, forming several massive roaming bands that pillaged and burned villages and attacked non-Jewish regional capitals from the Mediterranean to well east of the Jordan River. Josephus is our key source for what happened to these cities during the revolt, and his talent for exaggeration shines through his narrative—he would write his book *The Jewish War* for a mostly Roman audience and under the patronage of a Roman emperor, so it literally paid him to exaggerate the excesses of Rome's enemies, the Jewish rebels.

Josephus gives us a list of the Gentile cities and towns in Judea, Galilee, Idumea, and the province of Syria now overrun and totally destroyed by rampaging Jewish war parties. Some of the places he names, such as Ptolemais and Kedasa, were before long being used as staging posts for Roman military operations, while others, such as Gischala and Gadara, would be used as major centers of resistance by the rebels, who reinforced their walls, as Josephus himself tells us, which seems to rule out these cities' total destruction in the first stage of the uprising as described by Josephus.

Certainly, the villages around principal cities and towns, unprotected by walls as they were, would have easily fallen prey to Jewish attackers. And suburbs of cities that overflowed beyond the protection of old city walls would have been set ablaze by the rebels. Josephus also includes the southern coastal cities of Ascalon and Gaza among those "entirely demolished" in this first blush of the revolt, only to describe, several pages later, how Ascalon remained intact and in Roman military hands and only came under rebel attack months later.

The majority of rebel raids were in fact mostly confined to inland centers east of the Jordan River in what today is Jordan. Cities such as Philadelphia (the modern-day Jordanian capital Amman), Gerasa (Jerash), Gadara, Sebonitis, and Pella were attacked. In the Golan Heights, named for the biblical area of Golan, centers such as Hippos and Caesarea Philippi came under Jewish rebel attack. In today's West Bank, Sebaste in Samaria and Gaba (al Jab'a) were surprised. The outskirts of Ptolemais (Acre) in

Phoenicia, a major Mediterranean port serving the province of Syria and home to numerous retired legion veterans, were raided, as was a village subject to the nearby port of Tyre. At the approach of rebel bands, Gentile women and children fled to nearby woods. Their men attempted to defend their homes and were subject to "an immense slaughter" by the Jews, says Josephus.

West of the Jordan lay Scythopolis—Beit She'an in today's Israel—the largest of the ten cities that made up the Decapolis. This league of cities had originally been established through today's southern Syria, Israel, and Jordan by Greek colonists. At Scythopolis, equal numbers of Jews and Gentiles fought for control of the city, although the Greek population gained the ascendancy. Some Jews there even took up arms in support of their Greek neighbors, only for the Greeks to suspect their motives and put them to the sword.

At Alexandria, capital of Egypt and considered one of the three great cities of the Roman Empire after Rome itself and Antioch, there had long been tensions between the Jewish minority and the majority Greek population, tensions that often exploded into violence. Alexandria had been founded four hundred years earlier by Alexander the Great, who was subsequently buried there. It had always been essentially a Greek city, with large Egyptian and Jewish minorities. News of the revolt in Judea and surrounds led to conflict between Jews and Gentiles in Alexandria, which soon became all-out civil war.

The Jews had once occupied two of Alexandria's five residential quarters. Since conflict between Jews and Gentiles in the city in AD 38–41, Jewish residents had been confined to the Delta Quarter, the fourth quarter, and, under an AD 41 edict of the emperor Claudius, a cap had been put on the Jewish population via a ban on Jews migrating to the city from Upper Egypt. Nonetheless, Jews still represented some twenty percent of the city's half million people.

To quell the violence in Alexandria and to restore order, the Roman prefect of Egypt, Tiberius Julius Alexander, sent troops of his garrison into the Delta Quarter. Alexander had only been in his post since May, after the emperor Nero had summarily dismissed his predecessor, Gaius Caecina Tuscus, and sent him into exile for having the temerity to bathe in a luxurious new bath installed at the palace at Alexandria in advance of a planned visit there by Nero the following year. Tiberius Alexander was an Egyptian Jew who not only held Roman citizenship but was a member of Rome's Equestrian Order, which required a net worth of four hundred thousand sesterces—coincidentally the equal of the annual salary of the prized post of prefect of Egypt.

Alexander's father had been a senior Jewish official in Alexandria, an alabarch, imprisoned at Rome by the emperor Caligula, while his uncle Philo of Alexandria was a noted Jewish philosopher who'd led a delegation to Rome to put the case for Alexandrian Jews after conflict between his people and Gentiles in the city in AD 38. Alexander's sister-in-law was the Jewish Queen Berenice, sister of King Herod Agrippa II—her first husband had been Alexander's late brother Marcus. Alexander himself had served as Roman procurator of Judea between AD 46–48, an appointment made by the emperor Claudius, who counted Alexander's father among his friends. Determined that Nero not perceive him to be soft on his fellow Jews, Alexander now gave his legionaries open slather in the Delta Quarter. Those soldiers were authorized to kill Jews who resisted, and pillage their homes to their hearts' content.

At this point, Alexander had twelve thousand legionaries under his command, based at a military camp on the outskirts of Alexandria. Of these men, five thousand filled the ranks of Egypt's resident 3rd Cyrenaica Legion (Cyrenaica's 3rd Legion). Another five thousand marched for the recently arrived 15th Apollinaris Legion (Apollo's 15th Legion). The 15th had been transferred to Egypt after active service in Armenia under Rome's top general Domitius Corbulo several years earlier, during which time Tiberius Alexander had been Corbulo's chief of staff. The 15th Apollinaris had been sent to Egypt because it was due to take part in Nero's planned military campaign from southern Egypt into Sudan, or Ethiopia as the Romans called it, which was due to be launched in the fall of AD 67.

The remaining two thousand legionaries in Alexandria were new citizen recruits from Libya destined for the 18th Legion in Germany. Another three thousand men recruited in Europe for the 18th were currently training with the Army of the Upper Rhine. This legion had been recently reformed by Nero after it, along with the 17th and 19th Legions, had been wiped out in the Teutoburg Forest during what Romans called the Varian War fifty-seven years earlier. Nero's plan seems to have been that, once all its five thousand men were trained and united, the new 18th would take up garrison duties in Egypt, freeing up the 3rd Cyrenaica, 15th Apollinaris, and 5th Macedonica (5th Legion of Macedonia) for the Ethiopian operation. The latter unit had been based in Pontus on the Black Sea since the Roman annexation of that former independent kingdom in AD 62 but was scheduled to travel to Alexandria at the start of the spring of AD 67 to link up with the other legions assigned to the Ethiopian invasion.[11]

The legionaries unleashed by Prefect Alexander in Alexandria marched to the Delta Quarter, then advanced at the dash along its narrow streets. On their heels came thousands of Gentile residents of the city, intent on grabbing their share of the loot. The Jews resisted, pitting their best fighters and what weapons they had against the legionaries, and for a time they held the troops back in the narrow streets and even caused some Roman casualties. But it didn't take long for highly trained legionaries to break Jewish lines. Soon the Jews were fleeing, and legionaries were going from house to house, killing anyone they found, ransacking the contents, then setting fire to houses before moving on.

Only when Jewish leaders prostrated themselves before the Romans and begged for mercy did Prefect Alexander halt the slaughter and give the order for his men to cease their punitive actions and withdraw. Being disciplined legionaries, says Josephus, the troops immediately complied. The Gentile civilians weren't as disciplined, and they continued to strip the bloodied bodies of Jewish men, women, and children piled in the streets until Alexander had his legionaries put a stop to it.

Josephus was to estimate that fifty thousand Jews died in Alexandria during this phase of the revolt. As palls of smoke from the fire-ravaged Delta Quarter filled the sky, an uneasy calm fell over Alexandria. Prefect Alexander had snuffed out the revolt in Egypt, but to the northeast, in Judea and Galilee, Jewish rebels were in control.

IV

THE IMPENDING STORM

In the northwest of the province of Syria lay Antioch, Syria's bustling capital, which had a population of more than half a million people. Here, at
his palace on an island in the middle of the Orontes River, which passed
through the famously beautiful city, the province's Roman governor for
the past year, Proconsul Gaius Cestius Gallus, had been vacillating over
what to do about the Judean problem for weeks. Josephus refers to him as
Cestius; for continuity's sake, he is referred to here by his last name, Gallus.

A senator, and a consul of Rome twenty-four years before this, Gallus
was likely to now be aged well into his sixties. His family, the Cestii, came
from humble origins, and his father had been the first family member to
obtain a consulship. His surname, and that of his father, Gallus, usually
indicated a Roman whose family origins lay in Gaul. But as Gallus's father
is believed to have come from Latium near Rome, the appendage would
have derived from its other meaning—*gallus* is Latin for "cockerel." So
Gallus, like his father, may have been seen as a strutting rooster.

Gallus's job as proconsul of Syria was the highest-paid and most sought
after provincial gubernatorial post in the empire. Apart from attracting a
large salary, the role had entitled Gallus to hand out appointments on his
provincial staff to relatives as well as to his other "clients" and the sons and
nephews of clients, making him a very popular patron. As a result, he was

keen to do nothing that shortened his term as governor and reduced his power and influence.[12]

On receiving word of the unrest and protest in Jerusalem that spring and early summer, before the massacre of Roman troops at Masada, Jerusalem, and elsewhere, Gallus had called his senior civil and military officers together for a conference at his Antioch palace. When they came together, most of his officers, who included the commanders of the four legions then based in Syria, advised Gallus to lead a military expedition into Judea to put down the unrest. But Gallus, although he had served as a legion commander himself many years before, was not a militarist. He was in fact a timid man. Instead, he chose to send an envoy to Jerusalem to carry out an inquiry into the causes of the unrest.

The Jewish superintendents of the Temple and Queen Berenice had separately written to Gallus laying the blame for Jewish discontent firmly at the feet of Procurator Florus, who had also written to Gallus. In his report, Florus predictably blamed the Jews for the problems in Jerusalem and absolved himself of any wrongdoing. Even though Florus was Gallus's subordinate, Gallus was intimidated by the procurator and reluctant to either dismiss him or attribute any blame to him. This was because Florus's wife, Cleopatra (not *the* Cleopatra, but another noblewoman of the same name), was a close friend of the emperor Nero's wife, Poppaea Sabina, and through the empress's influence Nero had personally given Florus his Judean post.

The direct connection with the emperor had given Florus the confidence and the arrogance to act abominably toward his Jewish subjects from the start of his tenure in AD 64 and to not care a bit what Governor Gallus thought. Florus had continued his outrageous behavior even though the empress had died, apparently due to a miscarriage, in AD 65. Florus believed he still had the emperor's blessing, and so, too, did Governor Gallus.

The man Gallus chose to conduct his Judean inquiry was a Tribune Neapolitanus, who was "one of his intimate friends" according to Josephus. In other words, Neapolitanus was one of Gallus's clients, from a family he knew extremely well, and was therefore a man he could trust. Neapolitanus's rank of *tribunus laticlavius*, or tribune of the broad stripe, was a military one, referred to as that of "military tribune" to distinguish the holder from the civil post of tribune of the plebeians at Rome. The equivalent of a colonel today, the military tribune of the broad stripe was significantly more senior than the *tribunus angusticlavius*, tribune of the thin stripe, who was merely an officer cadet and of such unimportance that his six-month appointment, which was like an internship, didn't appear on the official biographies of Roman officers.

A native of today's Italian city of Naples, Tribune Neapolitanus was a member of the Equestrian Order and was likely in his mid-twenties—he would qualify for senatorial rank at age thirty. In the first century, men of military tribune rank served as second in command of legions; however, it's likely Neapolitanus occupied an administrative post on Gallus's staff at Antioch and held the rank of supernumerary military tribune. This relatively new rank had come about because, with less than thirty legions, there had only been the need for an equivalent number of military tribunes, creating a bottleneck on the Roman civil service promotional ladder. To correct this, the emperor Claudius had permitted the appointment of more than the required number of military tribunes, thus pushing larger numbers of talented young men through to the Senate. As a result, a provincial governor might have several military tribunes on his staff in administrative positions.

As a matter of "good form," Gallus had avoided giving the Judean investigative post to an officer who outranked the procurator of Judea. For the same reason, the officers commanding the legions currently stationed in Judea and Egypt were tribunes, so as not to outrank their superiors, the Equestrian Order procurator of Judea and prefect of Egypt. Most importantly, to the weak Gallus, the appointment of Neapolitanus would not give Procurator Florus grounds to complain to the emperor about his actions.

Accompanied by an escorting cavalry troop and wearing a white cloak and ornate bronze armor over his white tribune's tunic, Tribune Neapolitanus hurried south from Antioch to carry out his inquiry. In telling us about Neapolitanus's mission, Josephus makes no mention of him consulting with Procurator Florus or even visiting Caesarea. Gallus had Florus's written report giving his side of the story; all that the proconsul required from Neapolitanus was the other side of the story, through impartial non-Jewish eyes.

Once the tribune reached Jamnia in Judea, today's town of Yavne, midway between Jaffa and Aschod on the southern coastal plain and four miles inland from the Mediterranean, the tribune met up with King Herod

Agrippa II and the king's sister Berenice. Neapolitanus was also met by members of the Great Sanhedrin who had come down from Jerusalem to escort him to the city. All swore that the Jewish people had no rebellious intent. Together, Neapolitanus, Agrippa, Berenice, and the Jewish elders turned inland to climb up into the hills and make for Jerusalem. On arriving outside Jerusalem, they were met by throngs of weeping women who called for Procurator Florus's removal and punishment, as their husbands had been killed earlier on Florus's orders.

Tribune Neapolitanus found Jerusalem peaceful, with the Roman garrison seemingly in control of affairs—this was months before the massacre of Roman troops at Jerusalem and Masada. At the behest of Agrippa, Neapolitanus walked around the center of the city accompanied by just a single servant, and saw the wreckage of the city marketplace and the ransacked houses left in the wake of the earlier rampage by Florus's troops, before he'd replaced the offending 3rd Gallica cohort. All the Jewish people Neapolitanus saw in the city were calm, reverential, and acted friendly toward him. Going up to the Temple, he addressed the priests and a vast crowd that had assembled in the complex's outer Court of the Gentiles.

"I highly commend you for your faithfulness to Rome," the tribune declared, "and I earnestly exhort you to keep the peace."[13]

After courteously taking part in those aspects of the Temple's religious observances that were permitted to foreigners in the Court of the Gentiles, Neapolitanus and his escort departed the city and made their way back to Antioch. On his return, the tribune reported to Governor Gallus that all was peaceful in Judea, and that the Jews blamed Procurator Florus for the previous unrest. The peaceful state found in Jerusalem by his investigating officer had led Gallus to believe that all was now well in Judea, that the problem had sorted itself out.

King Herod Agrippa II was not as easily fooled as the tribune. He was aware of the underlying discontent in the city. Following Neapolitanus's departure from Jerusalem, Agrippa had remained in the city, where he was approached by Jewish elders who urged him to allow them to bypass Governor Gallus, who they believed would support Florus no matter what, and send Jewish envoys to Rome to put their case for the removal of Procurator Florus direct to the emperor Nero.

The Jewish king felt this would only worsen the situation; young Nero had neither the compassion nor the understanding of his predecessor Claudius, who had more than once ruled in favor of the Jews. Besides, Governor Gallus would be furious that the Jews had gone over his head and would likely punish Judea as a result. In a long speech addressed to a massive public meeting in Jerusalem, Agrippa spelled out the might of Rome and her vast empire and the fate of those who opposed Rome.

"Why not," he said at one point, "just kill your children and your wives with your own hands, and burn your beautiful native city? At least, as a result of such madness, no one can reproach you for having been defeated! My friends, it's best to foresee the impending storm while the ship is still safe in the harbor, and not set sail out onto the middle of the hurricane. Do you imagine that when the Romans have got you under their power again they will act toward you with moderation? Or will they rather burn your holy city, and utterly destroy your whole nation, as an example to other nations? Even those of you who survive the war won't be able to find a place to flee, for, all men have the Romans for their masters already, or are afraid they will."[14]

In tears, and with his watching sister Berenice also in tears, the king begged the people to pay the outstanding tax to Rome, to repair the broken bridges between the Temple and Antonia Fortress, and to make the most of Roman occupation and the concessions that Jews enjoyed, rather than take a confrontational approach to mighty Rome—an approach which, he predicted, would only end badly for all Jews across the world.

His words made sense to a moderate minority, but for the majority, sense had taken flight on the wings of the dream of independence and self-mastery promised by Jewish religious texts. The people had angrily responded to Agrippa that their argument wasn't with Rome, it was with the arrogant, brutal Florus, and if Agrippa didn't help them they would take matters into their own hands. It was following this meeting that the king and queen had been driven out of Jerusalem and the revolt had turned to violence at Masada and the Antonia Fortress.

Weeks later, with Jerusalem and much of Judea and Galilee in rebel Jewish hands, Governor Gallus finally realized that he had no alternative but to lead an army south to put down the revolt. From the Syria garrison he took one complete legion, the 12th Fulminata, known as the Thundering Twelfth, and four cohorts from each of the other three legions, the 4th Scythica (4th Legion of Scythia), 6th Ferrata (6th Ironsides Legion), and 10th Fretensis (10th Legion of the Strait). By using men from all four legions of the Syria station, Gallus seems to have wanted to share the glory and the spoils of the Judean operation. To these legionary units Gallus would add three thousand men of six cohorts of auxiliary light infantry based in Syria.

He would also incorporate into his force a quartet of five-hundred-man wings of auxiliary cavalry, taking three with him from Syria and collecting the fourth from its station at Caesarea once he reached that city. The balance of the legionary and auxiliary cohorts in Syria would remain at their bases, continuing to face east, confronting the recently pacified Parthian Empire beyond the Euphrates.

Gallus's choice of the entire 12th Fulminata to lead the Judean task force, or even to participate in it, was, to say the least, unwise. This was a legion that had performed badly in an AD 62 campaign in Armenia, when the inept Roman general Lucius Caesennius Paetus had surrendered a fortress to the Parthians, then led the 12th and the 4th Scythica on a humbling retreat out of Armenia. It had taken Rome's best general, Corbulo, to reverse the situation, leading other legions in a swift campaign that had in turn humbled the Parthians and led to the king of Parthia, Vologases I, submitting to Roman control of Armenia.

Roman historian Tacitus says that in AD 62, after their Armenian disgrace, the 12th Fulminata Legion, "from the loss of their best and bravest men and the panic of the remainder, seemed quite unfit for battle" as they marched out of Armenia and down to Syria, where they were based for the next four years. Tacitus adds that the legion was suffering from "numerical feebleness" at this time—the unit was significantly under-strength.

Unlike modern army regiments, which receive a regular flow of new recruits to bring their battalions up to or near full fighting strength, with only a few exceptions following major battle losses, Roman legions of the first century only had their losses made up when they underwent mass discharges and recruit intakes every two decades. This was when the twenty-year enlistment of its legionaries expired and a large proportion of its troops went into retirement, with a small number of the old enlistment reenlisting to march beside the new recruits.[15]

At the time the Jewish Revolt broke out, the 12th Fulminata Legion was still suffering from that numerical feebleness mentioned by Tacitus, which would only be reversed when the legion undertook its scheduled new intake of recruits, due to take place in AD 67/68. The legion's current

soldiers, who were now aged in their late thirties, forties, fifties, and sixties, were worn out and looking forward to their looming retirement. Perhaps the fact that the entire legion seems to have numbered little more than two thousand men fit for action dictated that the entire legion would join the two thousand men assigned to Gallus's Judean task force from each of the other three Syria-based legions. Commanding the detachment from the 6th Ferrata was Camp Prefect Tyrannius Priscus. As for the two other detachments of four cohorts each from the 4th Scythica and 10th Fretensis Legions, a Tribune Longinus is known to have commanded one, and a camp prefect may have commanded the other.

Gallus may have thought the operation would offer the 12th Fulminata's men the opportunity to regain their reputations before they retired and allow them to amass proceeds from the sale of Jewish booty to add to their retirement funds. As the men of the under-strength legion marched out of Antioch when Gallus's army set out in October of AD 66, we know that the 12th Fulminata's commander was a legate by the name of Gallus. He was quite possibly a relative of Governor Gallus—although Gallus was a relatively common Roman name. We also know that the 12th Fulminata's second in command was a tribune by the name of Placidus; later events suggest his first name was Julius. As for Governor Gallus's client, Tribune Neapolitanus, the young man would accompany Gallus as a member of the governor's staff.

Gallus had sent messages to regional Roman allies calling for sixteen thousand additional troops to bring his army's overall numbers to around thirty thousand men, although he didn't wait for the allied forces to join him in Antioch. Instead, probably worried that Nero would be angry if he put off his punitive Judean expedition any longer, Gallus hurriedly departed the Syrian capital with his legions and sent orders to three kings to have their troops link up with him at the Syrian port of Ptolemais.

King Herod Agrippa II joined him from Beirut, bringing 3,000 of his own light infantry and 1,000 cavalry. King Sohaemus of the autonomous Syrian city-state of Emesa set off in the wake of the large Roman column, bringing 1,500 of his personal cavalry and 2,500 foot archers. King Antiochus of Commagene, to the immediate north of Syria, whose force would take the longest time to reach Ptolemais, sent 3,000 light infantry, 3,000 foot archers, and 2,000 cavalry.

Ptolemais had been used in the past as the staging point for an earlier operation against rebellious Jews. In 4 BC, amid the political instability that had followed the death of Herod the Great, Judea had been rent by Jewish unrest and protest against Roman influence. The then proconsul of Syria, Publius Quinctilius Varus—the same Varus who would lose three legions and his own life in the Teutoburg Forest massacre of AD 9—had promptly brought several legions down to Ptolemais from Syria. Using the city as his base of operations, he had thereafter rapidly marched on Jerusalem, where he crucified two thousand Jewish agitators en masse and snuffed out the nascent revolt.

Ptolemais had been granted Roman military colony status by the emperor Claudius, who had settled numbers of retired legion veterans there. In addition to offering Governor Gallus loyal citizens and port facilities, Ptolemais contained grain and a significant water supply, both of which were essential to a campaigning army. There, King Herod Agrippa II joined Gallus with his troops, becoming the governor's chief adviser on Judea and the Jews for the campaign.

Establishing a vast, tented military camp outside Ptolemais, Gallus, while he waited for the last of the allied troops to arrive, led part of his army inland, into the territory of Zebulon. This was in southeast Galilee, bordering on the Sea of Galilee—like the Dead Sea, a lake; in fact, the lowest freshwater lake on Earth. Jewish partisans in the area fled to the mountains of Galilee, leaving their villages to be plundered and burned by Gallus's troops. After Gallus withdrew back to Ptolemais, local Syrians lingered behind, sifting through the ruins of the pillaged villages as they looked for spoils the legions had missed, only for Jewish partisans to return and put them to the sword.

Once King Antiochus's and King Sohaemus's troops arrived, Governor Gallus led the combined army from Ptolemais, leaving Syria and marching into northern Judea. Large numbers of locals had gathered from throughout the region to support the Roman army, and these camp followers swarmed along behind the army as Gallus led it down the coastal highway to Caesarea. At Caesarea, Gallus was greeted by Procurator Florus. Here, too, he took part of the Caesarea garrison into his army—four of the six cohorts of the 3rd Gallica then at the Judean capital and the one wing of auxiliary cavalry that formed part of Florus's garrison.

That cavalry wing was commanded by a prefect, Aemilius Jucundus. The rank of prefect of auxiliaries was, like that of military tribune, the equivalent of a colonel today. Like tribunes, prefects were officers of Equestrian rank. Appointment as prefect was at that time the next step in

the career of a Roman officer after service as a military tribune.[16] Jucundus, who was likely in his late twenties, was a member of one of the most noble of Roman families, the Aemilii, which could trace its lineage back to the second king of Rome. Jucundus's name means "delightful," suggesting he'd been a charming child—Romans' last names were sometimes acquired when they were children.

For the past two years, Prefect Jucundus had been stationed in Caesarea with his cavalry wing. Procurator Florus had frequently used Jucundus and his troopers in brutal policing actions against the Jews in Judea, and, as events were to prove, Florus had secured Jucundus's personal loyalty, no doubt by boasting of his direct connection with the emperor and promising Jucundus favored treatment in the future. Another prefect with the family name of Aemilius, Aemilius Secundus, commanded one of the cavalry wings that Governor Gallus brought with him to Caesarea from Syria. With the name Secundus often applied to a second-born son, this cavalry prefect may have been Jucundus's brother; he would later join Jucundus in talking Governor Gallus into rash action.[17]

Governor Gallus now based himself at Caesarea, delegating the task of subduing the region to subordinates. He began by sending two forces down the coast to the Jewish-held city of Joppa, today's Jaffa. One force traveled via the coast road while another took an inland route, so that they approached Joppa from two different directions. Surprising and overwhelming the partisans there, the Roman troops killed 8,400 and set the city on fire. Gallus also dispatched a large force of cavalrymen to range through the toparchy of Narbatah several miles east of Caesarea, killing all Jews they found and looting and burning their villages.

Meanwhile, the general commanding the 12th Fulminata Legion, Legate Gallus, with Tribune Neapolitanus attached to his staff, was sent by Governor Gallus into Galilee with a large force of infantry and cavalry. Legate Gallus made straight for Sepphoris. Three miles north of the village of Nazareth and largest of all the 250 cities, towns, and villages of Galilee, Sepphoris had housed a palace of Herod Antipas during the lifetime of Jesus Christ and possessed Greco-Roman refinements such as a drama theater seating four thousand. By the time Gallus and Neapolitanus reached it with their troops, Sepphoris's Gentile residents had been holding out for weeks against besieging Jewish Sicarii partisans, and they now joyfully welcomed the Roman relief force.

The Sicarii rebels who had been threatening Sepphoris fled from the area to Mount Asamon to the north, and with the bulk of his force, Legate Gallus pursued them to the mountain. As legionaries pushed up the slopes in pursuit, they were ambushed by rebels who lay in wait for them. Throwing short, metal-tipped, lead-weighted javelins called darts, the Jews killed two hundred Roman troops caught in the open below. In response, the Roman general divided his legionary forces. While some troops kept the rebels busy, two detachments outflanked them. Having worked their way around the partisans, legionaries surprised them from above, and in close-quarters fighting they easily dealt with the lightly armored Jews. These partisans fought bareheaded and with nothing more than thick leather vests for body protection, which, while it made them more fleet of foot than the heavily armored legionaries, meant they were massively disadvantaged in close quarters fighting.

Any rebels who fled to the plain were cut down by Gallus's waiting cavalry. A handful of the partisans escaped up into the more remote parts of the mountain, but the vast majority, more than two thousand of them, were killed by the general's infantry and cavalry. Seeing no more threat from rebels in Galilee, Legate Gallus led most of his men back to Caesarea, leaving Tribune Neapolitanus in command at Sepphoris accompanied by the 120 troopers of the 12th Fulminata Legion's own legionary cavalry troop, with orders to hold the city against future rebel attack. To ensure that Sepphoris remained loyal to Rome and supportive of the tribune and his men, Legate Gallus took members of the families of the city's leading men to Caesarea with him as hostages. These hostages were soon sent to the coastal town of Dora, today's Israeli village of Dor, just to the north of Caesarea. They would sit out the rest of the war there in comparative safety.[18]

Once these detachments rejoined him at Caesarea, Governor Gallus gave the order for the army to march. First reaching Joppa, then turning east into the dry hills, the strung-out army, with its thousands of pack animals plodding along near the rear, tramped up the dusty road toward Jerusalem, following the Yarkon River to its head, where springs bubbled to the surface at the town of Antipatris. Word had reached Gallus that a large body of rebels had gathered at the Tower of Aphek near Antipatris, so he sent a force in advance of the main army to deal with them. The rebels had disappeared by the time the Roman advance force reached the Tower of Aphek, leaving their camp for the Romans to destroy.

From Antipatris, Gallus's army marched south to Lydda, today's Lod. Only fifty Jewish men were found there, and they were swiftly killed. Before they were put to death, they revealed that the rest of the town's Jewish population had gone to Jerusalem for the Feast of the Tabernacles. Leaving Lod in flames, Gallus again turned left, directing his army along the ascending road toward Jerusalem to the east. Destroying deserted villages en route, the Romans followed the road as it continued to climb steeply through the Beth Horon Valley, a place that would before long be etched in Roman memory.

After passing through the deserted villages of Beth Horon Inferior and Beth Horon Superior, the leading elements of the column reached another village, Gaba, which lay just nine miles north of Jerusalem. Here, Governor Gallus gave orders for a marching camp to be built, and as surveyors laid out the camp and legionaries began to toil in their armor, digging entrenchments and throwing up an earth wall around the campsite, several thousand auxiliary infantrymen from the column's vanguard stood guard in ranks that faced Jerusalem, and cavalrymen foraged for fodder and firewood.

At Jerusalem, word arrived that a Roman army of thirty thousand men was winding up the road from the coast and setting up camp at Gaba. Despite the fact it was a Saturday, the Jewish day of rest, Jewish men left their feasting and took up arms on the Sabbath. Tens of thousands of armed men, perhaps hundreds of thousands, rushed out of the city, disorganized, yelling, angry, and ignoring calls from more levelheaded men not to act rashly.

Among prominent partisans hurrying to do combat with the Roman foe were a number of men from outside Jerusalem's priestly class. Silas the Babylonian had previously served as an officer in King Herod Agrippa II's army. Niger, a native of the Perea district east of the Jordan River, which had once formed part of Herod the Great's kingdom, had left his post as governor of the district of Idumea, south of Judea. Also among the rebel leaders were two noble sons of King Monobazus of Adiabene and Erbil—today's Urfa in Turkey and Erbil in Iraq—whose royal family had converted to Judaism and had two palaces at Jerusalem.

Within a few hours the excited, exhilarated partisan horde arrived at Gaba and swept onto the stationary Roman sentry lines in their path. Led by the likes of Silas and Niger, the rebels threw themselves onto the locked oval shields of the auxiliary light infantry who stood between them and the camp building works. By their very numbers, the Jews overwhelmed auxiliaries at one point and broke through their ranks, hacking left and right as they went.

Roman cavalry on foraging duty wheeled about and came at the gallop to stop Jewish fighters before they reached the camp works, and more auxiliary infantrymen came at the run from the still arriving column. Eventually, Roman troops succeeded in driving off the partisans, but not before four hundred auxiliary infantrymen and one hundred and fifteen cavalrymen had been killed. The partisans, who had lost just twenty-two of their men, withdrew to Jerusalem congratulating themselves on stinging the nose of the Roman beast.

Meanwhile, a Jewish peasant by the name of Simon bar Giora, a native of the city of Gerasa in southern Samaria, today's West Bank town of Jurish near Nablus, had taken a large party of fellow peasants and skirted the Jerusalem road north through the hills until they reached the Beth Horon Valley. Here they found the rear of the Roman column on the road, with its drawn-out baggage train of thousands of mules and donkeys loaded with equipment. The Roman army used one baggage animal for every eight soldiers, to carry their tents and grinding stones, plus more animals for camp material and supplies, officers' chattels, dismantled artillery pieces, and ammunition. Gallus's army was using more than four thousand pack animals.

Sending unarmed civilian muleteers fleeing in panic, Simon and his men rushed down the slope, cut out the mules carrying some of the legions' dismantled artillery pieces and ammunition, and led them away into the hills before the column's rearguard could stop them. Hours later, Simon and his men triumphantly led the mules into Jerusalem, showing off the captured Roman artillery and gloating over their success.

These two partisan attacks on his army unnerved Governor Gallus. By nightfall that day the marching camp at Gaba was erected, and as the next day dawned Gallus was reluctant to leave its protection. He had clearly thought he would shock and awe the Jews by his troops' ruthless rampage through Galilee and coastal Judea and seems to have been hoping the Jews of Jerusalem would capitulate once his army drew near. The stiff resistance encountered outside Gaba had suggested otherwise. As Gallus and his army sat in the camp at Gaba for two days and did nothing more than cremate their dead outside the camp walls, King Herod Agrippa II, seeing Gallus's reluctance to push on to Jerusalem, offered a suggestion.

The king's idea was to send two of his own chief aides, Borceus and Phebus, men well known to the Jewish leadership, to Jerusalem as peace envoys. They would go with two objectives—to convince all the rebels to lay down their arms in return for a full pardon from Gallus, or at the very least convince the more moderate Jews to desert the revolt and leave Jerusalem. Governor Gallus jumped at this idea. So, Borceus and Phebus set off for Jerusalem on their mission, mounted, but unarmed and unescorted.

By this time the rebels had organized themselves. They occupied the elevated parts of the city with lookouts and placed guards at all the entrances to Jerusalem, implementing a system of regulated watches. When Borceus and Phebus arrived at the northern entrance to the city, they were stopped by Jewish sentries, and a crowd quickly gathered. The Zealots in the crowd, who immediately recognized the king's men, feared that moderates would capitulate in fear to the envoys. So, they never let lead negotiator Phebus open his mouth. They speared him as he sat in his saddle, then turned on Borceus. Although wounded, Borceus was able to turn his horse back the way he had come, push through the crowd, and gallop to safety. The moderate Jews in the crowd were furious with the Zealots for killing the king's envoy when he'd come in peace, and drove the Zealots back into the city with sticks and stones. But the damage had been done.

To Gallus, the message brought by the wounded Borceus was clear: there was no negotiating with the most extreme of the rebels, and he would have to conquer Jerusalem, the jewel in the Jewish crown, by brute force. Reluctantly, Gallus gave the order to march on Jerusalem. Three days after establishing the Gaba camp, the army moved out. Normally, marching camps were destroyed as a Roman army moved on, to deny it to the enemy, but as a fallback position, Gallus left the Gaba camp essentially intact.

Some partisans came out to attempt to harry the advancing column, but Roman cavalry soon put them to flight, enabling the main army to arrive unmolested at Mount Scopus, the ridge to the north of Jerusalem, where it began to build its latest camp. From the summit of the ridge, 2,710 feet above sea level, Governor Gallus, King Herod Agrippa II, and their aides and officers were able to look out over the city below as legionaries dug their camp's defenses and erected their tents.

Immediately below Mount Scopus stood the narrow stone-paved streets and flat-roofed houses of the northern sector of Jerusalem. Called the Bezetha, or New City, it was a sector unprotected by city walls. Beyond Bezetha lay the Lower City, the fire-blackened Antonia Fortress, and the impressive Temple Mount with its Second Temple complex. South of the Temple Mount spread the Upper City, in the west of which rose the walls of the Palace of Herod. The palace's three ornate towers, previously the location of the last stand of Centurion Metilius and his doomed men, were now occupied by rebel Jewish lookouts. All the older parts of the city were protected by ancient stone walls thirty feet high, known as the First Wall and Second Wall.

Gallus had visited Jerusalem before in more peaceful times and stayed at the grand Palace of Herod, which was like a five-star hotel to its high-ranking guests. It may have been tempting to secure the palace first, but Agrippa would have advised Gallus to aim all his efforts on taking the Temple Mount. Secure the Temple and all its treasures, he would have said, and rebel resistance would crumble to nothing.

Still Gallus hesitated. He ordered his cavalry to scour the countryside around Jerusalem and empty surrounding villages of their grain supply but otherwise instructed the remainder of his troops to stand down from offensive operations and stay within the protection of their new camp's walls. With the imposing Roman army now on Jerusalem's doorstep, weak-kneed Governor Gallus was hoping the sight would intimidate the rebels into backing down. He was giving the Jews yet another opportunity to capitulate.

V

A ROMAN DISASTER

On the morning of November 1, AD 66, the fourth day since his Roman army had encamped on Mount Scopus, Governor Cestius Gallus finally commenced an attack on the city of Jerusalem.[19] Leaving auxiliaries to guard the Mount Scopus camp and his baggage, and with legionary infantry leading the advance in close battle formation, his army marched down off the ridge astride the Damascus Road, the highway that led into the north of Jerusalem.

The northern suburb of Jerusalem, the New City, then had no defensive wall. In the early AD 40s, the last king of Judea, Herod Agrippa I, had laid the foundations for a Third Wall that encompassed the New City, inclusive of at least sixty towers and several gateways. Agrippa, as he was familiarly known, had ceased work on this wall when he became worried that his patron, the Roman emperor Claudius, would construe this as a preparation for a revolt against Rome. In 2016, construction workers would make the first modern discovery of part of Agrippa's abandoned Third Wall foundations, involving a six-foot-wide wall and the base of a tower, in Jerusalem's present-day Russian Compound northwest of the Temple Mount.

Gallus's legionaries entered the streets of the New City in tight formation and with their long, rectangular, curved shields locked together. Partisans who attempted to stand in their way in narrow streets were confronted by what appeared to be an unstoppable machine advancing at a steady mechanical walk, and they soon gave way without offering resistance, retreating behind the city's Second Wall and closing the gates.

Gallus's troops now set fire to all the buildings in the New City and to Jerusalem's timber market, which was in this sector and would burn well, before withdrawing. As the New City blazed, instead of attacking the city walls, Governor Gallus sent legionaries around the western side of the city to build a new camp outside the wall in the Valley of Gihon, opposite the Palace of Herod.

"Had he only at this moment attempted get within the walls by force," wrote Josephus, who was in the city at this time, seeing the panic engendered by the Roman push into the New City among the hundreds of thousands of Jewish men, women, and children around him, "the war would have been terminated at once." But, on the verge of victory, Gallus had preferred the security of a new camp closer to the city rather than pressing home the advantage.[20]

As the day passed with nothing but building work in the Gihon Valley, one of the senior priests, Ananus bar Jonathon, persuaded leading moderate men of the city to secretly send envoys to the Roman commander extending an invitation to come into the city to conduct peace talks. Expecting Gallus to accept, they prepared to open the Valley Gate to him. But Gallus, ever cautious and fearful, and unaware of both the dissension within the ranks of the Jewish leadership and the widespread support in the city for a peace deal, suspected a trap and failed to take up the invitation. Once again Gallus let success slip through his fingers. Instead, he changed strategy and ordered preparations made for an assault on the Temple Mount to the north.

Meanwhile, Eleazar and his Zealots came to hear of this invitation to Gallus and angrily sought out Ananus and his peace party colleagues. Finding them on the wall awaiting the anticipated approach of Governor Gallus, they threw them from it and then rained stones down on them. Somehow, Ananus and his companions survived this, although probably with broken bones. Escaping to their homes, they barricaded themselves inside.

Having witnessed this dissension among the rebels, Gallus changed his mind yet again and gave a new order, to attack now from the west. This sent troops with scaling ladders against the First Wall opposite the Palace of Herod. With limited support from their remaining artillery pieces, legionaries went against the wall for five days, with the rebels fighting off each attack from the walls with spears, darts, and stones. When, by the fifth day of fighting, some Roman troops succeeded in coming over the wall, they were picked off by rebels using the dart-firing ballista artillery captured by Simon bar Giora, operating from the nearby towers of the Palace of Herod. Once again, the Roman assault was beaten off.

On the morning of the sixth day, Gallus called off this attack and shifted operations to the north, to the Second Wall at the Temple Mount, around the Sheep Gate, close to the Antonia Fortress. For this new assault, the Roman tactics were dramatically different. This time, Gallus employed all 5,500 of his allied archers, putting them behind the cover of the shells of burned-out houses. From there, they provided barrage after barrage of arrows to cover troops going against the wall. With rebels on the wall restricted by these clouds of arrows, this tactic succeeded in getting hundreds of legionaries close in under the wall.

As protection, these legionaries employed the famous Roman testudo, or tortoise formation—the men of the first rank held their shields at body height while those of the following ranks interlocked their shields overhead and at the flanks, creating a protective roof, like the shell of a tortoise. As the legionary testudo approached the wall along city streets, they were met by rebel missiles, which only glanced and bounced off the interlocked shields. Once the front-rank men were at the wall, while protected by the testudo created by their comrades, they lay aside their shields and set to work undermining the wall with their pickaxes. For generations, Roman military engineering had often held the secret to winning wars, and the Roman legionary's dolabra, or pickax, was, in the view of leading general Corbulo, "the weapon with which to beat the enemy."[21]

The legionary cohort that went against the wall had come prepared with lumber and fire-making material, which was inserted into the hole they dug beneath the wall and piled beside the gate. Seeing this, a number of Sicarii rebels, believing it only a matter of time before the Romans burned down the gate and burst in, fled out other gates and departed the city. Moderates regained hope of terminating the revolt and began talking of opening the Sheep Gate to Gallus and surrendering. But then Providence, and the weakness of Cestius Gallus, combined to save the day for the Jews.

Even as commanders on the spot reported it would only be a matter of time before they had the Sheep Gate alight, Gallus ordered all his troops to withdraw immediately—from the gate and from the city—to the camp on Mount Scopus. Gallus had been talked into this stunning retreat by a group of his own officers. While the 6th Ferrata Legion detachment had been briefly in Caesarea during the slow advance down the coast, the detachment's commander, Camp Prefect Tyrannius Priscus, had been corrupted by Procurator Florus. The procurator wanted Governor Gallus, his superior, to fail. If the Jews at Jerusalem were seen to foil Gallus's attempts to conquer Jerusalem and terminate their revolt, it would be Gallus, not Florus, who would be facing the wrath of the emperor Nero and recalled, and Florus's earlier provocation of the Jews would be forgotten. Or so Florus hoped.

Now, Florus's instrument, Camp Prefect Priscus, combined with cavalry prefect Jucundus, who was already in Florus's power. They brought in Prefect Aemilius Secundus and the prefects of the force's other cavalry wings, plus all their decurions—the Roman warrant officers who commanded cavalry troops—to petition Gallus to call off the assault and withdraw from Jerusalem to the coast.

In the city, Josephus, who watched the Roman withdrawal in astonishment, could not fathom the reason for it and would only much later learn of the key role Priscus and the cavalry prefects had in talking Gallus into pulling out. What grounds Priscus, Jucundus, and the other prefects and decurions had for convincing Gallus can only be speculated on. It was true that Roman armies traditionally ceased campaigning and went into winter camp in the middle of October every year, and that deadline had passed. Perhaps it was the threat posed by the weather that caused Gallus to lose heart. November rains were expected to lash Jerusalem. Winter snow was even a possibility in the coming weeks. Perhaps Priscus and his colleagues convinced Gallus that he risked being cut off and surrounded in enemy territory. The disgrace suffered by Roman general Paetus in Armenia just a few years before this, when he'd allowed his army to be surrounded and cut off, forcing him to surrender his base and retreat from the country, would have been fresh in Gallus's mind.

Many rebels, seeing the Roman army depart up the Damascus Road to Mount Scopus, gleefully gave pursuit, harassing the Roman rearguard and causing casualties to both infantry and cavalry. That night, Gallus kept his army behind the protective walls of the Mount Scopus camp. At dawn the next day, after just nine days at Jerusalem, the Roman force marched out of the camp, six men abreast and in close formation, heading north through the hills along the Damascus Road toward the village of Gaba and away from Jerusalem.

Sicarii rebels watching from the hills were hardly able to believe their luck. Emerging from their hiding places, they swarmed around the army as it marched north, attacking the column's rear and flooding along the slopes on both sides of the road, throwing darts at the marchers from both flanks. The helmeted legionaries had their shields on their left arms and their baggage poles on their right shoulders. To each pole were tied two stakes used on the top of their marching camp palisade, plus a javelin or two, their pickax, and other entrenching tools. From the poles hung each man's bedroll, a cooking pot, a sickle, a bag containing their personal items, military decorations, and helmet crest for parades.

Encumbered with all this equipment and under strict instructions from bellowing centurions to keep formation, totally prevented from firing back or launching counterattacks, all the Roman troops could do was keep step while trying to protect themselves with their shields as darts came flying from all directions. Legionaries were forever struggling to close ranks to fill gaps, conscious of the threat of agile, lightly armored Jews dashing in to exploit those gaps.

The rear of the Roman column suffered worst, with heavy casualties and a number of baggage animals abandoned. Mounted men, on their horses sitting above the column, presented especially juicy targets to Jewish dart throwers. Roman officers rode when on the march, and senior Roman officers, who didn't carry shields as a rule, were now particularly vulnerable. Camp Prefect Priscus, commander of the 6th Ferrata contingent, fell dead from his horse, impaled by darts. His mounted colleague Prefect Aemilius Secundus was also killed. Ironically, Priscus and Aemilius had led the call for Gallus to withdraw the army, and that withdrawal had led directly to their deaths. Another mounted senior Roman officer killed on this stretch of road to Gaba was Tribune Longinus, who commanded either the 4th Scythica or 10th Fretensis legionary contingent. The bodies of most of the fallen had to be abandoned where they fell, to be stripped and defiled by their killers.

Even worse, as far as the Romans were concerned, the 12th Fulminata Legion, apparently at the rear of the column, lost its golden eagle standard to Jews. Josephus wrote that the Jews were ever "ready for making incursions upon them," while, saying of the Roman troops, "their ranks were put in disorder, and those that were put out of their ranks were killed." The standard bearer of the 12th would have died trying to defend his eagle, as did the *primus pilus*, the chief centurion of the legion. To lose its eagle was the greatest disgrace to a legion, which would carry the stain of it forevermore.

In the space of a few miles, Gallus lost an eagle and three of his most senior officers. First-rank centurions stepped up to take the places of these officers, but the impact on the morale of their troops can only be imagined. Governor Gallus himself was in shock. Once the bloodied column reached the safety of the walls of the old marching camp at Gaba and took refuge there, Gallus refused to proceed any further. For two days he kept the army stationary. This only allowed thousands more partisans to arrive from Jerusalem to join the Sicarii in surrounding the camp.

Seeing the numbers of rebels growing by the hour, Gallus's remaining senior officers were able to convince the governor that they had to move on or risk being trapped here. Clearly, the baggage train was slowing the army, so Gallus ordered all baggage animals other than those carrying artillery to be slaughtered and their loads destroyed, to prevent everything falling into enemy hands. On the third morning since reaching the Gaba camp, the army resumed its march toward the Beth Horon Valley.

Where the army's route passed through flat country, rebels melted away. But where the road descended sharply five hundred feet into the valley, it passed through several narrow passes, so the rebels hurried ahead and lay in wait on the heights either side of each pass. When the column passed beneath them, the Jews rained missiles down on the Romans and their allies. Several times the column was halted as these passes became death traps. The dead piled up on the road, and wounded Roman troops wailed in pain and fear as their assailants above whooped with joy. Only with raised shields and more casualties was the army able to push on through.

Normally, a legion would march eighteen to twenty-one miles in a day, marching in the morning and building their overnight camp in the afternoon. Because of the delays in the passes, and despite having disposed of much of its baggage, Gallus's army only made feeble progress of a few miles on this day. By nightfall it had reached the two villages of Beth Horon, where the Romans built a marching camp that incorporated the village houses. The rank and file had to sleep under their blankets in the open, as their tents had been destroyed back at Gaba when there were no mules to carry them. As for the rebels, they retired to the surrounding hills to get a good night's sleep before resuming the attack the next morning.

That night, Cestius Gallus chaired a conference with his officers. All agreed that their situation was desperate. So, an assembly of the legionaries was called. Standing before his troops in the darkness, Gallus asked for volunteers to remain at this camp as a rearguard, to delay the enemy while the remainder of the army made its escape. It was clearly a suicide mission, but that didn't prevent volunteers stepping forward. Four hundred of the four legions' best men were chosen—probably one hundred from each legion represented in the column. Gallus then ordered the remainder of his men to lighten their personal loads of everything that would slow them down. The surviving mules carrying the artillery were also to be left behind; it was hoped this would delay booty-hunting rebels.

Gallus's units then drew lots for the order of march, and in the early hours of the morning all but the four-hundred-man rearguard slipped quietly from the camp and proceeded down the road in the darkness, with every man taking pains to avoid making any noise that could alert the rebels. As dawn broke over the valley, the army was close to four miles away from the Beth Horon camp and upping its pace in the increasing daylight. At the Beth Horon camp, the four hundred volunteers raised standards as usual and sounded the trumpet calls of the dawn change of watch, attempting to give the impression that the entire army was still in camp.

Watching from the hills where they had slept, the rebels saw into the camp and knew that something wasn't right. So, in their tens of thousands, they launched attacks on the camp from all sides and soon fought their way into it. The Roman legionary volunteers fought to the last man from the camp ramparts and the roofs of the village houses. But they were all soon overwhelmed by the rebels, who, realizing they had been tricked, gave chase to the escaping army along the Damascus Road.

The Jews pursued Gallus and his column almost all the way to Antipatris. But the Romans had too great a start and reached the town. Soon they would be down on the plain, where their cavalry, operating freely at last, would make mincemeat of Jewish foot soldiers. So, the rebels retraced their steps to Beth Horon, where they stripped the Roman dead and looted the camp of its artillery pieces, standards, and items jettisoned by the retreating army. They then returned to Jerusalem with their booty, running in through the city gates and singing elatedly.

As many Jews at Jerusalem dared to think that they had defeated almighty Rome and gained their freedom, Governor Gallus withdrew to Caesarea, where he returned to quarters the troops of the regular garrison that had participated in the hellish march to and from Jerusalem. To offer some semblance of Roman authority in Galilee, Gallus left Tribune Neapolitanus and his cavalry inland at Sepphoris for the time being, although, changeable as ever, he later withdrew them and left Sepphoris to fend for itself.

Meanwhile, King Herod Agrippa II dispatched a force to surround and besiege the partisan-held Galilean citadel at Gamala and control the surrounding countryside. This force was made up of some of his own infantry under Equiculus Modius, the king's longtime friend and companion, and a troop of Roman cavalry under a Decurion Ebutius. Modius's numbers would prove insufficient for the task, and after an unsuccessful siege of seven months, he and his force would also withdraw.

Departing Caesarea, Gallus then marched the balance of his army north up the coast to Ptolemais. There, he left Tribune Placidus with two cohorts of his humbled 12th Fulminata Legion and a troop of cavalry, with orders to hold the walled port city against rebel attack. Gallus then proceeded all the way back up the coast to Antioch, taking his legions with him. En route, King Herod Agrippa II and his troops departed Gallus's column at Beirut, where the king's sister Berenice had awaited his return and where Agrippa set up temporary headquarters. Beirut had a predominantly Roman character, with a number of its residents being the grandchildren of veterans of the 5th Macedonica and 8th Augusta Legions who had retired to Beirut in the reign of Augustus.

Gallus arrived back at the governor's palace at Antioch around the end of November. He would, at some point, have to glumly dictate a report to a secretary informing the emperor Nero that he had failed him. It was an admission that was likely to cost him his career. During his disastrous expedition into Judea and Galilee, Gallus had lost 5,300 foot soldiers, 380 cavalrymen, and the eagle of one of Rome's legions, all for nothing—Jerusalem and much of Judea and Galilee were now firmly in the hands of Jewish rebels.[22]

But for now, Gallus, in shock, did nothing. He knew that it would take a week or ten days for his report to reach Nero by sea, putting it in the young emperor's hands just as he was preparing to celebrate his birthday on December 15. Perhaps Gallus told himself that such bad news on this occasion would only make Nero even more irascible and arbitrary than normal. Perhaps the governor used the excuse that, as the Mediterranean sailing season had ended in October, he could not safely send a ship carrying the ill tidings across the stormy sea. That same termination of the sailing season saw the Mediterranean merchant fleets tied up in port until March, meaning word could not reach Nero of Gallus's failure via a gossipy captain or passenger of a cargo vessel until the spring.

Gallus could send his report overland via the horse-drawn carriages of the official Roman government courier service, the *Cursus Publicus Velox*—literally, the state's very fast way. That could take weeks, meaning the report might not reach the emperor until the new year. But, dreading what Tacitus describes as Nero's "savage temper," Gallus could not bring himself to confess his failure. Apparently hoping that some miraculous event would intercede to save him, he put off the inevitable and kept news of his disastrous expedition from his emperor.[23]

VI

LIKE A VOICE FROM THE GRAVE

Despite Governor Gallus's reluctance to inform his emperor of what had happened, news of the Roman retreat from Judea soon spread throughout the Middle East. The city of Damascus in the south of the province of Syria had a large Jewish minority of some ten thousand people among its population, but prior to this, the Gentile anger against Jews that had seen the wholesale slaughter of Jewish people in Judea, Galilee, Egypt, and other Syrian cities had not manifested itself in Damascus.

To enable the Roman authorities to keep an eye on them, the Jewish population of the city had been forced from their homes and concentrated in the open gymnasiums of Damascus, where the locals normally did their daily exercise, but otherwise they had been left unmolested. Word of Governor Gallus's disastrous expedition changed that. In a rage for revenge for the loss of Roman troops and in particular the loss of Syrian-born legionaries, a number of whom would have had family and friends in Damascus, the Hellenic population of Damascus rose up against their Jewish neighbors, and in just an hour they rampaged through the gymnasiums and cut the throats of all ten thousand Jewish men, women, and children.

In Jerusalem, while extremists crowed that the Romans had been ejected from Jerusalem for good, moderates among the leading priests warned the people that the Romans would be back, and they must prepare for that day throughout the region. Two moderates, Joseph ben Gorion and Ananus, the former high priest, were popularly elected to head a new governing council in Jerusalem. This council organized stonemasons and work parties to resume construction of the Third Wall on the city's northern perimeter, construction that been terminated more than twenty years earlier. The priest Josephus watched as a spirit of preparedness for an eventual return of the Roman army swept throughout the city, and young men now every morning undertook physical exercise in the open spaces of the city—they did it individually, not as a group, Josephus observed. He also heard the sound of hammer on anvil ringing throughout Jerusalem as men bent their backs to fashioning weapons, ammunition, and armor without being asked or told to do so.

The governing council also appointed generals to take charge of partisan efforts in different regions. Joseph and Ananus took care to appoint fellow moderates to these posts, keeping power out of the hands of men who had lately shone in the defeat of the Romans but who were not of the priestly class. John the Essene, a priest of the Jewish Essene cult, was sent to take command in Thamna, Lod, Joppa, and Emmaus. Joseph bar Simon was sent to Jericho. John bar Matthias was given command in the Acrabatene and Gophnitica toparchies. To control partisan affairs in all of Galilee, the governors appointed Josephus, giving him a pair of priestly subordinates.

Josephus strapped on a bronze cuirass—the type of molded upper body armor worn by Roman officers—and slung a belt containing a sword over his shoulder. Then, leaving his wife; mother; father, Matthias Sr.; and elder brother, Matthias Jr., at the family home in Jerusalem, Josephus hurried to Gamala, the strongest city in Jewish hands in his districts of Upper and Lower Galilee. From there he sent out a call for partisan volunteers for an army he intended to train along Roman lines.

Josephus had never served with the Roman army, but he had witnessed the comings and goings of Roman cohorts while growing up in Jerusalem and had a rudimentary knowledge of their structure. When he'd journeyed to Rome in AD 64 to advocate the freedom of Jewish prisoners, he had seen close up the City Guard's freedmen soldiers, the haughty bearded imperial guardsmen of the German Guard, and Rome's feared military policemen, the Praetorian Guard. On that trip, he had won an audience with the empress Poppaea Sabina through a Jewish actor friend who was one of her favorites. Not only had Josephus obtained the freedom of the Jewish prisoners via the influence of the empress, he had come back impressed by the military might he had seen.

Tens of thousands of Jewish men answered Josephus's call. Choosing sixty thousand of the youngest and fittest as foot soldiers, he appointed six hundred of them to be his personal bodyguard. He put 240 others on the few horses he could acquire—the donkey being the most common mode of transport in Judea. Josephus divided his recruits into infantry units of ten, one hundred, and one thousand. Appointing officers over them, arming them with weapons accumulated in the revolt so far, he began training them to emulate the Roman legions by marching in formation and responding to orders conveyed by trumpet calls.

To lead partisan forces in Idumea, the Jerusalem governors appointed Jesus bar Sapphias, one of the members of the Great Sanhedrin, and Eleazar bar Ananias, chief of the Zealots and son of the former High Priest Ananias, who had been killed by Menahem and his Sicarii. The appointment of Zealot leader Eleazar seems to have been designed to get him away from the seat of power. Niger of Perea, governor of Idumea, was meanwhile instructed to follow the orders of Jesus and Eleazar.

While some of these appointees, such as Josephus, assiduously went about their appointed tasks, petty jealousies caused others to decide to do their own thing. The Samaritan peasant leader Simon bar Giora, who'd made a name for himself capturing Roman artillery in the Beth Horon Valley, returned to his native territory and with a band of armed peasants ravaged the Acrabbene toparchy on the border of Samaria and Judea, raiding outlying farm villas and villages and torturing his victims.

When the rebel leadership at Jerusalem sent forces to counter this banditry, Simon and his men escaped south to the fortress at Masada. There, young Sicarii commander Eleazar ben Ya'ir gave them sanctuary. Since taking the fortress, Ben Ya'ir and his men had raided the oasis town of Ein Gedi, north of Masada. Apart from its Jewish residents, this town housed seven hundred women and children who were apparently the de facto wives and illegitimate children of the Syrian troops of the 3rd Gallica cohort that the Sicarii had wiped out on taking Masada. Separating these women and children from the Jewish men of the town, Ben Ya'ir and his men had mercilessly massacred the lot because of their connection to the Roman army.

Meanwhile, the former governor of Idumea, Niger of Perea, angry that others had been appointed over him, decided to take back control of Idumea for himself. He allied with Silas the Babylonian, who'd also been overlooked when the rebel commands were handed out, and John the Essene, who was apparently then based at Joppa on the Mediterranean coast. This trio independently put together an army to take over Idumea, starting with the Idumean coastal city of Ascalon, south of Joppa, which remained in the hands of a small Roman garrison.

At the time, Ascalon had a population of some fifteen thousand people, mostly Gentiles. Herod the Great had built public baths and fine colonnaded public areas in the city at his own expense, even though the thriving little metropolis was more Greco-Roman than Jewish. In the twentieth century, archaeologists would uncover examples of the statuary that adorned the city forum during this period—statues of Apollo, a war god, and Victoria, the Roman goddess of victory, both of whom had been favored deities of Rome's first emperor Augustus, as well as a statue of Pax, goddess of peace, with an olive branch in her hand. She was a favored deity of Vespasian.[24]

Ascalon was important to the Romans because this ancient Canaanite and Philistine port was a safe haven for the fleets of vital cargo ships carrying grain from Egypt to Italy every spring and summer. Those ships "coasted" from Alexandria to Italy's ports, following the Mediterranean coastline all the way, and should a storm brew, they sought the safety of the nearest port. Ascalon was conveniently located between Egypt and Syria on this route. The city's importance to Rome was such that when, in 6 BC, Judea became a Roman sub-province answerable to the proconsul of Syria, Ascalon separately reported to the proconsul in Antioch, not to Rome's Judean procurator in Caesarea.

The rebels had a double interest in Ascalon. It offered rich pickings in terms of arms and booty and was the last Roman-occupied city south of Caesarea. So, the three go-it-alone partisan leaders put together a force of twenty thousand of "the most hardy" rebels, then marched on the city at the double.[25]

Ascalon was well protected against attack. The high, thick city wall curved inland from the coast in a half-moon shape that eliminated corners. At the seafront, the city sat on a high precipice, with a ramp ascending the cliff face from the dock to a single seaward entry gate.

The city's six-hundred-man Roman garrison was made up of 480 Syrians of a cohort of the 3rd Gallica Legion and a squadron of auxiliary cavalry, which Josephus tells us were mounted archers—Syria provided the Roman army with several wings of mounted archers, who were armed with a powerful and accurate composite bow as well as the standard cavalry broadsword.

In charge of the Ascalon garrison was the 3rd Gallica cohort's Centurion Antonius. We know little about him other than the fact he possessed fine military strategic skills, which he was about to demonstrate. The centurion would have been on high alert for weeks ever since receiving news of the fate of the Jerusalem and Masada garrisons, and although the partisan force that descended on Ascalon moved rapidly across the coastal plain, he was ready for it, closing the city's narrow gates. Leaving his legionaries stationed around the curve of the city walls, Antonius took his cavalrymen out and lined them up before the city as the attackers advanced from the northeast.

Excitedly, the thousands of partisans swarmed up to the waiting Roman cavalry, which stood its ground, then charged. Soon, the Jews were being driven back by Antonius's sword-wielding riders. Leading from the front, two of the rebel leaders, Silas the Babylonian—the only rebel with any military experience—and John the Essene were both quickly cut down. Panic then set in among their leaderless men. Rebels at the front turned and tried to flee in panic, trampling comrades who were pressing up from behind.

Throwing away their weapons, rebels ran in all directions. On the flat plain, there was nowhere to hide. Roman cavalrymen chased down fleeing partisans and herded them back to the city as prisoners. There, the Jews were stripped and then run through by the swords of Antonius's legionaries. Out on the plain, other cavalrymen hunted down and bunched together terrified partisans, then "killed them easily with their arrows," according to Josephus.[26]

The slaughter lasted until nightfall, when the Romans' arms ached from all the killing and they could lift them no longer. Josephus says that ten thousand Jews were killed by Antonius and his few hundred men that day, while the Romans suffered nothing more than several wounded. The surviving Jewish commander, Niger of Perea, led wounded survivors to an Idumean village called Sallis in the foothills of the Judean Mountains— identified by some scholars as the village of Kefar Shihlayim—where they took refuge as Antonius and his cavalry withdrew.

Niger and his rebels spent some days recovering before Niger sent out a call for reinforcements. When thousands of fresh fighters arrived, he led them back toward Ascalon. Centurion Antonius had been expecting this and lay in wait for the rebels with both infantry and cavalry, ambushing Niger's force as they came though several narrow hill passes. Rebels who escaped this ambush onto the plain were mown down by the waiting Roman cavalry. A further eight thousand Jewish partisans were killed in these engagements.

Niger and a few of his men escaped to a village Josephus calls Bezedeh, which is likely to have been today's Beit Guvrin, due east of Ascalon and seven miles further inland from Kefar Shihlayim. Beit Guvrin is renowned for its caves, and in the second century it would become the Roman military base of Eleutheropolis. Here, Niger and his companions took refuge in a town watchtower, which was apparently made of wood.

The Romans pursued these last rebels, and, surrounding the Bezedeh tower, Antonius and his men set fire to it. As the tower burned furiously, the Roman troops withdrew, expecting no one to survive the inferno. They returned to Ascalon, unaware that there was a network of caves beneath the tower. Three days later, relatives sifting through the burned-out tower wreckage looking for Niger's body to give it a decent burial heard Niger calling for help from beneath the ground—like a voice from the grave. Niger, the sole survivor of his rebel force, had escaped into a cave beneath the tower and survived the fire, only to be trapped beneath the wreckage. Amid cries that Niger's preservation was a miracle and he had been chosen by God to lead his people, he was hauled out.

This ended rebel efforts to take Ascalon from its Roman garrison. The city would remain in Roman hands for the remainder of the revolt. But the disastrous campaign to take Ascalon was not the end of Niger's career as an influential rebel commander. Jerusalem would before long feel the heat of his passion for power.

VII

ENTER VESPASIAN
AND TITUS

One day in February, AD 67, a middle-aged Roman general was receiving his regular morning back and neck massage in the bathhouse of a rented seaside villa. His name was Titus Flavius Vespasianus. For convenience's sake, modern historians would shorten his name to Vespasian. This particular morning, Vespasian lay on a massage bench in an out-of-the-way town on an island in the Aegean Sea.[27]

As friends and members of his staff listened with worried frowns, Vespasian's secretary read him a short letter from the emperor Nero, summoning him to an urgent meeting at the Greek city of Corinth, where the emperor had based himself for the past few months. Should Vespasian go to Nero? Vespasian knew that his colleague, the renowned general Domitius Corbulo, brother-in-law of the late emperor Gaius also known as Caligula, had similarly received a summons from Nero recently. And as Vespasian knew, that summons had led to Corbulo's death.

When Corbulo stepped ashore from a fast warship at Cenchreae, the port of Corinth, he'd been met by senior freedmen on Nero's staff, who had given him a blunt option—take his own life or face execution as a traitor. His daughter Domitia's husband, Lucius Annius Vinicianus, had just committed suicide at Rome on the emperor's orders, after being discovered plotting against Nero.

Although no evidence linked Corbulo with his son-in-law's treasonous plot, Nero considered him guilty by association. The emperor had long harbored fears about the loyalty of his best general. Eight years earlier, when Centurion Arrius Varus, now chief centurion of the 3rd Gallica Legion, had carried messages to Rome from Corbulo while leading a vexillation of 3rd Gallica cohorts campaigning in Armenia with the general, Centurion Varus had whispered in Nero's ear that Corbulo privately spoke in unflattering terms about his emperor. Nero had promoted Varus and filed his information away in the back of his mind. Now, the paranoia engendered in Nero by a plot against his life the previous year, led by a senator named Piso, caused him to eliminate all potential threats, even though his late chief secretary, Seneca, had once warned him that a man can never eliminate his successor—because there will always be one.

If Corbulo had insisted on his innocence and subsequently been condemned and executed, his estate would have been forfeited to the emperor, leaving his wife and family destitute. If he took his own life, his estate and his family would be preserved. So, Corbulo drew his sword, and crying "Axios!"—which meant "I am worthy (of such a noble death)!"—he literally fell on his sword, dramatically taking his own life.[28]

Did Nero also suspect Vespasian of complicity in this plot? Vespasian was on good terms with Corbulo's well-connected family, as he would demonstrate by marrying his son Domitian to Corbulo's youngest daughter Domitia Longina in AD 70. Thoughtfully now, and wearing his habitual dour expression, Vespasian sat up, put on his shoes, then came to his feet and dressed himself without the help of servants, as was his habit. He was of moderate height, solidly built, with a paunch and the hint of a double chin. Round-faced, he was balding, with his remaining hair silvering. Born near Reate in Latium, central western Italy, in AD 9 (the same year as the massacre of Varus's legions in Germany), he was the son of a tax collector and banker, and grandson of a centurion in the senatorial forces of Roman general Pompey the Great that had been defeated by the rebel senator Julius Caesar. "They were admittedly an obscure family," says Vespasian's Roman biographer, Suetonius, "none of whose members had enjoyed high office."[29]

Vespasian's elder brother Flavius Sabinus had been the first member of the Flavian family to enter the Senate. Sabinus had gone on to command a legion in the reign of Claudius, after which Nero had appointed him to the powerful post of city prefect at Rome, making him the capital's combined police and fire chief. Sabinus still held that very post at this moment. Surely Sabinus would have alerted his brother if he'd heard anything that suggested Vespasian was likely to share Corbulo's fate? Vespasian and Sabinus were close. When proconsul of the province of Africa three years back, Vespasian had fallen into debt, and Sabinus had bailed him out, taking mortgages on Vespasian's properties.

When Vespasian had arrived in Greece in the emperor's vast entourage the previous October, he'd been high in Nero's favor. Nero had come to Greece intending to stay a year and compete in all four classical Greek games, including the Olympic Games, changing the dates of several of the competitions (which were normally staged two years apart) so that he could do all four in twelve months. Nero considered himself an expert driver of racing chariots and an accomplished actor, singer, and lyre player. The Roman elite secretly ridiculed him when he competed in public competitions, and the much later myth that Nero fiddled while Rome burned in the AD 64 Great Fire of Rome grew from this criticism. He had in fact been competing in a singing contest on the west coast of Italy when that fire broke out, and had hurried back to Rome to supervise firefighting efforts.

Nero, who became emperor at the age of sixteen, had progressively seen the deaths of the three figures who'd restrained him from indulging his passions for racing and the stage. First, he'd had his manipulative mother, Agrippina the Younger, murdered in AD 59. In AD 62, Burrus, his prefect of the Praetorian Guard, had died from throat cancer. Burrus's colleague Seneca, who had served as Nero's tutor and then chief secretary, had retired following Burrus's death, but in AD 65 he'd been implicated in the Piso Plot, as a result of which the emperor had forced Seneca and numerous others to commit suicide.

The removal of this trio had left Nero free to play, and, says Cassius Dio, he came to Greece intent on being crowned "Victor of the Grand Tour," the title bestowed on the winners of consecutive Olympic, Pythian, Isthmian, and Nemean Games, much as the winners of consecutive US, Wimbledon, French, and Australian tennis championships today are said to win the Grand Slam.[30]

Just the same, Nero was not as blind to his public image as his uncle Caligula, who had also endeavored to be a chariot racing and theatrical star, in the process alienating his senior military officers. Caligula's bookish successor, the emperor Claudius, had seen the need to impress his legions with martial success and had gone forward with the invasion of Britain that Caligula had previously toyed with. As it happened, Vespasian and his brother Sabinus had commanded two of the four legions that undertook that AD 43 British invasion. In emulation of Claudius's military success, following his Grand Tour of AD 66–67, Nero intended to launch not one but two conquering military campaigns to give him a macho reputation as a soldier.

According to Roman writers Tacitus and Cassius Dio, one of Nero's campaigns was to be a push to the Caspian Gates, also known as the Wall of Alexander and traditionally said to be iron gates built by Alexander the Great to keep out barbarian tribes from the Russian Steppes. Several locations have been suggested for these otherwise unidentified gates, including a pass between Russia and Georgia on the Caspian Sea, and south of the Caspian, not far from Armenia.

Like his mentally unstable uncle Caligula, Nero was clearly intending to emulate Alexander the Great—Caligula had worn Alexander's armor, retrieved from his mausoleum in Alexandria. For his Caspian Gates mission, Nero created a new military unit, grandiosely calling it the Phalanx of Alexander the Great. With a minimum height of six feet, its exclusively Italian recruits were armed as Greek hoplites, with twelve-foot-long spears. This five-thousand-member "phalanx" raised in Italy in the second half of AD 66, was the first military unit composed of Roman citizens, apart from the Praetorian Guard, recruited in Italy south of the Po River in the imperial period since the reign of the emperor Augustus. Within two years it would be renamed the 1st Italica Legion (1st Italian Legion), and be equipped in the traditional legion fashion.[31]

In preparation for the Caspian Gates operation, an existing legion, the 14th Gemina Martia Victrix, had been transferred from Britain to Carnuntum on the Danube in AD 66. The Phalanx of Alexander the Great was due to join it in the spring of AD 67 for a summer campaign. With Corbulo's reputation as a crack general and his experience in Armenia, close to the Caspian, it would have been logical to have expected him to be put in command of the Caspian Gates operation, and he probably went to Greece hoping this appointment was the reason for the emperor's summons.

Nero's second military campaign was to be the previously mentioned push south from Egypt into Ethiopia. Vespasian was a leading contender for command of this operation. His military credentials were strong. After he'd served as a military tribune in Thrace in the early AD 30s, in AD 41, through the influence of Narcissus, the emperor Claudius's secretary of correspondence, Vespasian was appointed a legate and given command of the 2nd Augusta Legion on the Rhine, which he'd subsequently led in the AD 43 invasion of Britain.

During this period Narcissus had even arranged for Vespasian's son Titus to be schooled alongside the imperial children at the Palatium, the emperor's palace on the Palatine Hill at Rome. Titus had become the best friend of Claudius's son Britannicus; he'd even been right beside Britannicus the night the prince was poisoned at dinner in a plot by Nero's mother, Agrippina the Younger. That assassination had made Nero heir to Claudius's throne.

In the invasion of Britain, Vespasian had commanded his legion with distinction, fighting thirty battles in today's southern England and capturing twenty British towns and the Isle of Wight as he pushed all the way to Cornwall. He and his brother Sabinus had both been awarded Triumphal Decorations by Nero for the British campaign, the highest military award a Roman general other than a member of the royal family could then attain.

After a consulship in AD 51, Vespasian had lost his influential friend Narcissus in AD 54 when Agrippina engineered the correspondence secretary's death. Without friends in high places, and careful not to antagonize Agrippina, Vespasian had thereafter kept a low profile while she still lived. Once before, he'd incurred the wrath of the imperial family, and he had no intention of repeating his mistake. That had been during the earlier reign of Caligula, when serving as Aedile of the Alleys, a city official responsible for keeping Rome's alleys clean, which Vespasian failed to do. After being humiliated by the emperor for his failure, he had worked hard to regain Caligula's favor, and as a novice senator in January of AD 40 had made a sycophantic speech in the Senate in support of the wayward young emperor, going on to boast that Caligula had invited him to dinner at the imperial palace prior to setting out on an AD 39–40 tour of Gaul.

During Caligula's reign, too, Vespasian had cultivated the friendship of Praetorian Prefect Clemens, later marrying his boy Titus to Clemens's daughter, Arrecina Turtulla. Vespasian only made a career comeback once Agrippina was dead and Burrus and Seneca were out of power with appointment as governor of the province of Africa in AD 63, a post that covered today's Tunisia and Algeria. He'd been in Nero's favor ever since and, as a feted general and one of a handful of ex consuls in the emperor's Greek touring party, was justified in anticipating appointment to command Nero's planned invasion of Ethiopia.

The Ethiopian operation was due to be launched in the fall of AD 67. This timing was to allow the march south along the Nile to take place after the crushing heat of summer. That same heat had defeated previous attempts to conquer the region that went all the way back to the sixth century BC and Cambyses II, son and successor of the creator of the Persian Empire, Cyrus the Great. It was also designed to permit Nero to base himself in Alexandria to "oversee" the operation once he had completed his Greek Grand Tour.

Although not yet explicitly offered to him by Nero, Vespasian seems to have prepared for the Ethiopian command, for he brought along on the tour a personal party that included his eldest son, Titus, and a number of clients who might take up posts in his command team. It seems likely that the three legions earmarked for the invasion of Ethiopia were intended to remain there as the Roman garrison of the conquered territory, with the operation's commander serving as governor of the new province of Ethiopia, as had been the case with the invasion of Britain.

But several months into the Greek tour, Vespasian had blotted his copybook with the emperor and been banished from his presence. Vespasian was an earthy man. He ate and dressed conservatively and was not a fan of the theater. All the members of the emperor's touring party were expected to attend when Nero gave speeches and appeared at the hippodrome or in the theater, and in October–November Vespasian had sat on the terraces at Olympia with the others of the imperial entourage along with excited, starstruck locals when the emperor predictably won the Olympic Games chariot race and the Games' contests for singing, tragic acting, and heralding.

He'd been present, too, when Nero had given a speech on November 29 at Corinth, a Roman military colony since the days of Julius Caesar, and declared that he wished to reward all Greece for its goodwill and piety toward him by liberating the Greek provinces from the obligation of paying taxes to Rome in the future. Overnight, a not insignificant portion of the Roman treasury's income was eliminated by Nero's desire to please the

Greek populace with this blanket tax immunity. The Greeks adored him for it, with their cities sending him pledges of undying loyalty and calling him Zeus the liberator.

Vespasian did not approve of this imperial generosity. His own checkered record with personal finances had seen him become extremely careful with money. As his financial fortunes were restored he'd invested in mule farms, which held contracts to supply the Roman army and were a license to mint money. As governor of Africa he'd resisted the temptation to make money via corruption, a temptation to which many in his position yielded. He returned to Rome from Africa no richer than when he left, according to Suetonius, who knew Vespasian from a distance as a child and later had access to the imperial archives, which included Vespasian's later lost memoirs, *Commentaries of Vespasian*. Vespasian had become such a miser when it came to the public purse in Africa that he'd been pelted with turnips in one African city after imposing a new local tax.

Vespasian may have winced on hearing the announcement of Nero's tax relief for the Greeks, but he said nothing. He knew better. But then, in December, while in the audience for one of Nero's musical performances, the bored Vespasian had fallen asleep. His son Titus had probably nudged him awake, with both men sighing with relief when the emperor seemed not to have noticed.

Alas, early the next morning, when Vespasian went to pay his respects to Nero, as he and the other members of the imperial party did every day, he was barred from entering the audience chamber by Phoebus, the imperial freedman who served as doorkeeper to the emperor. Phoebus told Vespasian to go away, as the emperor did not wish to see his face. Clearly, someone on Nero's staff had seen Vespasian nod off.

"But, what shall I do?" Vespasian asked. "Where on earth shall I go?"

"Oh, go to Morbia!" responded Phoebus with a shrug. There was no such place as Morbia. This was Phoebus's sarcastic little joke. Morbius was the Latin word for distress and illness. It was a joke that would rebound on Phoebus three years after this, as will later be related.[32]

Hoping to be recalled by Nero, and leaving his son Titus with the imperial retinue to continue to pay daily obeisance to the emperor, Vespasian had gone to the villa at the out-of-the-way town and waited for weeks. Now, the call had come. But was it a call to service, or a call to his death?

With his son Titus a veritable hostage at court, Vespasian had no choice but to take a ship back to Achaea to answer the emperor's call.

As Vespasian would later tell Josephus the historian, Nero received him graciously, as if there had never been a falling out between them. For the emperor was at last aware of the disastrous fate of Cestius Gallus's punitive Judean operation. The information had come to him via the agency of King Herod Agrippa II. Two leading Jewish priests, the brothers Saul and Costobarus, had slipped out of Jerusalem in the wake of Gallus's retreat and gone to the king at Beirut. The king had recently welcomed his cavalry commander Philip bar Jacimus back into his fold after retrieving him from Gamala, where he'd been hiding under the noses of the rebels since his escape in disguise from Jerusalem. So, Agrippa had sent Philip, Saul, and Costobarus to Cestius Gallus at Antioch, where they offered to go to Nero in Achaea and tell him that the revolt in Judea was all Procurator Florus's fault.[33]

Grabbing this opportunity to absolve himself of blame for the Judean calamity, Gallus had sent the king's delegation to the emperor along with a member of his own staff who carried his report of the operation, a report which stressed the deficiencies of Florus and the insane courage of the rebellious Jews who had dealt the Roman army such a bloody defeat. Nero had not been fooled. Or at least his chief advisers had not been fooled. By the time that Vespasian came to this meeting, the emperor was fully aware of the cause of the predicament that now prevailed in Judea.

"What has happened was rather due to the negligence of the commander than to the valor of the enemy!" twenty-nine-year-old Nero angrily declared as he paced back and forth in front of Vespasian. "Well, I, who bear the burden of the Empire, despise such misfortunes," he added, trying to appear nonchalant about the affair.[34]

Vespasian would tell Josephus that he could see beyond the pompous facade of the tall, thin, young Caesar that day. He could see that, while he wanted to appear the big man and stand above such petty annoyances, Nero had been shaken by the news from Judea. Gallus's inglorious and costly Judean retreat had exceeded Paetus's disastrous Armenian expedition in its ineptitude. It rivaled Varus's defeat at the hands of the Germans in AD 9 in terms of the loss in Roman military numbers and prestige. Beneath the emperor's puffed-up exterior, says Josephus, Vespasian saw consternation and fear.

"I've been deliberating as to whom I should commit the care of the East," the emperor went on, "and who might punish the Jews for their rebellion, and might prevent the same sickness from also seizing upon the neighboring nations." Now, Nero must have broached a smile. "I have found no one but you, Vespasianus, equal to the task, and able to undergo the burden of so mighty a war."[35]

And so the general was able to inwardly sigh with relief and listen in respectful silence as Nero rattled off Vespasian's military record, as if he knew it by heart, and lavished him with "great praises and flattering compliments," according to Josephus. The same source tells us the emperor did remark that, although the fifty-seven-year-old Vespasian was now "growing to be an old man in the [military] camp," his life ever since his youth had been filled with military success, right up to the British campaign, via which Vespasian had allowed the emperor Claudius, Nero's late uncle and adoptive father whom Nero despised, "to have a Triumph bestowed on him without any sweat or labor of his own," in Nero's words.

Nero spoke as if he felt the need to talk Vespasian into accepting the appointment, as if the incident with Phoebus might incline Vespasian to turn down the proffered post of Roman commander in chief in the East. But Vespasian knew the Judean opportunity could remake his reputation and his fortunes. More importantly, Vespasian was to tell Josephus, he knew that Nero "had his sons as hostages for his faithfulness"—apart from Titus, who was here in Achaea with him, his youngest son, the fifteen-year-old Domitian, was being schooled back at Rome, in the care of Vespasian's brother Sabinus but within easy reach of Nero's chief freedman, Helius, who had been left in charge at Rome with all the emperor's powers over life and death.

There was also the matter of Vespasian's mistress, Antonia Caenis. She had been the young freedwoman secretary of Antonia the Younger, daughter of Mark Antony and mother of Claudius and his famous soldier brother Germanicus. In AD 31, when Vespasian was twenty-one, Caenis had carried a secret message from Antonia at Rome to the emperor Tiberius on the Isle of Capri, a message that revealed Tiberius's Praetorian Prefect Sejanus was plotting against him. That warning had resulted in Sejanus's execution. Vespasian had commenced his affair with Caenis when a young man but had ended it when he married Flavia Domitilla the Elder around AD 36. After the death of Domitilla sometime in AD 50s, Vespasian had resumed the relationship with Caenis, and he now kept her in her own villa on the Via Nomentana in the northeastern outskirts of Rome. Vespasian never married Caenis, but he dearly loved her, as all Rome knew. She would remain his devoted mistress until the day she died. Vespasian would have appreciated that, like his sons, Caenis, far away in Rome, was also a hostage to Nero.

So it was that, for a variety of reasons, Vespasian accepted the job of putting down the Jewish Revolt in Judea. Nero had no interest in military affairs. Considering himself an athlete and an aesthete, following his meeting with Vespasian he would have gone off to drive a chariot, to rehearse a song with his homosexual lover, Sporus, or to have a theatrical costume fitting with his wardrobe mistress, Calvia Crispinilla.

To discuss the military details of his mission, Vespasian would have had a detailed briefing meeting with one of Nero's two Praetorian prefects, Gaius Ofinius Tigellinus. In effect the emperor's defense secretary, Tigellinus was heading up the military branch of the Palatium staff traveling with the emperor. Tigellinus, who was roughly the same age as Vespasian, had succeeded Burrus as prefect of the Praetorian Guard in AD 62 after serving as prefect of the Cohortes Vigilus, Rome's seven-cohort Night Watch, whose former slaves stood duty through the night hours as both a nocturnal police force and fire brigade. Tigellinus gained his first important post through the influence of Agrippina the Younger. His freedwoman mother had served in the house of Antonia the Younger, where Antonia's granddaughters, Agrippina and her sisters, the daughters of Germanicus, had grown up. Tigellinus had even been sent into exile for a time after being accused of sexual relations with Agrippina. Despite a far from glorious military track record, Tigellinus nonetheless had a reasonable grasp of strategy.

Vespasian began his new appointment by making his son Titus his deputy for the Judean operation. Titus, the same age as the emperor but possessing the military skills and experience that Nero lacked after serving as an active and efficient tribune and prefect with legions and auxiliary units on the Rhine and in Britain, looked much like his father—round-faced, muscular, with a tendency to paunchiness. But he was also handsome—some say even cherubic—could sing well, and could play the harp. Titus was a fine horseman and skilled with sword and javelin. He was deadly accurate with a bow, an unusual skill for a Roman gentleman. And, says

Suetonius, Titus had a phenomenal memory. He had mastered Roman shorthand and claimed he could imitate any handwriting, joking that, if all else failed, he could become the most celebrated forger in existence. After his military service, Titus had worked as a lawyer at Rome and had just served an annual term as a quaestor, a junior Roman magistrate, when his father included him in his party for the Greek tour.[36]

With Titus at his side, Vespasian ironed out the military details of the Judean mission with Tigellinus. To allow Vespasian to be commander in chief in the East, Nero invested him with imperium, equaling the emperor's powers. This gave him authority over all other Roman generals and governors and gave him the right to march Roman troops over provincial borders, which no general or governor was ordinarily permitted to do under pain of being declared an enemy of the state by the Senate, as Julius Caesar had been in 49 BC.

Vespasian's plan was to begin by quashing all opposition in Galilee and Samaria, isolating Jerusalem, before setting out to conquer the city. Tigellinus told Vespasian that he could use the legions already stationed in Syria as he saw fit, but after their thrashing under Gallus, Vespasian demanded fresh blood. The two legions and supporting auxiliary units that had been assigned to Egypt for Nero's Ethiopian operation were ideal. Clearly, Nero must be informed that that Ethiopian operation had to be suspended, at the very least until Judea was firmly back in Roman hands.

The 15th Apollinaris Legion was already in Alexandria for the Ethiopian expedition, and as Vespasian and Tigellinus were speaking, the 5th Macedonica Legion was en route there. Vespasian wanted both these legions, which had relatively fresh enlistments, were up to strength, and possessed strong reputations. Josephus referred to the 5th Macedonica as one of Rome's most esteemed legions. Its fame went back to its defeat of the war elephants of Julius Caesar's senatorial opponents at the 47 BC Battle of Thapsus in North Africa. Ever since, the legion had carried the elephant emblem on its shields. The 5th Macedonica had earned its title from a victory won while serving in Macedonia between 30 BC and AD 6. More recently, in the early AD 60s, the legion had undergone its twenty-year discharge and enlistment of new recruits at its then station in Moesia on the Danube. All its new recruits had been from Moesia, and as a result its men were frequently referred to by their legionary colleagues as the Moesians, and the unit itself as the Moesian Legion.

Vespasian was told he could have both these legions, but in exchange the Palatium wanted the six cohorts of the 3rd Gallica Legion currently garrisoning Caesarea for service on the Danube. Ever since the 5th Macedonica had been transferred from Moesia to Pontus, the Germanic and Sarmatian tribes beyond the Danube, which formed the province's northern border, had been restive. The Syrians of the 3rd Gallica, stung by their losses to the Jews, would be given the opportunity to show their mettle in Moesia as they filled a gap in Rome's defenses there.[37]

This transfer of the 3rd Gallica to Moesia would be facilitated by a piece of logistical coincidence. Everything points to Rome's new Pontic Fleet, formed in AD 64, conveying the 5th Macedonica by sea from its base at Trapezus on the Black Sea to Alexandria at the very moment Vespasian, at Corinth, was discussing troop dispositions for his Judean campaign. On its return to the Black Sea, the forty-ship fleet would be calling at Caesarea. There, it could collect the three thousand men of the six 3rd Gallica cohorts and transport them to the western side of the Black Sea, from where they could march to their new base on the Danube. And this appears to have been what took place. Meanwhile, Centurion Antonius's seventh cohort of the 3rd Gallica, which was currently cut off at Ascalon, was left where it was for now, holding that city, and would not be involved in the transfer to Moesia.

The six 3rd Gallica cohorts transferred to Moesia would very quickly make a reputation for themselves there. Shortly after arriving at their new station they would be called out in wintry weather after ten thousand fierce mounted warriors of the Roxolani tribe crossed the Danube and began raiding Roman territory in Moesia. The Roxolani were expert horsemen who sheathed their immense broadswords down their backs, drawing them two-handed over their shoulders. One icily cold day, the 3rd Gallica men would catch the Roxolani in an encampment protected by nothing more than an encirclement of wagons. The three thousand Syrian legionaries would slaughter all ten thousand Roxolani in one bloody surprise attack. Theirs was a victory that would resonate around the Roman world at a time when Romans had been rocked by the news of the losses in Judea, and would give the 3rd Gallica men a fearsome reputation among fellow legionaries and civilians alike.

With these legion transfers agreed, Vespasian dispatched his son Titus to take a Liburnian, the fast frigate of the Roman navy with a narrow profile and a single bank of oars, from Achaea across the Mediterranean to Alexandria to fetch the two selected legions there up to Judea, braving the rough seas of the late winter that still kept the shipping lanes closed to wind-powered cargo ships. As a member of the Equestrian Order, Titus could legally enter Egypt without specific permission from the emperor, and in Egypt the 5th and 15th were currently both commanded by tribunes, meaning they would take Titus's orders without demur. Titus would then march the two legions, plus a number of auxiliary units also being withdrawn from Egypt, and up the Mediterranean coast to meet his father in Ptolemais, which would once again serve as the Roman army's staging point.

There was one small irritation, which Vespasian would have to live with. As expected, both Cestius Gallus and Procurator Florus were now summarily removed from their posts by Nero. As the new proconsul of Syria, Nero appointed Gaius Licinius Mucianus. Like Vespasian, Mucianus was a former consul and a member of Nero's touring party in Greece. Roman biographer Suetonius claimed that Mucianus had long shown jealous hostility toward Vespasian, which he made no effort to hide. Meanwhile, Vespasian considered the unmarried Mucianus "a notoriously immoral fellow" who "treated him disrespectfully." Mucianus liked pretty boys and was known to don a dress on occasion, interests he shared with the emperor, which endeared him to Nero. Vespasian never publicly said an unkind word about Mucianus other than on one occasion when an acquaintance mentioned his sexual predilections. "Personally," Vespasian responded, "I'm content to be a male."[38]

Despite their mutual dislike, the two men knew they had to not only work together but travel overland together to reach Syria with their retinues. Mucianus, once based in Antioch, would take orders from Vespasian even after the general moved on to Judea. So, to get the job done, they buried the hatchet. As the pair set off from Greece, the Palatium sent out letters to the same three kings who had provided allied forces to Gallus's army, commanding them to send troops to reinforce Vespasian in Judea in preparation for a new campaign against the Jews in the late spring. A new ally was also approached for reinforcements for this campaign, King Malchus of Arabia, who would send six thousand Arab archers to join Vespasian's gathering army at Ptolemais.

As the Roman war machine slowly but methodically creaked into motion, official word reached Cestius Gallus at Antioch that he'd been dismissed. All Gallus's clients also lost their jobs and dejectedly went home to Rome, among them Tribune Neapolitanus and Legate Gallus of the disgraced 12th Fulminata Legion. Governor Gallus himself died in Antioch before he could return home, probably as a result of a heart attack, although the historian Tacitus suggested he died of shame.[39]

VIII

FIRE AND BLOOD
IN GALILEE

When Vespasian and Mucianus arrived in Antioch from Greece in the spring of AD 67, they were greeted by the waiting King Herod Agrippa II, who was ready for the renewal of the Judean War. Vespasian would have met Agrippa and Berenice on their visits to Rome, where the king's father had a palace on the Palatine, which the king and queen would also have used. Vespasian would have known how loyal the Jewish king was to Rome, and the pair soon became firm friends.

Agrippa had once again brought troops in support of the Roman war effort—a thousand cavalry and a thousand foot archers this time. Commanding all his cavalry was none other than Philip bar Jacimus, the cavalry commander who'd escaped the clutches of the rebels in Jerusalem and then escaped Gamala to lead the king's delegation to Nero. Agrippa had received reports from Jewish enemies of Philip that he had betrayed the king at Jerusalem and sided with the rebels, but Agrippa didn't believe a word of it. After Philip's return from Greece, the king gave him a large force of cavalry and sent him to bring the royal servants trapped at Gamala to him and to restore the families of the "Babylonian Jews" who served in his army to their home in Batanaea in the Perea district east of the Jordan. In accomplishing this task, Philip left his own young daughters at Gamala, apparently thinking they would be safer there.

Vespasian arrived in Antioch with a legion. The 10th Fretensis Legion had joined Vespasian's party as it passed through the city of Cyrrhus, just to the north of Antioch, en route from Greece. Cyrrhus was situated on a hillside between Commagene and the plain of Antioch in today's northern Lebanon, not far from a tributary of the Orontes River. The flourishing Greek-style city was on the long-established trading route from Commagene to the Euphrates at Zeugma, via Antioch. The 10th Fretensis had been stationed at Cyrrhus for decades. The city's amphitheater, which can still be seen today, had been built as the legion's training arena and to keep its five thousand legionaries entertained.

Historian Josephus was later told that the 10th Fretensis, along with the 5th Macedonica, was among Rome's most esteemed legions. As with the 5th Macedonica, the fame of the 10th Fretensis went back to Julius Caesar. The 10th had been personally raised by Caesar in western Spain and had served as his preferred legion throughout the civil war that Caesar eventually won to become dictator of Rome. The legion's title, Fretensis, referred to a 48 BC sea battle in the Otranto Strait between Italy and Greece. After Caesar's then deputy Mark Antony put the legion aboard warships, it had boarded and captured many of the ships of the Senatorial fleet that had been harassing Caesar's staging point at Brindisi. Ever since, the legion had carried a warship emblem on its shields, along with the original bull emblem that signified its origin in Spain.[40]

Despite the 10th Fretensis Legion's vaunted reputation, by AD 54, when Corbulo came upon it lazing at its base at Cyrrhus, the men of the 10th had become so lax through lack of action that some of them had sold their helmets, and their equally lax officers had allowed them to do it. Corbulo had very quickly punished the helmet sellers and reintroduced tough discipline to the unit.

For his Judean campaign, Vespasian appointed one of his accompanying clients to take over command of the 10th Fretensis. This was Marcus Ulpius Traianus, or Trajan as later historians came to call him. His son of the same name, who was thirteen years old at this time, would one day become emperor of Rome. Marcia, sister of General Trajan's wife, had married Vespasian's son Titus in AD 63 following the death of Titus's first wife Arrecina, making Trajan and Titus brothers-in-law. Titus had recently divorced Marcia, but Vespasian continued to be a patron of General Trajan. It was common to retain clients after a marriage tie had been severed—Vespasian retained relatives of his late wife Domitilla as clients following her death.

Marcus Trajan was of praetor rank, making him the equivalent of a major general today. It was rare for praetors, who served as senior judges at Rome, to revert to the command of a legion, a post they had filled on the way to becoming a praetor. But Trajan's past experience of military command would prove invaluable to Vespasian, and Trajan would repay Vespasian's patronage with steadfast service.

Another of Vespasian's clients was given the command of the 5th Macedonica Legion, taking up the post once both he and it reached Ptolemais. With the rank of legate, this new commander was Sextus Vettulenus Cerialis, a senator whose family hailed from the Sabine tribe in central Italy, which was looked down upon by natives of Rome. His father had been chief centurion of the 11th Claudia Legion, but an enlisted man nonetheless, and Cerialis would show his gratitude to Vespasian for this opportunity to shine as a legion commander by dedicated loyalty. Following the Judean War, Vespasian would promote Cerialis further, with a consulship and a provincial governorship.

Leaving Proconsul Mucianus in charge of civil affairs at Antioch, Vespasian continued on down the Mediterranean coast accompanied by his generals and King Herod Agrippa II, taking the king's Jewish troops with him along with the complete 10th Fretensis Legion and five wings of cavalry that were normally based in Syria. One of those wings was the Ala Gaetulorum Veterana, made up of mature retired Berber cavalrymen from today's Algeria, serving behind the standard of the Gaetulian Lion. The Gaetulians were a desert people, natural riders known for horse rearing and capturing animals for Roman spectacles. They were famously hardened, skillful fighters.

The newly appointed commander of this Gaetulian cavalry wing was also a retiree—Gaius Valerius Clemens, a former legion chief centurion. Clemens, who'd been born at Augusta Taurinorum, present-day Turin in northern Italy, had spent decades serving with various legions before going into retirement less than five years before this at the city of Heliopolis in the west of Syria province—today's Baalbek in Lebanon. Heliopolis was a major religious center, home to one of the largest temple complexes in the Roman world and to a famous oracle. With his former military rank, Clemens was one of the city's leading citizens. He would have served on the town senate and played a leading white-robed role in Heliopolis's annual sun god festival parades, for which he shaved his head and embraced chastity and abstinence, as custom required.

On leaving his last legion, Chief Centurion Clemens had joined the part-time Evocati militia at Heliopolis. Evocati membership for five years after discharge was then one of the terms of legion enlistment, and as a result Clemens had been called up for service in the current emergency and put in charge of the Berber troopers. Clemens would die sometime over the next two years during this Judean campaign under Vespasian. He was apparently a popular leader, because ten subordinate decurions from his Gaetulian ala would pay for a memorial to be erected to him at Heliopolis following the war.[41]

As Vespasian marched out of Syria, he left the 4th Scythica Legion in the province. It was busy building a new base for itself on an escarpment at Zeugma overlooking a crossing of the Euphrates, due east of Antioch. The 6th Ferrata Legion also remained in Syria, at its Raphanaea base farther south. As for the 12th Fulminata, the shattered legion that had lost its eagle to the Jews, eight of its heavily depleted cohorts, minus the two cohorts currently stationed at Ptolemais with Tribune Placidus, were sent to the port city of Laodicea, just to the south of Antioch, where the unit was to undergo its discharge of veterans and enlistment of new recruits later in the year.

While Vespasian came south with his forces, his son Titus marched north from Egypt with the two fresh legions and twenty-three cohorts of auxiliaries—ten of the auxiliary cohorts were 800-man double-strength *miliaria* units, with the remainder being of normal strength, with 480 men. In Titus's column, the 5th Macedonica and 15th Apollinaris Legions were both led by their tribune second-in-commands. We don't know the name of the 5th Macedonica's tribune, who would soon be superseded as commander of the legion by Cerialis, the legate appointed by Vespasian. The 15th Apollinaris was now commanded by the tribune Domitius Sabinus, who would continue to command the legion through the coming campaign.

Using the Liburnian frigates of the Alexandrian Fleet to ferry his troops across the branches of the Nile, Titus made several halts in Egypt, and following the Via Maris coastal highway, paused at Gaza in southernmost Idumea. His force of fifteen thousand troops, including thousands of screening cavalry, was enough to daunt Idumean rebels, who had lost eighteen thousand of their comrades to Centurion Antonius's thousand men. This meant that the progress of Titus's force up the coastal road through Idumea and Judea was unopposed.[42]

Passing through Ascalon, Titus not only congratulated Centurion Antonius and his men for their valiant efforts against the rebels, he added Antonius and his 3rd Gallica cohort to his force and left auxiliaries to garrison Ascalon. Another centurion from Titus's legions would take charge of the city. Noted American archaeologist William F. Albright, who came to world attention by authenticating the Dead Sea Scrolls in 1948, had decades earlier discovered an inscription at Ascalon thanking a centurion of the 10th Fretensis Legion, Aulus Instuleius Tenax, for his service to the city, and in 1922 Albright expressed the belief that it was Centurion Tenax who took over the Ascalon garrison command from Antonius at this time.[43]

With speed the essence, after leaving Ascalon, Titus's Roman column skirted Joppa on its way north. This port was again held by Jewish rebels, who operated ships from the city to threaten shipping up and down the coast. Joppa would be dealt with by the Romans in due course. For now, Titus marched on by. By the time his column reached Caesarea, the six 3rd Gallica Legion cohorts had already departed by sea for Moesia, led by the legion's chief centurion, Arrius Varus. Ahead lay that unit's appointment with destiny and the Roxolani beside the Danube.

As these six cohorts of the 3rd Gallica sailed away, Tribune Nicanor joined Titus's staff at Caesarea for the coming campaign. There are several reasons to believe that Nicanor had commanded the 3rd Gallica for the past few years, and an event that was to soon take place at Jotapata and which is detailed in the following chapter lends added weight to this belief. While Titus was in Caesarea, and before he continued north, he further denuded the city's garrison by adding the five auxiliary cohorts and wing of cavalry normally stationed there to his force. In addition to light infantry, we know that at least one auxiliary cohort now in Titus's column was made up of slingers from Syria.

In Ptolemais, weeks after they had separated in Achaea, Titus and his father reunited, with Vespasian surprised but delighted by the speed with which his son had made the overland journey from Egypt with his troops. By this stage, the remaining allied troops had arrived at the Ptolemais assembly camp—the archers from Arabia, the cavalry and archers from Emesa, and, led by King Antiochus's eldest son, Epiphanes, troops from the Kingdom of Commagene.

While Vespasian was waiting for all his forces to join him, he answered a plea from the people of Sepphoris. Prior to this, Vespasian had heard good things about Tribune Placidus, who'd been left, if you remember, by Governor Gallus at Ptolemais with a garrison of his 12th Fulminata men and cavalry. So, Vespasian now gave Placidus a mission—take his thousand 12th Fulminata legionaries and a cavalry force of a thousand troopers and push rapidly into Galilee to relieve Sepphoris, which was being hounded by rebels.

Retaining their loyalty to Rome, partly because the Romans continued to hold their family members as hostages at Dora, the leading citizens of Sepphoris had sent envoys to meet Vespasian at Ptolemais and beg for the protection of a Roman garrison. Sepphoris had twice been in the hands of Josephus and his rebel army in recent months. Josephus had even given community leaders permission to leave to visit their family members at Dora.

As Tribune Placidus and his troops moved quickly to secure Sepphoris, Josephus and his partisans withdrew three miles from the city to the hill village of Garis. There, they threw up a large defensive earth wall all the way around the hill. Placidus was also under orders from Vespasian to clear the plains of Galilee of rebels, so, leaving his infantry garrisoning Sepphoris, which would now remain in Roman hands for the remainder of the Judean War, Placidus led his cavalry in applying a coldly efficient scorched-earth policy across Galilee.

Ignoring rebel-held walled cities and towns of the region, and "according to the rules of war," says Josephus, Placidus swept the surrounding lush farmlands, killing or capturing everything that moved, human and animal, and burning everything that didn't—village and farm buildings, utensils, supplies, food, anything that could sustain the rebels. "Galilee was all over filled with fire and blood," says Josephus.[44] Old and infirm Jews captured in this sweep were killed. Healthy young male and female Jewish captives were led off in chains to be sold as slaves. Agrippa was offered those Jews captured in his territories by Vespasian, but the king also sent them to the slave markets.

When Placidus and his cavalry drove into central Lower Galilee and approached the hill city of Jotapata, today's Yodfat, east and a little south of Ptolemais, tens of thousands of rebels in the city flooded out onto the plain and did battle with them. Placidus and his troopers, heavily outnumbered, lost seven men and were in risk of being surrounded, so made a strategic retreat, returning to Vespasian at Ptolemais and leaving the rebels to withdraw behind the walls of Jotapata. Across Galilee, the rebels and their commander, Josephus, readied themselves for the inevitable approach of Vespasian and prepared for the fight of their lives.

IX

THE SIEGE OF JOTAPATA

At dawn one day in May, AD 67, the massive Roman camp at Ptolemais came to life as "Prepare to March" was sounded by the trumpets of each cohort. More than thirty thousand soldiers rose, packed
their personal equipment and dismantled their tents. Again "Prepare
to March" was sounded, and the troops loaded their tents and grinding stones onto mules, which were led away by their drivers. When
"Prepare to March" was sounded a third time, the troops assembled
in marching order on the camp's parade ground, where they waited in
disciplined silence.

As Titus, King Herod Agrippa II, Prince Epiphanes of Commagene,
and Vespasian's subordinate officers stood watching, Vespasian stepped up
onto his tribunal, a reviewing stand made of earth. Another Roman officer,
the "announcer," probably a tribune of the legions, followed his general
and stood to his right. Vespasian cast a severe eye around the troops in
their neat ranks and files. If he was pleased by the sight, he didn't show it.
Vespasian frequently bore a constipated expression. Once, when a noted
wit was making jokes at the expense of the other members of his party,
Vespasian asked him to make a joke about him. "I will," said the jokester,
"when you've finished relieving yourself."[45]

Now, the announcer spoke, bellowing to the assembled troops. "Are
you ready for war?"

"We are ready!" was the massed response, with legionaries and auxiliaries punching the air with their fists.

"Are you ready for war?" the announcer repeated.

"We are ready!" the army responded a second time.

"Are you ready for war?" the announcer asked a third time, in a demanding tone this time.

"We are ready!" the Roman troops came back, with a deafening roar now, enthusiastically punching the air yet again.[46]

Vespasian nodded, and the trumpets sounded. The camp gates opened, and the troops began to march out of camp. Allied cavalry and infantry went first. As was the rule in Roman camps, the cavalrymen led their horses until they were outside the camp; only then did they mount up. Even Vespasian and King Herod Agrippa II mounted their steeds once outside the camp gates.

The legions had drawn lots for where they would march in the column. On the march, their standards were carried in a bunch at the center of the column, which was where Vespasian and the other commanders were located. Vespasian was surrounded by several hundred men chosen from all of his legions to form the Commander in Chief's Guard. These men were armed with round shields and long spears as opposed to the regular long, curved, rectangular shield and shorter javelins of the legions' rank and file. At the very end of the column, trailing the last mules of the baggage train, came the officers' servants, thousands of them, unarmed and on foot. Josephus was to put the number of men in Vespasian's force at sixty thousand, excluding noncombatants and camp followers such as servants and booty and slave traders, but the details he provides of the units involved make approximately thirty-two thousand fighting men a more likely number.[47]

Heading east, Vespasian's column crossed the border between Syria and Galilee, with allied foot archers fanning out ahead into woods on the army's route to ensure no partisans lay in ambush. At this point, rebel commander Josephus was at the fortified Lower Galilean hill village of Garis, not far from Sepphoris, with an army of thousands of partisans. Apart from fighting the Romans, Josephus had of late been contending with rival partisan leaders who'd attempted to get their hands on him and kill him. Several times he'd discovered betrayers in his own ranks. Rather than execute them all, he'd had the hand of one betrayer chopped off. He'd threatened to chop off both hands of another but then gave him the option of chopping off his own left hand, an option the man had taken. These tactics had served to keep his fractious underlings in line, but at the news of the approach of Vespasian's army, many of his men melted away from Garis. Josephus was to say that, at this point, he began to despair of winning this war.

With those partisans who remained loyal to him, Josephus withdrew farther east to the rebel-held city of Tiberias, on the western shore of the Sea of Galilee. This Romanized, Greek-speaking city, complete with drama theater near its south gate, had been built in AD 18–20 by Herod the Great's son Herod Antipas, who featured in the last days of Jesus Christ. Tiberias was the capital of Antipas's tetrarchy, or governate. Named by Antipas for Roman emperor Tiberius, the city had, after his death, become part of Herod Agrippa II's realm. Despite the fact that Josephus's rebel forces now controlled it, the city's majority Gentile population retained loyalty to Agrippa.

Vespasian ignored Tiberias for now. Marching his army southeast, he headed for the rebel city of Gadara, which he knew was only lightly defended. Near today's Umm Qais in northern Jordan, Gadara was one of the ten cities of the Greek Decapolis and had been in rebel Jewish hands since early in the revolt. With a protective wall and sitting on a ridge facing north, from which it was possible to see the Sea of Galilee, Tiberias, and the southern tip of the Golan Heights, Gadara was considered highly defensible.

With the Romans expected to first attack the larger city of Jotapata to the northwest, not far from Ptolemais, the approach of Vespasian's army caused many partisans at Gadara to panic and flee, leaving few rebels to defend the town and no time to summon reinforcements. It took just a day for Vespasian's troops to storm over the walls and into Gadara. After all the young Jewish men in the city were killed, Vespasian had Gadara and all surrounding villages and country villas put to the torch. Any Jews found in the district were dragged off into slavery.

Now Vespasian sets his sights on Jotapata to the northwest, closer to Ptolemais, which meant doubling back. Jotapata, he knew, had a much more formidable rebel presence and was a threat at his back that must be removed before turning south to Judea. To give the Roman army a direct route, cavalrymen and foot soldiers became road-makers, and after four days' toil they turned a path through the hills into a straight and solid road. As they worked, Vespasian waited with the remainder of his encamped army.

Urging his men to work harder and longer, Vespasian was a strict taskmaster. His troops didn't seem to mind. They had found that their new commander in chief was a man without airs and graces, a man who ate the same rations as themselves and regularly visited them as they toiled. A century earlier, the consul Marius had taken much of the personal equipment of the legions off the backs of mules and transferred it onto the backs of legionaries. As a result, legionaries had come to refer to themselves as Marius's Mules. Now, knowing Vespasian's background as an investor in mule farms, legionaries who still considered themselves mules coined a nickname for their general—the Mule Driver.

On the day after the new Roman road to Jotapata was completed, Josephus arrived at Jotapata from Tiberias to take rebel command at the city. His arrival, he was to later say, "raised the drooping spirits of the Jews."[48] One Jew whose spirits weren't raised slipped out of Jotapata and hurried south to find Vespasian, offering information in return for a pardon. When the Roman general learned from this deserter that there were more than forty thousand Jews in the city, and that the rebel commander for all of Galilee was now in charge at Jotapata, he became doubly determined to take and destroy the city. Giving the industrious Tribune Placidus a thousand cavalry and, as his deputy, the equally active Decurion Ebutius, Vespasian sent him ahead at the gallop with orders to quickly surround the city to prevent any rebels getting in or out. Meanwhile, Vespasian marched the rest of the army over the hills toward Jotapata via the newly built road.

When his army arrived outside Jotapata in the late evening of June 2, Vespasian added a double row of infantry to Placidus's line of cavalry surrounding the city. Legionaries then dug entrenchments and pitched camp on a hill a little under a mile north of the city, deliberately in full view of the Jewish defenders to daunt them.

When the Romans awoke the next morning, they found that Josephus and thousands of his rebel fighters had encamped outside the city walls on the northern side of Jotapata. The city's long, thin ground plan looked like the imprint of a north-facing left foot. The ground east, west, and south of Jotapata's walls, which curved around natural gradients, sloped away steeply, making the northern wall the easiest to assault and most difficult to defend. With no prospect of escape, Josephus had convinced his partisans to take the initiative and fight outside the wall, catching the Romans in the open. "Nothing makes men fight so desperately in war as necessity," Josephus was to later say.[49]

Vespasian clearly thought that Jotapata would fall as easily as Gadara. Instead of having his legions raise firing mounds for his artillery pieces, he simply arrayed his thousands of archers and sent massed ranks of Roman legionaries marching toward the wall under the cover of swarms of arrows. But Josephus and his men didn't stand still to receive the arrows. They dashed at the legionaries and threw themselves at the slowly advancing Roman wall of locked shields, forcing the archers to suspend their fire rather than hit Romans.

Soon, there was hectic hand-to-hand fighting as the Jews dove in and out against the wall of shields. As annoying as bees to a bear, they kept this up all day, harassing the Roman front line and preventing it from moving forward. Hostilities ended at sunset, with both sides withdrawing. This first day of the battle had cost just thirteen Roman lives and seventeen Jewish lives, although six hundred rebels were wounded. But the Romans had made no progress.

For another three days this was repeated, with the Roman infantry stopped before the north wall by the continual harassment of Josephus and his men, who had gained great courage and enthusiasm from their success with these tactics on the first day. So, five days into the assault, and no further advanced, Vespasian called a council of war with his senior commanders. At his camp praetorium, or command center, on the hill outside Jotapata, he sought their input.

The upshot of this meeting was a decision that two of the three legions, the 5th Macedonica and 10th Fretensis, would build earth ramps against the city's north wall. Once they were completed, Roman troops could advance up the ramps to mount the fortifications and enter the city. This would take time, but Vespasian curbed his impatience and gave the order for the ramps' construction.

While some Roman troops maintained the encirclement of Jotapata, others ranged the surrounding hills, chopping down every tree and quarrying and rounding stones to be used by the legions' heavy artillery pieces. Those stones were cut to the same size and weight. Josephus says each weighed a talent, which was around sixty pounds. The standard weights for legion catapult stones ranged from two pounds to a massive 360 pounds—the latter being known as the "wagon stone" because it needed a wagon to carry it. At the same time, at a range of no more than 220 yards from the wall, stable earth mounds were built for the artillery so that it could fire over the heads of Roman troops in front of it. In addition to one heavy-stone-throwing catapult per legion cohort, there could be as many as fifty-five lighter Scorpios and Carroballistas per cohort. According to Josephus, Vespasian deployed a total of 160 catapults against him at Jotapata.[50]

These catapults opened up a barrage of metal-tipped darts, ordinary stone balls, and burning balls that had been dipped in sticky black pitch. All these weapons let fly with a *whoosh* that could be heard within Jotapata. These missiles were joined by arrows of the archers from Arabia, and this rain of projectiles not only kept the rebels off the north wall, the Jews were cleared from all the open spaces in the north of the city. As an added precaution, two mantlets, wheeled wooden sheds with protective hide coverings, were moved into position ahead of the artillery. Under the cover of these, legionaries began piling earth dug in the rear to commence the pair of earthen ramps some yards apart, aiming for the northwestern section of the wall—using the earlier analogy of the left foot imprint, they were heading for the middle toes.

To hamper this construction work, Josephus sent out raiding parties who caught the workers in their mantlets and set fire to the woodwork at each ramp. To counter this, Vespasian linked the mantlets to each other with wooden palisades and stationed troops to closely protect the work teams. As the ramps continued to creep closer to the north wall, rising higher as they went, Josephus came up with another strategy.

In the dark of night, Josephus's men installed poles on top of the city wall. Between these poles they stretched the hides of oxen freshly killed in the city, creating a leather barrier. When the Romans resumed artillery fire in the morning, darts and stones bounced off this barrier. The hides, dripping with oxblood, even resisted the flames of fireballs. Under the cover of these hides, Josephus and his men increased the height of their wall by piling up more and more stones and earth until the wall was eighty feet high, and mounted a number of wooden towers offering cover to defenders.

This clearly frustrated the laboring Romans, as did the fact that Josephus's men resumed their hit-and-run raids on the ramp workplaces, setting fire to woodwork wherever they could. Annoyed by the rebel tactics, Vespasian had work on the ramps suspended and ordered his troops to settle in for a long siege. Bringing in water and food from the coast, the Romans could sit pat, intent on starving out the Jews. As it turned out, food was not a problem for Josephus and his partisans in Jotapata, but water was. Water collected in basins on city rooftops normally supplied the people of Jotapata through the dry summer, until the spring rains. But this normal supply was nowhere near enough for the more than forty thousand people now crowded into the city.

Josephus implemented water rationing, but even then people going to rooftops to collect their daily cup of water had to be careful not to be picked off by Roman artillery. Josephus responded by having people wash clothes, using their scanty water supply, then hang the dripping clothes on the wall to make their besiegers believe they had water to spare. The Jewish commander even resorted to sending men over the western wall at night and down the steep escarpment beyond it, covered in sheepskins so they could escape to other rebel-held towns in quest of water. Once these men neared the Roman lines, they got down on all fours and pretended to be dogs to avoid the sentries, but the ruse didn't fool the Romans.

As hot days passed and the water supply continued to run low, Josephus convened a meeting with his lieutenants to discuss whether they should try to escape. But the rest of the people in the city got wind of their meeting and a crowd gathered, some demanding, others begging, that they not leave. So, to show that he was dedicated to remaining, Josephus led a surprise attack outside the city. Breaking through the Roman lines, Josephus and his men reached Vespasian's camp a mile away, ripping down tents, setting fire to equipment, and causing general consternation before withdrawing to the city again, outdistancing the chasing legionaries, whose heavy armor slowed them down. For several days Josephus kept up these sallies, in daylight and darkness, until the Romans stationed Arabian archers and Syrian slingers to pelt the Jewish raiding parties as soon as they appeared in the open. The slingshot was more than an annoyance. Modern experiments have shown that Roman lead slingshot could travel at 100 mph and had a stopping power almost equal to that of a .44 Magnum handgun cartridge, with an accurate range of 130 yards.[51]

Rather than sit and let the rebels take the offensive day after day, Vespasian now ordered a resumption of ramp construction. The artillery and archers were moved closer to the north wall, and as the ramps grew higher, and closer to the wall, they were linked up to form one large ramp. We know that this ramp even used concrete revetments—they have been unearthed in recent times by archaeologists working at the Jotapata site. Eventually, the now single, broad ramp reached the wall. Two massive battering rams had already been prepared. Josephus spotted them lying in the open field behind Roman lines. The rams were now installed inside two wheeled mantlets, suspended from an overhead beam and with just a small opening at the front of each mantlet to allow the ram's iron head to protrude.

With the ram operators stationed inside, the mantlet built by the 5th Macedonica Legion was run up against the ramp to the top of the recently elevated wall. The ram was swung back and forth, and soon the iron head was pounding into the stones and compacted earth of the wall, which had been shored up with timber during construction. Immediately, the wall shook, and a wail of alarm went up from people inside the city. As the ram continued to pound, Josephus had men fill sacks with chaff and then attach the sacks to ropes. Via the ropes, the sacks were hung down over the wall where the ram was working. Lowered to sit in front of the ram's head, they softened its blows.

To counter this, the ram was moved to a new location on the ramp, where it started pounding afresh. But the defenders simply moved their chaff bags to the new location. Roman ingenuity finally overcame Jewish ingenuity when a razor-sharp scythe was strapped to the end of a pole. A Roman volunteer emerged from the mantlet with the pole. Reaching up, he sliced the ropes holding the bags of chaff, which fell to the ground.

Two rams were soon at work, side by side on the ramp, with the second operated by the 10th Fretensis. As the rams pounded away, Jewish defenders became desperate. One Galilean, naked to the waist and perspiring heavily, appeared on top of the wall directly above the ram being operated by the 10th Fretensis. He was holding a massive rock. Roman artillery quickly zeroed in on him, but despite sustaining five wounds from Roman darts, the man held his position. Raising the rock above his head, he flung it down with such accuracy that it broke the head off the ram. Then he jumped down among legionaries at the mantlet and fought them hand to hand. A pair of Galilean brothers jumped down to join him, and together they drove the 10th Fretensis men from their ram. Josephus and his fighters now rained burning brands down on the two mantlets, although the mantlets' hide covers resisted catching alight.

With one ram knocked out, the Roman troops withdrew until night-fall to strategize, leaving the mantlets and the one still functional ram in place on the ramp. After dark, Moesian legionaries returned to the 5th Macedonica's ram and resumed pounding where the wall had first shaken. Vespasian personally oversaw operations here, and while standing to the rear of the mantlet he was hit on his toe by a dart launched by a rebel on the wall. Men came running from all around to aid their general, and Vespasian was quickly carried to the rear, where he was attended by physicians and joined by his anxious son Titus. Learning that word of his injury had quickly spread, and Roman morale had consequently taken a dip, as soon as his foot was bandaged Vespasian returned to the action and urged his men to fight all the harder.

With their general hale, hearty, and full of determination, albeit with a limp, men of the 5th Macedonica let out relieved cheers, and shouting encouragement to one another, they again set the ram to work pounding the already weakened wall. All the while, the Roman artillery continued its barrage of balls, knocking the parapet from the wall and the corners from its defensive towers. In the darkness, defenders continued to appear on top of the wall with burning brands, in the process making targets of themselves. Countless rebels were cut down holding brands. Others, wounded, jumped down to attack the Romans at the mantlet, only to die in the effort.

Josephus was standing atop the wall watching all this when a Roman ballista ball cannoned past him. Looking around, he saw that the man who'd been standing immediately to his right had been hit, and with such velocity that his head had been cleaved clean from his shoulders. In daylight, the man's head would be found in the city, more than six hundred yards from the wall. Elsewhere, a pregnant woman hit by a ballista ball inside the city was ripped open by the impact, with her unborn infant cast onto the ground.

The noise the Roman artillery made as it fired, and the groan the balls and arrows made in flight—like the groans of the decomposing dead, Josephus said—were as frightening to people in the city as the missiles themselves. Terrified women and children cried so much at this horrific din that Josephus ordered them all to block their ears and be locked in their houses so that their lamentations didn't affect the morale of the Jewish fighting men.

In the night, a section of the wall gave way to the 5th Macedonica's ram. Vespasian now ordered preparations made for an all-out assault through the gap created at dawn, when his men could see what they were doing. The mantlets were rolled back, and scaling ladders and a siege tower that had been built in the rear readied for the attack. Vespasian's plan was simple. While the 5th Macedonica used the siege tower to attack the breach in the wall, which was where Vespasian's main hopes lay, the 10th Fretensis and 15th Apollinaris would use scaling ladders at other locations to force the wall's defenders to split their efforts over the multiple locations.

Inside Jotapata, Josephus and his lieutenants knew what was coming and weren't idle. Defenders labored through the night to build another, inner wall around the breach in the outer wall. Older men were then stationed with Josephus on the wall's tallest, soundest parts. The younger, fitter men were placed to defend the breach. Women and children locked away in the city's dwelling places were ordered by Josephus to remain quiet—and none cried or screamed, none besought their men to come to them. Josephus then joined the five men assigned to the front rank of the defense of the broken wall, opposite the ramp of the 5th Macedonica Legion.

On the other side, Vespasian made his troop dispositions with care. Volunteers from among his cavalry were dismounted and equipped with long, pointed poles, then formed up in three ranks on the ramp. Their task was to use the poles to jab rebels who appeared on the wall, to prevent them raining missiles down on the best men of the two legions who lined up behind the cavalrymen with scaling ladders. All remaining cavalrymen were placed on their horses all the way around the east, west, and south walls of the city to intercept Jews who attempted to escape. Archers and slingers formed a second line behind the cavalry.

At the appointed time, all the trumpets of the legions sounded "Attack!" and the entire army roared a unified war cry that boomed around the hills. Josephus, who was on the receiving end of this war cry, described it as "a terrible shout." And now the Roman artillery let fly. Legionaries and the dismounted cavalry rushed forward, some up the ramps, others to the wall. On the other side, Josephus had instructed his men to drop to one knee and hold their shields above their heads, forming a solid roof over them all. He knew that the artillery would cease firing as soon as Roman foot soldiers had reached the wall. Once missiles stopped falling, the Jews cast aside their shields, which were peppered with darts, and rose up to fight.

The struggle at the wall lasted all day. Climbing legionaries came up the siege tower and ladders in endless streams. When some Romans were knocked away, there were always others to fill their places. Jewish defenders had no such reinforcements, and as more and more of them fell, and Romans succeeded in reaching the top of the wall in one place, Josephus called on a new desperate weapon. Several caldrons of oil—apparently lamp oil—had been simmering over fires. These were hauled up the wall and, sizzling and smoking, were poured over climbing Moesian legionaries of the 5th Macedonica below.

The effect was startling, and horrifyingly effective. The boiling oil covered Roman soldiers from head to foot, got in their eyes, seeped beneath their armor, and ate into their skin. Screaming, they fell like lemmings. And when they hit the ground, they could only rip off helmets and "leap and roll about in their pain," according to Josephus, who witnessed their agonies, or run blindly, howling, into the path of the next wave of legionaries coming to take their turn at the wall. Enraged by this barbaric treatment of their comrades, the following legionaries bellowed their determination to get their hands on the dealers in boiling oil and give them a taste of their own medicine, and began climbing.[52]

Josephus had one more defensive card to play. As the day was drawing out, vats of a greasy oil produced from the seeds of the herb fenugreek, which was used by Jewish cooks to make a relish, were poured down onto the woodwork of the siege tower and ladders, making them impossibly slippery. To the delight of the defenders, legionaries slipped and fell left and right. The Roman assault was becoming a farce. With the sun setting, Vespasian had "Withdraw" trumpeted, and his attacking troops pulled back to camp, taking their wounded with them. Jewish casualties had been relatively light, and the Romans had failed to exploit the breach in the wall to get inside Jotapata. The honors remained with the rebels.

Vespasian now ordered the construction of three massive wheeled siege towers. Each was to be fifty feet high, made from wood covered with iron plates that would both fend off missiles and make the towers impervious to fire. This would take several days to accomplish, leaving the majority of Vespasian's men idle in camp. So, seeing his troops impatient for Jewish blood after the injuries and frustrations of the last few days, Vespasian called in two of his generals and gave them assault missions to accomplish. These were designed to keep a portion of his troops busy and potentially give them plenty of booty—under the laws of war observed by Rome, if an enemy city surrendered, the Roman commander could determine the fate of its residents and contents, whereas if legionaries took it by storm they were entitled to a share of the proceeds from the sale of booty and from the sale into slavery of inhabitants.

Trajan of the 10th Fretensis was ordered to take two thousand of his legionaries and a thousand cavalry and storm the rebel-held town of Japha, not far from Jotapata. Cerialis of the 5th Macedonica was to take three thousand legionaries and six hundred cavalry south into Samaria to occupy Mount Gerizim. Vespasian had learned that thousands of Samaritan Jews had gathered on that mountain, which was a holy place to them—Samaritans believed that it was there that Abraham the Patriarch had taken his son Isaac to execute him as per the wishes of God, whereas the Jews of Jerusalem believed that Abraham had taken his son to Mount Moriah, which became the Temple Mount in Jerusalem.

Japha had been surrounded by two relatively low defensive walls by its Jewish defenders, and General Trajan's troops soon stormed the outer wall. As the Roman assault troops came over this, rebels fled toward the inner wall. But their compatriots at that inner wall, fearful of allowing the pursuing Romans inside the town, locked the gates, shutting out their retreating Jewish comrades and refusing to let them in, even when the refuge seekers called out to friends and relatives by name, begging to be saved.

When the Romans closed the gates in the outer wall, thousands of rebels were trapped between the inner and outer walls. The legionaries proceeded to slaughter the now panic-stricken men caught in the trap, running them through with their swords if they stood up to them, slitting their throats if they turned their backs and tried to escape. According to Josephus, twelve thousand Jewish rebels died in this slaughter.

Trajan now sent word to Vespasian that he had all but taken Japha. Estimating that few partisans remained inside the surrounded town, Trajan suggested that his brother-in-law Titus might like the honor of completing the Japha assault. Vespasian agreed and sent his son to the doomed metropolis accompanied by another thousand legionaries and five hundred cavalry. Once Titus reached Japha, he joined his troops to those of Trajan, and with Trajan in charge on the left wing, Titus stationed himself on the right wing and took command of the assault. At a trumpet call, the Roman legionaries surged forward with scaling ladders, all the way around the encircled town.

Rebels resisted from Japha's inner wall for a time, then withdrew into the town. When Roman troops flooded over the wall, they were to find that the partisans and their women had stationed themselves on the town's flat rooftops. As the legionaries tried to force a passage down Japha's narrow streets, they were pelted from above with darts by partisans and with anything that came to hand by their women—roof tiles, bricks, broken furniture. Forced to fight from house to house, Titus and his men took six hours to clear the town.

Any adult male Jew the legionaries found in houses or in the open, armed or unarmed, was assumed to be a rebel and killed on the spot. In this final Roman assault, a further 3,000 Jewish men were killed, while 2,130 Jewish women and children were rounded up and led away in chains to be sold by the slave merchants. With very few Roman casualties, Titus's first battle of the campaign had proven a cheap and easy victory.[53]

Meanwhile, in Samaria, General Cerialis was dealing with the problem posed by the thousands of Samaritans massed on Mount Gerizim. Arraying his 3,600 troops at the foot of the mountain, Cerialis sent the Samaritan leaders a message vowing to spare the lives of all if they surrendered peacefully. But the Samaritans feared they would be sold into slavery if they surrendered, so they turned down Cerialis's offer. Two days after Titus had stormed Japha, Cerialis sent his 3,000 infantry up the mountain with orders to take no prisoners. According to Josephus, 11,600 Samaritans were killed that day.

Missions accomplished, Titus, Trajan, Cerialis, and their troops returned to Jotapata, where work had continued to further elevate the assault ramps as the massive siege towers were constructed to the rear. On July 19, the forty-seventh day of the Roman siege, these ramps were higher than the city wall. That same day, a Jewish deserter came to the Roman lines and offered Vespasian information on how to take the city.

Vespasian didn't entirely trust this fellow. Previously, a Jew had been captured while attempting to escape Jotapata, and he had defied torture by fire, refusing to reveal anything about the state of the rebel defenses inside the city. That man had died crucified on a cross, smiling down at his Roman tormentors. Now, without coercion, this latest Jewish deserter was advising the Romans how to take the city, telling Vespasian that he'd seen the exhausted Jewish sentries of the last watch before dawn always nod off to sleep, making this the ideal time to launch a stealthy surprise attack on the city. Do that, said the deserter, and Jotapata would fall.

Although Vespasian feared a trap, he ultimately felt that little would be lost if he tested the man's information. Keeping the informer in custody for now, Vespasian gave his son Titus the task of leading a commando raid on the northern wall, to see whether the Jewish sentries were indeed asleep leading up to dawn. The 15th Apollinaris Legion had yet to figure prominently in the Jotapata assault, so as his companions in the commando raid, Titus chose the tribune commanding the legion, Domitius Sabinus, and a group of his best 15th Apollinaris legionaries.

In the darkness, and with the added cover of a thick mist that descended on Jotapata in the early hours that night, Titus, Sabinus, and their men crept up a ramp and dropped down onto the city wall. Not a creature stirred nearby. The deserter had not lied—the Jewish sentries were indeed asleep at their posts. Creeping up to them, Titus and his men slit their throats. Then, quietly descending into the slumbering city, Titus's party tiptoed to the nearest gates, then flung them open. Thousands more Roman troops who had been lying in wait by the ramps silently rose up and came jogging to the gates before pouring into the city.

As cohort after cohort of legionaries flooded through Jotapata with flashing swords, every Jew encountered was cut down. Thousands of men, women, and children screamed with terror as they fled down the slopes of the citadel in the north of the city and into the suburbs of the south, with Roman soldiers on their heels. Jewish commander Josephus awoke to the cacophony and, grabbing his sword, emerged to find that he had no chance of organizing resistance now that his enemy was inside the walls. He instead turned and ran to a hiding place that he would have previously reconnoitered. The hill of the citadel was pitted with caves, which were essentially shallow holes in the ground, and Josephus jumped down into a pit among these caves. This pit, he knew, opened into a cavern that, uniquely among those on the hillside, was invisible from above. Inside the cavern he found forty leading people of Jotapata, men and women, and he joined them in cringing in its dark concealment.

With the coming of daylight, the Roman slaughter grew to its height. No one was spared. The Romans, incensed by the way some of their comrades had been killed and maimed by the desperate Jewish defense via boiling oil, had blood lust. Even if their commanders had wanted to stop them as the massacre continued, they couldn't. Josephus, in his *Jewish War*, estimated that forty thousand Jews died in Jotapata during the siege and its bloody last day. Some today question that figure, considering it exaggerated and accusing Josephus of inflating the number to gain sympathy for his fellow Jews, putting the actual figure at more like seven thousand.

One reason for suggesting Josephus inflated the number of dead stemmed from the fact that, when a mass grave was unearthed by archaeologists at the Jotapata site during the 1990s, the number of human remains indicated far less than forty thousand victims. However, the Romans left the Jewish dead at Jotapata in the open and forbade the burial of the bodies for another year. After Jewish relatives of the dead came to the site in AD 68, it's probable that remains that could be identified were removed for burial elsewhere, with unidentified remains going into the mass grave. Certainly, that mass grave would not have been dug by the Roman army; they always left enemy dead where they fell.

Not all Jewish casualties occurred in the first flush of the Roman surge through the city. Some Jews fled to the caves, where most could be seen from above. Those who refused to surrender were incinerated in their holes by fires lit by the legionaries. But they were first given the chance to surrender, with the slave market their destination. It was here that Centurion Antonius again enters the story. Josephus doesn't identify him as the same Centurion Antonius of the 3rd Gallica Legion who was the Roman hero of the defense of Ascalon, but neither does he say that he wasn't the same man.

Centurion Antonius reached his right hand down to a partisan who had been hiding in one of the holes and had agreed to surrender, to haul him out. With the centurion off guard, the Jew thrust a spear up between his legs. Entering Antonius's groin, the spearhead passed up into his vital organs, and he died instantly. If it was the Centurion Antonius from Ascalon, we can't escape the irony of the fact that the man who had led the slaughter of eighteen thousand Jewish rebels there perished at Jotapata extending his hand to help a rebel. We aren't told of the fate of his assailant. Antonius's compatriots would have ensured it was horrific—incinerated alive, probably.

Once the killing had ceased, Vespasian ordered the utter destruction of Jotapata, first by fire and then via the tumbling down of the brick and stone shells that remained. On July 22, two days after the city's fall, a Jewish woman was discovered in the ruins searching for food. On being questioned by Vespasian, the woman revealed her hiding place and identified the forty people hiding with her, including Josephus, the Jewish rebel commander for all of Galilee. Vespasian, seeing the possibility of rebel resistance across Galilee crumbling if it became known that Josephus was in Roman hands, immediately sent two of his tribunes to the pit. They called down to Josephus that Vespasian wished to offer him his life if he surrendered.

These two officers, Tribunes Paulinus and Gallicanus, were likely the second in command of the 5th Macedonica and 10th Fretensis Legions. But they were unable to convince Josephus to trust them, even though they assured him that Vespasian admired his courage and leadership skills and only wished to talk with him. So Vespasian sent a third officer, Tribune Nicanor, to try to convince Josephus to give himself up. This tribune was Syrian, and Josephus says in his *Jewish War* that Nicanor had been his "familiar acquaintance in time past."

As previously discussed, it's probable that Nicanor had been in charge of the 3rd Gallica Legion at Caesarea for at least several years prior to the recent departure of six of its cohorts for Moesia. Titus and Vespasian would have retained his services because of his intimate knowledge of Judea and Jerusalem, and in AD 64 Nicanor and Josephus would have become acquainted after Nicanor organized his passage to Rome and back from Caesarea for the hearing in which Josephus successfully represented several Jews of Judea. Travel between Roman provinces by noncitizens required a pass approved by the Palatium at Rome and issued by the local governor, and if a military escort was involved it would have been organized by the local military commander—in this case, Tribune Nicanor.

Calling down into the pit, Nicanor assured Josephus that he and his fellow Roman officers didn't hate Josephus; they admired him. As for Vespasian, said Nicanor, he had nothing but the best motives for seeking Josephus's surrender. "The general is very desirous to have you brought to him, not to punish you," Nicanor went on. "For he could do that anyway, if you didn't come voluntarily. He is determined to save a man of your courage."[54]

Josephus trusted Nicanor more than he trusted most Romans. As he wavered over his answer, Roman legionaries, impatient with this stubborn Jew, crowded around the pit with incendiary material, declaring that if he didn't come out of his own accord they would burn him out. When Tribune Nicanor angrily ordered them away, Josephus's trust in him grew. After offering up a prayer, Josephus called to Nicanor that he was coming up. But Josephus's fellow Jews in the cave were horrified that he would even contemplate giving up and swarmed around him with drawn swords.

"Are you so fond of life that you can bear to see the light in a state of slavery?" one demanded.

"How many have *you* persuaded to lose their lives for liberty?" growled another.[55]

They had all committed to dying rather than capitulate to the Romans, and several of Josephus's companions raised their swords to ensure that Josephus kept to that commitment. Quickly rethinking his plan to immediately surrender, he sweet-talked his companions.

"Since it is resolved among you that you will die," he said, "come on, let's commit our mutual deaths to determination by lots."[56]

Josephus himself later wrote that he had no intention of dying when he made this suggestion. He arranged for his companions and himself to pair up, then the members of each pair drew lots. The bearer of the second lot was to execute the holder of the first lot, then kill himself. Josephus deliberately chose a weak-minded individual as his partner in death, then convinced him to wait until all the others had killed themselves. Then he talked the man into preferring life to death. Josephus was then able to climb out of the pit after all, and offer his wrists to Nicanor for binding.

As Tribune Nicanor led Josephus away to the Roman camp, heading for Vespasian's headquarters, word quickly spread among legionaries that the Jews' general was being brought in alive, and thousands soon surrounded the pair. Some of the troops were merely curious and wanted to clap eyes on the man who'd defied them for so long. Others, more passionate and angered by the loss of friends to partisans, called for his immediate execution. Nicanor attempted to cool tempers, but it took Titus arriving on the scene to calm the situation.

Josephus was then led before Vespasian by Titus, who expressed sympathy for the young Jewish commander, a man much the same age as himself. Titus, who was to later demonstrate a compassionate side, imagined himself in Josephus's shoes, but Vespasian was much less kindly than his son. A practical man, he was a soldier first and foremost, and after all the tricks that Josephus had pulled while leading the resistance against him, Vespasian didn't trust him an inch. When he seemed inclined toward ordering Josephus's immediate execution, Titus succeeded in convincing his father not to kill Josephus but instead to keep him under close guard. It seemed to

Josephus that Titus's plan was to convince his father to send him to Nero to allow the emperor to decide his fate.

As Josephus was about to be led away, he took a gamble, one that would both save and change his life. Having learned that Vespasian was known to seek the prophesies of oracles, he now boldly told the general that he had something to tell him, if permitted to speak with him alone. It was something to the general's advantage, he said. Vespasian, suspicious but curious, ordered everyone to leave his praetorium apart from Titus and two of their friends—almost certainly Vespasian's clients, the generals Trajan and Cerialis. Josephus then proceeded to prophesy that both Vespasian and his son Titus would become emperor of Rome and urged Vespasian to keep him close, for his own benefit, and not send him to Nero. Vespasian considered this prophesy nonsense, an invention to buy the prisoner time. Impatiently, he ordered Josephus taken away, but kept in chains for the time being. A centurion was appointed Josephus's personal jailer.

One of the two friends of Vespasian who'd been in that meeting—later events suggest it was Cerialis, because he and Josephus would go on several missions together and have the opportunity to talk—subsequently asked Josephus why, if he possessed the gift of prophesy, he hadn't told the people of Jotapata that it was pointless to resist the Romans, as the city was destined to fall. In response, Josephus told the general that he had indeed prophesied this to the Jotapatans, even predicting the city would fall after forty-seven days of siege—we don't know whether he did make such predictions, or not, but Josephus claimed that several among the 1,200 Jewish captives at Jotapata would confirm them.

Vespasian, like many Romans, was indeed a deeply superstitious man, guided by auspices, influenced by omens, and awed by the forecasts of oracles. As Josephus's prediction played on his mind over the coming weeks, he softened his attitude toward the man. While still maintaining Josephus under close arrest, Vespasian had fine new suits of clothing and other expensive gifts sent to him. Titus also paid him various honors. And all thoughts of sending the Jewish priest to Nero evaporated.

X

TAKING TIBERIAS AND TARICHEAE

Once Jotapata had been leveled, Vespasian marched his army back to Ptolemais on the coast, and from there he took it down the coast road to enter Judea for the first time. As Vespasian and his troops arrived at Caesarea, the regional capital, they were mobbed by the overjoyed Gentile population. When the crowds heard that Josephus, the rebel Jewish general, was in Vespasian's party, they clamored for his death, but Vespasian had Josephus locked away safely in Caesarea's citadel, which lay close to the sea on the city's main east-west street.

It was August, and the height of summer. The traditional commencement of the legions' winter break was not due until mid-October, yet Vespasian now called a halt to major offensive operations and sent his legions into winter camp. The 15th Apollinaris Legion and the one remaining cohort of the 3rd Gallica were assigned to Caesarea, while Tribune Placidus's two cohorts of the 12th Fulminata marched up to Laodicea to join the rest of their unit for the legion's upcoming discharge. Placidus, whose name means "calm," having gained a reputation as a solid and dependable soldier, was retained by Vespasian as one of his staff officers.

Meanwhile, so as not to overtax the abilities of Caesarea to supply his troops, Vespasian sent the complete 5th Macedonica and 10th Fretensis

Legions inland to loyal Scythopolis for the winter. These troops would have to suffer through that city's notoriously stifling summer heat before they enjoyed the pleasantly mild months of winter. Many of the auxiliary cohorts of Vespasian's army were spread between the two cities, as were some of the allied forces, although King Herod Agrippa II's troops accompanied him back to his old capital inland, Caesarea Philippi.

Why Vespasian brought his campaigning season to such an early conclusion has not been explained. After the siege of Jotapata had unexpectedly taken a month and a half, perhaps Vespasian wanted to give himself a full campaigning season, commencing in the spring the following March, to tackle Jerusalem, a much larger and more formidable city. He was aware that Nero was still in Greece, playing and racing, and possibly also knew that Helius, the freedman the emperor had left in charge at Rome, had begun sending Nero increasingly frantic messages urging him to return to Rome and again take up the reins of government. Tidings of discontent were coming from Gaul and Britain, where the populations were resentful of high taxes imposed on them by Nero—all the more so once they learned that the emperor had freed Greece from taxation.

Everywhere, even at Rome, people were openly lampooning the emperor for his theatrical lifestyle and singing bawdy songs about him. But a physical revolt against Nero's rule in Gaul, which would be initiated in the late winter of AD 67–68 by his governor Julius Vindex, was still many months away. We know that by late AD 67, Vindex loathed the fact that Nero was more interested in playing entertainer than being emperor, and Vindex was writing to fellow governors around the empire complaining about the way Nero governed and urging concerted corrective action.

Greco-Roman biographer Plutarch, who would come to have dealings with Vespasian's son Domitian several decades later, was to write that some governors reported Vindex's letters to Nero. But not all did. It is likely that Vespasian, as commander in chief in the East, received just such a letter. But the summer of AD 67 seems a little premature for this correspondence, making the early pause in Vespasian's Judean campaign unlikely to have had anything do with Vindex.[57]

Vespasian didn't halt operations entirely. He was aware that rebels under the late John the Essene had partly rebuilt the Idumean coastal city of Joppa after Gallus's troops had burned it in AD 66. Basing themselves there, these rebels were ranging up and down the coast from Phoenicia to

Egypt in boats they built, playing pirate as they harassed Roman merchant shipping. To deal with this problem, Vespasian now dispatched a force of auxiliary infantry and cavalry from Caesarea. The Roman force reached Joppa in the early evening, but the rebels, alerted to their approach, were able to take to the water in their boats and escape.

The rebels remained anchored just offshore all night, out of range of the missiles of the Roman troops who lined the shore. But in the early morning hours a storm blew down from the north. Known in the region as "the Black North Wind," this storm threw some rebel boats against each other and drove others onto the rocks. One way or another, the entire rebel fleet was wrecked by the storm. Many partisans drowned. Others who swam to shore died in the surf at the hands of waiting Roman troops. Survivors clinging to wreckage used their own swords to end their lives before they were claimed by the waves or their enemies.

With the coming of daylight, Joppa was overrun and destroyed for the second time in less than twelve months by Roman troops. The Roman detachment had orders to then build a permanent base for themselves, based on the ancient Egyptian citadel of Joppa, ruins of which still stand today. With the infantry garrisoning this new Joppa base, the accompanying Roman cavalry ranged the coastal district, ravaging it and leaving nothing but desolation in their wake.

News meanwhile reached Jerusalem that Jotapata had fallen to the Roman army. It began as a rumor, which many in the city refused to believe. The defeat of Gallus the previous year had led many to be convinced that God was on their side and that Jewish cities were not destined to fall prey to their Roman oppressors. But as the reports increased, and messengers no longer came from Jotapata, the fate of the city and its defenders became obvious. As the hundreds of thousands of people of Jerusalem went into mourning for lost friends and relatives, it was even reported that their general Josephus was among the dead, and public mourning for him, with hired mourners and pipers, went on for days, with crowds coming to his house to console his family.

Meanwhile, for the winter break, Agrippa was able to convince Vespasian and his entourage to accompany him to his city of Caesarea Philippi, which had remained in the hands of the king's forces. In AD 61, the king, who had sycophancy down to a fine art, had renamed the place Neronias Irenopolis, Nero's City of Peace. The new name would die as soon as Nero died. At Neronias, Vespasian offered sacrifices at a local temple in thanks for his successful campaign to date—Herod the Great had built a Temple of Augustus in the city, and there was also a noted hillside shrine dedicated to Pan, god of the hunter, who was also considered a god of luck.

While the troops of Vespasian's escort relaxed for twenty days, the king and his sister Berenice wined and dined Vespasian, Titus, and their senior officers at the city's Palace of Agrippa. Titus had met the famously attractive Berenice before. But this sojourn was his first opportunity to spend an extended period in her company. Even though Berenice was eleven years older than he was, and Jewish, Titus fell head over heels in love with her. And she fell for him. Their affair, which began here, would last for years, but, as Romans could not legally marry foreigners, Titus would eventually end the relationship by sending Berenice back to the East from Rome, where she would live for some time through the AD 70s.

With Vespasian a captive audience over these three weeks of relaxation, Agrippa was able to convince him to take back nearby cities Tiberias and Taricheae, which had previously been part of the king's realm but were now held by Jewish rebels. Sending Titus back to Caesarea to collect the wintering 15th Apollinaris Legion, Vespasian himself marched with Agrippa to Scythopolis, where he collected the 5th Macedonica and 10th Fretensis—even though the legions would have had as many as one third of their men on winter furlough—and marched them and associated allied troops to within four miles of Tiberias. Deliberately, Vespasian camped in plain view of the city, which had been walled securely around in stone by Josephus when he was Galilee's rebel commander.

While waiting for Titus to join him with the legion from Caesarea, Vespasian sent a cavalry decurion named Valerian to Tiberias with fifty troopers. Valerian's orders were to talk peace with the people of Tiberias. Most of the city's residents had only turned against the king and Rome under duress from the rebels, or so Agrippa assured Vespasian, so this was their opportunity to prove him right and save their necks.

To show their peaceful intent, Decurion Valerian and five of his men dismounted outside the city walls, only for the city's rebel commander, Jesus bar Shaphat, to come dashing out the south gate leading an armed party of yelling partisans. With no orders to engage the rebels, Valerian and his companions fled on foot, abandoning their spooked horses. Collected by their comrades, the embarrassed cavalrymen returned to Vespasian, and Jesus triumphantly led the Roman cavalry horses back into the city as his trophies of war.

Fearing Roman retribution, the leading men of Tiberias fled the city, going to the Roman camp and to King Herod Agrippa II. The king then took them to meet with Vespasian. Falling down before the general, they begged him not to take out his anger on the entire city when only a few troublemakers were to blame. The general was furious; not so much because the city had resisted his offer of peace but because he'd lost six good cavalry horses. Overcoming his fury, he accepted the oaths of friendship and loyalty given by the leaders of Tiberias, and sent General Trajan with a larger cavalry force to tell the city of the oaths given by their leaders. With the mood in Tiberias quickly turning against them once this message was delivered, Jesus bar Shaphat and his partisans took this as their cue to leave, and they hurriedly departed for Taricheae, three miles around the Sea of Galilee to the north.

The people of Tiberias then threw open their south gate to welcome the Romans. On hearing this, Vespasian marched his army to the city. Finding the south gate too narrow to admit his legionaries marching in normal formation, the general had his men tear down the entire south wall, instructing the townspeople to leave the wall down from that time forward. Agrippa now gave his word on behalf of the city that it would remain faithful forevermore, a move that spared the inhabitants the wrath of Rome.

With the arrival from Caesarea of Titus with the 15th Apollinaris Legion and auxiliary units, Vespasian moved his now combined force north to build a larger camp for all three legions between Tiberias and Taricheae. Another Greek-founded town, Taricheae was a fishing community—its Greek name literally means "place of processing fish." Jews called the town Magdala, and the female disciple of Jesus Christ, Mary Magdalene, is believed to have come from there.

Vespasian was expecting a tougher tussle for Taricheae. A much larger Jewish rebel force than that at Tiberias, made up of "foreigners" in Josephus's words, had taken over the town, which was also bulging with Jewish refugees from throughout the region. In Josephus's estimation, there were at least forty thousand people there—as many as had been at Jotapata. The rebels had built defensive walls and collected a number of fishing vessels and fitted them out for war. Capitulation was clearly not an option for them.

Vespasian's men had just commenced to build the trench and walls of their latest marching camp outside Taricheae when rebel leader Jesus led a large raiding party that streamed out of the town and caught the digging legionaries unprepared. The diggers were forced to flee, allowing Jesus and his men to destroy the works. When a large Roman force hurried out to take on the raiders, the Jews turned and retreated. When Romans pursued them to the lake, Jesus and his men boarded waiting boats, which put out into the lake. From the water, the rebels exchanged missiles and taunts with the Romans onshore.

When Vespasian received a report that a force of rebel fighting men was massing on the plain outside Taricheae, he sent Titus with six hundred cavalry to deal with them. As Titus and his force arrived, they found thousands of rebels confronting them, so Titus sent a messenger galloping to his father seeking reinforcements. Titus's existing cavalrymen didn't want to wait to share the glory of victory with others, and seeing that he might not be able to constrain many of these men, a mixture of auxiliaries and soldiers of the kings, Titus gave them a brief pep talk, then extended his greatly outnumbered squadrons in a line across the plain, facing the yelling, gesturing rebels. Even as General Trajan was seen approaching with four hundred mounted Roman reinforcements, with three thousand foot archers marching along behind, Titus gave the order to charge, leading his original six hundred horsemen into battle.

The Jewish partisans soon had the worst of the fight against Titus's cavalry, and as many fell to lances and swords, the rest gave way and fled back toward Taricheae. Titus quickly led some of his troopers at the gallop to cut off the fleeing rebels. Getting between them and the walls of Taricheae, these troopers continued the slaughter while the remaining Roman cavalry pressed in from the direction of the plain, sandwiching hapless partisans between the two forces.

A small number of rebels succeeded in escaping back into the town, where they tried to force locals and refugees into taking up arms for them. Hearing dissension within the city, Titus led his cavalry into Taricheae via the lake. Many rebels were killed in the town; others fled out town gates and onto the plain, deserting their leader, Jesus. Yet others took to the water in boats and sailed away, remaining on the water because they felt safer there than on the land. They couldn't go far—the Sea of Galilee was just five miles wide at its broadest and little more than seventeen miles long. Titus now sent his father a message to say that rebels had been ejected from Taricheae and he had occupied the town.

Vespasian himself came to Taricheae the following day. Putting an auxiliary garrison in the town, the general gained the willing cooperation of local carpenters, who quickly repaired boats that had been laid up and completed others that had been under construction. These craft were not large. In biblical times, typical fishing boats on the Sea of Galilee were crewed by a handful of men. Vespasian put troops aboard the small craft, and personally taking command of this little fleet, set off across the lake in pursuit of the rebels.

As the Romans came up, the rebels threw stones at them only to receive darts in reply. Sailing into the midst of the rebel fleet, Vespasian's men killed them with flying javelins, then leapt onto Jewish boats, where they dealt death with their swords. When rebels fled to the shore, they were cut down by waiting troops. Vespasian's little navy entirely wiped out the maritime rebels, leaving the lake red with blood and filled with floating, bloating bodies and the wrecks of small boats. Josephus reported that, days after, "a terrible stink" hung over the lake. Between the battles outside Taricheae, in the town, and on the lake, says Josephus, a total of 6,500 rebel Jews perished.

Returning to the town, Vespasian sat in judgment on the tens of thousands of Jewish civilians in Taricheae. According to Josephus, he was inclined to be lenient toward them, but his generals Trajan and Cerialis and his tribunes warned that he could not risk having potential rebels at his back once he marched on Jerusalem. Even if they had not taken up arms before now, they said, these Jews might be radicalized in the future. It was better to be safe than sorry, they counseled.

In the end, Vespasian gave in to his officers, although he did not order the execution of all the prisoners. He had it announced throughout Taricheae that all Jews in the city must collect their valuables and be ready to be taken to the regional administrative center of Tiberias the following day for processing prior to return to their original homes in Gadara, Hippos, Gaulanitis, Trachonitis, and back to Taricheae itself. The following day, in a scene that is still familiar in the Middle East to this day, male, female, and child refugees set out from Taricheae along the road to Tiberias clutching those belongings they could carry. That three-mile length of road was lined on both sides by silent Roman troops, in place to ensure no one escaped into the countryside.

This September day of AD 67, believing that they were going home, these thousands of refugees went willingly, even happily, telling themselves that the grim-faced Roman soldiers at the roadside were there for their protection against rebel militants. The refugees were funneled to the Tiberias amphitheater, which was built into the lower slopes of Mount Berenice, today's Mount Bernike, on the outskirts of the city. Only rediscovered in 1990 and completely unearthed by 2009, this stadium, built for Roman gladiatorial contests and other blood sports, could seat seven thousand spectators.

With troops encircling the arena, the refugees were assembled on its sands. Vespasian watched the Jews arrive from the empty stone stands, and once they were massed before him, he ordered them separated into groups. One party of 1,200 was made up of old men and the maimed and useless. Six thousand fit young men were separated from the rest, and to their horror and the horror of their families, found they were being sent to Achaea in southern Greece as imperial slave labor on the Isthmus canal project that Nero had recently initiated in a ceremony where he'd turned the first sod. Of the remainder, 30,400 men, women, and children were set aside to be sold as slaves.[58]

A smaller number of prisoners, natives of Taricheae, were allocated to King Herod Agrippa II to do with as he wished. The king also sent these people to the slave traders. Once all the sobbing Jews destined for imperial slave labor and slave markets had been marched from the stadium, feeling the crack of centurions' vine sticks across their backs and forced to leave their belongings behind on the sand for sale by Roman traders, only the old and infirm were left standing plaintively there. Vespasian ordered the immediate execution of these 1,200, on the spot.

Now, Vespasian was convinced by Agrippa to cast his eyes across the Sea of Galilee. In the blue hills on the lake's eastern shore lay the city of Gamala, in the south of the Golan Heights. Agrippa told Vespasian that Gamala was a rebel hotbed that must be dealt with. On the eastern periphery of the king's realm, Gamala had resisted a siege by the king's own forces for seven months. Now, to remove yet another rebel thorn from his side before focusing on Jerusalem, Vespasian ordered his three legions to prepare to march on Gamala.

Tribune Placidus would not be taking part in the Gamala operation. Giving Placidus six hundred cavalry, Vespasian sent him to Mount Tabor, near Scythopolis, where large numbers of rebels had gathered. On his arrival there, Placidus sent word to the rebels that he had come on a peace mission and invited Jewish leaders to come down off the mountain to parley. Envoys came to meet the waiting tribune, intending to assassinate him. Placidus was expecting this, and when the Jews drew their hidden weapons, he and the few cavalrymen with him galloped away. When the rebels gave chase, Placidus led his pursuers into a trap. His cavalry, lying in concealment, surrounded the partisans and cut them to pieces. Rebels still on the mountain fled to Jerusalem, and civilians living on Mount Tabor agreed to peace terms with the tribune, who occupied the mountain with his troops.

Before Vespasian set off for Gamala, he had one more task that needed attention. For this, he dispatched his son Titus on a secret mission to Syria. Vespasian had apparently heard from Gaius Mucianus, governor of Syria. In all probability, Mucianus had by this time received one of the letters that Vindex, the restive governor of Gallia Lugdunensis, had sent to colleagues around the empire. At this time, too, Vindex had commenced to court Servius Sulpicius Galba, governor of the Roman province of Nearer Spain, suggesting that he would make a better emperor than Nero.

Titus was being sent to discuss with Mucianus what posture he and Vespasian would take in relation to the unfolding situation in Gaul and Spain. For, between them, Vespasian and Mucianus controlled nine legions, or elements of nine legions, in the East. And nine legions could make an emperor.

XI

GAMALA AND GISCHALA

Prior to the Jewish uprising, Gamala had been a wealthy little city in the hills in the south of the Golan Heights, looking west out over the Sea of Galilee. The surrounding hillsides were filled with olive groves that produced reputedly the best olive oil in the entire region and made the city an active trading hub. Gamala, or Gamla as it is known today, gained its name from the conical hill on which it spread—Gamala means "camel" in Aramaic, and the hill resembled a camel's hump. The site was fed by a freshwater spring, and it was this that had attracted the original settlers in the third century BC.

With a predominantly Jewish population, and previously subject to King Herod Agrippa II's rule, Gamala had welcomed a flood of Jewish refugees from Galilee, the Decapolis, and Judea, bringing its population to some nine thousand people. The refugees had filled every vacant space in the little hillside city. Even the Gamala synagogue had been pressed into use as a refugee accommodation center—excavation of the synagogue in modern times would find the north wall of the synagogue's prayer hall lined with the cooking utensils of those refugees.

Gamala's old circumventing walls had long ago tumbled down, so when Josephus was given rebel command in Galilee he had demolished some houses on the city outskirts and built walls between others to create a makeshift defensive wall around Gamala. The rebel leaders he left in charge in Gamala, Chares and Joseph, had maintained a thriving economy in the crowded city even while Agrippa's commander Mobius lay siege to it. They had even minted Gamala's own coinage. Those coins were inscribed "Deliverance to Holy Jerusalem," for, the rebel leadership saw the holding of Gamala as contributing to the much more important goal, to them, of maintaining the freedom and independence of the holy city of Jerusalem.

At the revolt's outset Gamala had become Josephus's headquarters and recruiting center for all of rebel Galilee. It was also the hometown of Menahem, late conqueror of Masada and butcher of a 3rd Gallica Legion cohort. And Gamala still harbored thousands of armed partisans. So, Agrippa was able to offer plenty of reasons for Vespasian to march against the city, reasons that motivated the Roman general even though it was well into the fall and the official end of the marching season was fast approaching. Now, retribution and revenge marched up to the walls of Gamala behind the eagles of the legions of Vespasian.

It was the second week of October when the Roman army reached the Golan Heights. On October 12, Vespasian's three legions pitched separate camps in the hills around Gamala. A natural ridge that dropped steeply away from the western side of the city made it unassailable from that direction, so Vespasian assigned the 15th Apollinaris Legion to the eastern side of Gamala, where the city's highest round defensive tower rose. Most of the 15th's men swapped shields and helmets for entrenching tools and immediately commenced work on an earth ramp against the eastern wall.

At the same time, the Moesians of the 5th Macedonica Legion set up camp opposite the center of the city to the south and also began work on a ramp. The Syrians of the 10th Fretensis Legion camped north of the city and began filling in a valley and defensive ditches before beginning their own assault ramp. To cover these operations, Vespasian had each legion set up its artillery.

While this construction work was commencing, Agrippa rode to one of the walls and called out to the rebels manning them, seeking a peace conference that might do away with the need for a siege. The Jewish response was a well-aimed sling stone, let loose from the walls, which struck the king a painful blow on the elbow. Agrippa's own men hurriedly surrounded him, and under cover of their shields he was escorted away. This treatment of a man who had gone to parley only enraged the Romans, and they set about their work with even more vigor, says Josephus.[59]

The rebels, low on food and water, with so many mouths to feed and feeling the need to improve morale in the city, made a sally outside one of the city walls, planning to harry the workmen. But the Roman artillery opened up such a withering fire of anti-personnel ballista bolts, darts, arrows, and, particularly, stone balls, partisans were cut down in swathes. The remaining rebels were driven back inside the city before they could reach the Roman earthworks.

In recent times, archaeologists working at the remains of one of ancient Gamala's outer walls unearthed 100 Roman iron ballista bolts, 1,600 iron arrowheads, and 2,000 ballista stones—all remnants of this very repulse of the rebel sally in October of AD 67. The ballista stones found here, mostly standard sixty-pounders, had been fashioned by hand from local basalt. They were perfectly round, like basketballs, as if made by machine. Yet basalt is notoriously difficult to shape.

It didn't take long for the Roman ramps to grow against the comparatively low walls, and before much more time had passed, mantlets were being run up against the wall, and battering rams went to work. Soon, the dry stone walls shook, and at a weakened point a Roman grappling hook was fired at the top of the wall. Called a *harpax*, this type of iron grappling hook had been adapted from Roman naval warfare for use in siege warfare on land. It was fired by catapult, after which the rope attached to the harpax unraveled and was mechanically winched in. Using this harpax, a section of the Gamala wall was quickly hooked and brought tumbling down. That breach can still be seen at the Gamala ruins today, while the harpax used to make it was found by archaeologists in the rubble of the fallen wall, below the breach.

Roman legionaries now formed up in their cohorts, probably assigned their positions for the assault by drawing lots. As they worked themselves up to storm the city, they rhythmically clashed their swords against their shields. Then the appointed hour arrived. Legion trumpets sounded "Charge," and with a roar the legionaries surged in through the gap in the broken wall and entered the lower part of the city. Getting into the city proved the easy part. Once inside, legionaries found themselves in narrow streets that inclined steeply up the hill. Slowly driving defenders back, Roman troops were able to push their way uphill to reach the upper city.

Partisans regrouped, and battling their opponents and gravity, Romans were driven back down into fellow soldiers coming behind. Some legionaries pushed their way into city houses to find refuge, or clambered onto roofs. But as these houses were built one against the other up the hill, the crush of soldiers caused wooden floors and tiled roofs to give way, and like a house of cards, whole residential sections collapsed in clouds of dust, killing, injuring, and burying numerous Roman troops. Several legionaries lost limbs in the destruction.

Cheering partisans took advantage of this Roman calamity, some using bricks and stones from the wrecked houses as weapons while others grabbed the weapons of legionaries trapped in the rubble, first using them to finish off their former owners and then charging the Roman troops who were trying to come to the aid of their comrades. In modern archeological digs, pieces of Roman legionary helmets, the brow and cheek-piece of an officer's helmet, pieces of Roman segmented armor, and Roman short swords would all be unearthed from this rubble.

Vespasian had personally entered the city for this assault, armed with shield and sword like his men, and with just a small bodyguard. He quickly found himself under heavy attack from higher up the hill. Vespasian had never run in his life, and he didn't intend doing so now. Calling the men around him to form a testudo, he and his comrades stood their ground protected by their raised shields until the rain of rebel missiles against them abated. Then, retaining the tortoise formation and without turning their backs to the enemy, the general and his men backed all the way to the city wall and out through the breach.

Among the many Romans killed on this disastrous day for Vespasian's army was Decurion Ebutius, the cavalry officer who'd gained a reputation for unequaled dash and courage during operations of the past months. He'd probably been a volunteer for the Gamala assault. The officer's helmet remnants since found in the ruins of Gamala may well have been his.

Another junior Roman officer, a Centurion Gallus, made his name this same day by living, not dying. Gallus, a native of Gaul if his name is a guide, had taken refuge inside a house in Gamala with ten of his men, and as night fell they found themselves trapped there, with rebels unwittingly on the floor either above or below them. Gallus and his men listened through the wooden floor as the owner of the house boasted over supper to his compatriots about what they were going to do to the Roman army the following day. Waiting until the early hours of the morning, Gallus and his legionaries crept out, cut the throats of their unwitting host and his sleeping friends, then slipped out of the city and returned to their own camp, where they were no doubt greeted as men who'd risen from the dead.

Vespasian went around his troops in camp the day following their reverse in Gamala, consoling them on their injuries and on the loss of friends and comrades, telling them that it was inevitable that the Roman army must suffer casualties in this war. Fate was to blame, he said, not any lack of Roman skill or superiority of Jewish valor.

"For myself," he went on to declare, "I'll continue to endeavor to go first before you against your enemies in every engagement, and to be the last to retire from it."[60]

For the time being, Vespasian resumed the siege, intending to starve out the rebels. But in late November, three legionaries of the 15th Apollinaris took it upon themselves to creep to the city wall where a large tower rose. In the early morning hours, during the night's last watch, they steadily worked on large stones at the base of this tower with crowbars. With no mortar to hold these stones in place, the legionaries succeeded in pulling out five of them. The base of the tower began to rumble, and the trio scurried back to Roman lines. And then with an almighty crash the entire tower tumbled down.

The rebel commander, Joseph, had come to investigate the ominous sounds from the tower, and along with the tower's Jewish sentries, he was brought down with it. As the injured Joseph struggled to escape the tower ruins, he was spotted by a Roman artilleryman, who let fly with a dart that claimed a direct hit and killed him. The rebels were now left without a recognized commander; Joseph's colleague, Chares, had been ill for some time—possibly suffering from dysentery in the unhygienic crowded city—and he passed away in his bed that same morning.

By this time Titus had returned from his flying visit to Syria for the meeting with Proconsul Mucianus, and he received his father's permission to lead two hundred of the best Roman cavalry, dismounted, plus a band of select legionaries, in a surprise night attack. This was to be launched via the new breach in the wall, where the toppled tower had stood. Titus and his men succeeded in creeping to the breach after dark, and were only spotted by Jewish sentries as they clambered through the breach. When Titus quickly met stiff opposition inside the city, Vespasian kept his word to his troops and personally led a much larger force to reinforce his son's party.

The two conflated Roman forces steadily forced partisan fighters back up the hill, as a violent windstorm blew up at the Romans' back. As if the

Roman gods had come to the attackers' aid, this storm seemed to blow Titus, Vespasian, and their men up the sloping streets, at the same time blinding defenders and blowing them from their precarious vantage points in the upper city. Losing heart in the face of this combination of wind and Roman steel, many partisans threw their wives and children off the highest precipices of the upper city, then made suicidal jumps after them. The Romans now raged through the city, and they, too, their blood lust raised, threw Jewish children to their deaths. Only two young women were spared. Dragged from their hiding place, they proved to be the daughters of Philip bar Jacimus, King Herod Agrippa II's cavalry general.

Josephus was to say that five thousand Jews perished by jumping or being thrown to their deaths, while four thousand had died during the fighting for Gamala, although some scholars feel the combined total of nine thousand Jewish dead another Josephus inflation. Vespasian ordered the city demolished so that it could be of no use to rebels again. The Roman army apparently didn't feel the need to retrieve war matériel used in the siege of Gamala for later use, for, as Vespasian's troops leveled the city, they made no attempt to gather up the two thousand ballista balls or the grappling hook that lay in the rubble. Gamala would never be rebuilt. The ruins of Gamala's synagogue, where rebel families sheltered during Vespasian's siege, have been unearthed by archaeological digs in modern times. The oldest surviving synagogue in Israel, it is the site of special Jewish religious services today.

With the Roman destruction of Gamala completed by early December, in all of Galilee only one small town, Gischala, or Gush Halav as the Jews called it, remained in rebel hands. Today the predominantly Christian/Muslim town of Jish, Gischala lay west of the Sea of Galilee and just to the north of Tiberias and Taricheae, on the slopes of Mount Meron, which was bedecked with olive groves and was another well-known olive oil production center. Despite its Greek name, Gischala contained several synagogues and a sizable Jewish population. According to Christian tradition, Saul of Tarsus, the future Apostle Paul, had lived with his parents in the town as a child.

The small number of rebels remaining at Gischala in December of AD 67 consisted of what Josephus described as a robber band. Yet their leader was no bandit. He was a wealthy local olive oil merchant, Yohanan bar Levi, who was to become known as Yohanan mi-Gush Halav, or John of

Gischala. He was "a cunning knave," in the words of Josephus, who considered him at times rash while at other times wise.[61]

Vespasian now withdrew the bulk of the Roman army to encamp once more for the winter, sending the 10th Fretensis Legion to Scythopolis and taking the 5th Macedonica and 15th Apollinaris with him to Caesarea. He left Titus in Galilee to deal with Gischala, and Titus diverted there with a thousand cavalry. On a December Saturday, Titus rode up to one of the town walls to offer peace terms to the rebels. Josephus says that Titus could see that the town would easily fall to him if he pressed forward with an assault, but he had tired of the often wanton bloodshed of the past months. Nowhere near as severe in his outlook as his father, Titus genuinely wanted to spare the people in the town, knowing that only a minority were rebels, while also knowing that once he let his troops loose on the town he would not be able to restrain them from killing guilty and innocent alike.

Titus called to the rebels on the walls that he offered a pardon—but for the pardon to be extended, all in Gischala must surrender, and the town must be handed over to him. John of Gischala called back that he was all for accepting Titus's offer and was prepared to force everyone else in the town to do the same. However, he said, it was the Jewish Sabbath, a day on which Jews neither took up arms nor discussed treaties. Titus, agreeing to return the following day to wrap up peace negotiations, withdrew with his cavalry to the walled village of Cydessa, or Kedesh as the Jews called it, which came within the administrative control of the port of Tyre, twenty miles away. Like Tyre, Cydessa had remained loyal to Rome.

Titus failed to leave a single Roman guard outside Gischala, and John took advantage of this to slip out of the town that night and head overland for Jerusalem. He not only took all his armed men with him, he took their wives and children as well—upward of nine thousand of them according to Josephus, although this is possibly another exaggerated figure. This band had not gone three miles when the fearful wailings of women and children in the party caused John to call a halt. The civilians were slowing him down, and he feared that their noise would attract their enemies and result in the deaths of them all. So, he convinced his men to go on without their families, who were left to fend for themselves.

As the heartbroken women and children attempted to return to Gischala, many became lost. John and his fighters, meanwhile, reached Jerusalem. They were welcomed into the holy city by a crowd of ten thousand, which thronged around them asking to hear of the state of affairs in Galilee. John didn't tell his fellow Jews that he and his men had fled Gischala and deserted their families. Instead, he boasted that he had bested the Romans and outwitted Vespasian's son and had come to add strength to the defense of Jerusalem. The Romans, he said, were struggling to take even the smallest villages in Galilee. As for Jerusalem, with its mighty walls, it was more than a match for the Romans and their engines of war, which, he said, were being broken against the walls of Galilean cities.

"Even if the Romans were to sprout wings," he declared, "they could not fly over the walls of Jerusalem!" Young men flocked around him, idolizing him and vowing to follow him in war. In this way, through lie and boast, John of Gischala became one of the leaders of the resistance at Jerusalem.[62]

When Titus returned with his troops to Gischala by the middle of the following day, it was to find the remaining people in the town opening the gates, receiving him as a savior, and informing him that John had tricked him and escaped to Jerusalem. Kicking himself for allowing John to dupe him, Titus sent part of his force galloping in pursuit of the rebel party and entered Gischala with the rest. Titus's cavalry failed to overtake the rebel fighters, but they did come upon their wandering families. The cavalrymen, who were likely to have been tough, mustachioed Gauls or bearded Germans, professional soldiers from the other side of the world with no time for fractious Jews of any age or sex, and who made up the bulk of Rome's cavalry, callously killed close to six thousand women and children, then drove another three thousand back to Gischala like cattle.

Giving these returnees and the remaining people of Gischala their lives, and leaving part of his force as a permanent Roman garrison in the town, Titus returned to Caesarea in time to join his father for the annual Saturnalia Festival. With all of Galilee now in Roman hands, Vespasian prepared for the campaign of the following year, AD 68, a campaign aimed at the ultimate prize, Jerusalem.

XII

NERO'S FATE CHANGES
EVERYTHING

In Greece that September, the emperor Nero had received the news of
Vespasian's summer successes in Galilee with impatience. Earlier in AD
67 he had competed at the Olympic Games at Olympia, where he had won
all the musical events and been awarded victory in the ten-horse chariot
event—even though he had fallen out of his chariot and failed to finish. He
had subsequently victoriously competed at the Isthmian Games at Corinth
in April–May, then the Pythian Games at Delphi in August, where he
had also visited the Oracle of Delphi, going to the head of the line of sup-
plicants for a prediction, the nature of which was never revealed. Then it
was back to Corinth to turn the first sods of his planned Isthmian Canal
project, for which Vespasian sent him the six thousand Jewish slave labor-
ers from Taricheae.

With the Roman conquest of Jerusalem clearly still a long way off, Nero
had unhappily canceled his planned Ethiopian operation to the south and
looked east. Deciding that he would instead focus on the Caspian Gates
offensive once Vespasian wrapped up the annoying Jewish problem, he
expected Vespasian to have the Judean counteroffensive completed as soon
as possible so that all resources could be focused on the Caspian Gates in
the new year.

In December, Nero's freedman Helius arrived in Greece from Rome to personally beg the emperor to return to the capital so he could be seen to deal with the problems simmering in the empire's western provinces. With the offensive against the Jewish rebels on hold for the winter, Nero unhappily acceded to Helius's requests and announced that he was going home. Sailing back to the west coast of Italy from Greece, by early January he had entered Neapolis (Naples), then Antium (Anzio), then Alba Longa in the Alban Hills outside Rome, finally entering Rome itself, always in triumphal processions as he returned home as victor at the Greek games. He had originally intended that these celebrations would combine his military, athletic, and artistic achievements, but as the ongoing Jewish War had robbed him of his planned Ethiopian and Caspian Gates military victories, the Triumphs were for his achievements in Greece alone.

For the Rome procession of his Triumph, part of the city wall was torn down to allow him a broader entry—the usual gate used by triumphants, the Porta Triumphalis, which was kept locked except when used for Triumphs, was quite narrow. For his Triumph, Nero rode through the streets of Rome in the golden chariot that Augustus had first used for his triumphal processions and had last been used by Germanicus and his brother Claudius in their Triumphs, in celebration of military victories. The rest of the time the chariot was reverently kept in the Temple of Capitoline Jupiter.

As he drove through the city, along streets lined with the cheering population, the beaming Nero wore a purple robe covered with gold spangles, and a crown of wild olive, the symbol of peace. In one hand he held up his laurel crown from the Pythian Games. Signboards held aloft by marchers in the procession proclaimed the names of each of the games won by Nero and the declaration: "Nero Caesar, first of all Romans since the beginning of the world, he won this."[63] The lyre player Diodorus rode in the chariot with him as the procession wound through the city, past adoring crowds in the Circus Maximus and the Forum, to the Palatine. The chariot was preceded by the senators of Rome and followed by troops of the Praetorian and German Guards, all chanting:

"Hail Olympian Victor! Hail Pythian Victor! Augustus! Augustus! Hail to Nero, our Hercules! Hail to Nero, our Apollo! The only Victor of the Grand Tour, the only one from the beginning of time! Augustus! Augustus! Oh, Divine Voice! Blessed are they that hear you."[64]

Even though Nero was back in Rome after an absence of over a year, he was still little interested in the affairs of state. When, at the beginning of April, news was brought to him of Julius Vindex's declaration of revolt in Gaul in late March—by some accounts on March 28, the anniversary of the murder of Nero's mother, Agrippina the Younger—Nero was more interested in discussing the workings of a new musical instrument, a water organ for the theater. Vindex, himself a native of Aquitania in Gaul, had attracted vast crowds of Gauls in Lugdunum (Lyon) with speeches about the rights of Gauls, and had now thrown off Neronian rule. Supported by leading men of Gaul, Vindex had enlisted thousands of willing young men into a Gallic army that he would march on Italy to dethrone Nero by force.

It was Praetorian Prefect Tigellinus who dispatched orders for a military response to Vindex and his Gallic army. From northern Italy, the recently formed unit originally named the Phalanx of Alexander the Great marched under the new name of the 1st Italica Legion to intercept the Gauls before they crossed the Alps. They were accompanied by the Taurine Horse, a cavalry wing from today's Turin in northern Italy, with the overall force commanded by the senator Junius Blaesus. Orders were also sent to Lucius Verginius Rufus, Roman proconsul of Upper Germany. Rufus, who commanded an army of four crack legions, was to march south into Gaul from his headquarters at Mogantiacum, today's Mainz, on the Rhine, with elements from all four legions, to likewise intercept Vindex on the march.

Taking thousands of legionaries and numerous auxiliaries with him, Rufus moved quickly. Heading south, he cut off Vindex's force of mostly raw recruits outside Vesontio, today's Besançon, at the foot of the Alps. Here in 58 BC, Julius Caesar had won one of the greatest victories of his Gallic War, and here, 110 years later, another Gallic army was to be routed. It is unclear precisely when the battle between the forces of Vindex and Rufus took place—it was apparently sometime in late May.

Vindex, in his forties, was well built and possessed a reputation as a fine soldier—a senator of Rome, he would have likely served as a legion commander while in his thirties, a posting that usually only lasted two to three years. His opponent, Verginius Rufus, on the other hand, was not a warlike man. He was a literary man, a noted author who was guardian to the writer Pliny the Younger. Rufus's funeral oration would in years to come be written and delivered by noted historian Tacitus.

In hopes of talking the Gauls into turning around and going home, Rufus coaxed Vindex to a parley, but, apparently, as the two leaders were talking peace, Rufus's experienced troops, who were chafing at the bit to teach the Gauls a lesson, launched an attack on Vindex's army of their own accord. The Gauls were slaughtered, and Vindex took his own life just two months after launching his revolt.

As Rufus's troops reasserted Roman control in Gaul, they offered to make Rufus their emperor, an offer Rufus would refuse, both then and when it was again made the following year. He and his legions returned to the Rhine, and when the 1st Italica Legion and Taurine Horse reached Gaul, they marched on up to the city that had briefly been the center of Vindex's revolt, Lyon, where they reestablished control of Gaul for Nero Caesar and the Senate of Rome, and Junius Blaesus took charge as the new governor.

Despite the destruction of Vindex and the threat he posed, the seeds of revolt had been sown, and at Rome, Nero was panicking. Five thousand freedmen sailors of the Roman war fleet at Misenum had been rapidly formed into a legion, promised Roman citizenship, and marched to Rome to protect their emperor. To further increase Nero's protection, orders were sent to Dalmatia for several cohorts of the 11th Claudia Legion and 15th Primigenia Legion to march at once for Rome. When they reached the capital by June, they were quartered in public buildings along with the seamen now serving as legionaries of the 1st Legion of the Fleet. These troops were joined by a number of retired legion veterans who were living in Italy and were recalled to their standards as part of their Evocati militia service.

By the first week of June, one of Nero's two Praetorian prefects, Nymphidius Sabinus, had forced the other prefect, Tigellinus, to resign, and convinced the Praetorian Guard to withdraw its support for the emperor. On June 8, it was announced in the Senate that Nero had fled to Egypt, and Servius Galba, seventy-year-old governor of Nearer Spain, was declared the new emperor. But Nero was still in Rome.

The following morning, Nero awoke in his fabulous new palace, the Golden House, built in the wake of the AD 64 Great Fire of Rome, to find that his German Guard bodyguards had disappeared. In a city swimming with troops—who had all been confined to barracks on the orders of the Senate—Nero was now the loneliest man in the world and the most unsafe of rulers. With four freedmen servants, he fled to the suburban home of one of those freedmen. There, about the middle of the day, as Praetorian cavalry were heard approaching and a terrified Nero feared being tortured and executed, he slit his own throat with the help of his freedmen.

So it was that on June 9, AD 68, after a reign of thirteen years, Nero Caesar, thirty-year-old fifth emperor of Rome and last member of the Caesar family, died by his own hand. A most unfit young man to rule an empire, Nero had always seen himself as a performer of enormous talent. His last words were said to be, "Oh, what an artist dies in me."[65]

*   *   *

Back in March, just as Vindex's revolt was gathering steam in Gaul, Vespasian had launched the campaigning season in Judea by leading two rested legions and supporting troops out of Caesarea and down the coastal plain. Climbing into the hills, he secured Antipatris, Lydda (Lod), and Jamnia, Gentile-controlled cities which gladly opened their gates to him.

Civilians loyal to Rome who had followed the general south were settled in these cities, with garrisons left in all three and also in the village of Adida—thought to be modern Al-Haditha, three miles east of Lod. Retaining his legionaries for offensive operations, Vespasian assigned auxiliaries and allied troops to these garrisons. In the larger towns the garrisons were commanded by centurions, while decurions were put in charge in the smaller centers.

Vespasian then established a new walled marching camp at the town of Emmaus, just nine miles from Jerusalem, as his forward base. There, he installed General Cerialis with the 5th Macedonica Legion and supporting auxiliaries, straddling the highway from the coast that the ill-fated Governor Gallus had used, and cutting off Jerusalem from the northwest. A tombstone discovered near Emmaus in modern times, of a thirty-year-old optio of the 5th Macedonica who had served nine years with the Roman army, probably stems from this period.

Vespasian then returned to Caesarea, where he received the news of Vindex's uprising in Gaul. Josephus was to claim that Vespasian now vowed to end the war in Judea as quickly as possible so that the emperor Nero had one less thing to worry about. To permit this, Vespasian sent orders to Trajan at Scythopolis to bring the 10th Fretensis Legion and meet him in June outside rebel-held Jericho, to the north of the Dead Sea, in the meantime tasking subordinates with wrapping up Jewish resistance east of the Jordan River and in Samaria.

The ever-reliable Tribune Placidus was given three thousand infantry and five hundred cavalry to pursue those partisans who had fled Gadara the previous year and were still known to be hiding out east of the Jordan River in the Perea district. Vespasian gave another large detachment of infantry and cavalry to an officer named Lucius Annius, with orders to neutralize Gerasa north of Jerusalem, the only city in Samaria still held by rebels. Annius, probably of tribune rank and likely a client of Vespasian, had lately joined Vespasian's staff.[66]

Annius's troops stormed over the walls of Gerasa at their first rush and overwhelmed the thousand young Jewish men defending the city, who were all put to death. Annius made captives and future slaves of all the family members of these slain rebels, then let his troops loot the town. Gerasa was burned to the ground, as were all the surrounding villages, before Annius rejoined Vespasian in Caesarea with his troops and captives.

Meanwhile, east of the Jordan River, Tribune Placidus's men would take longer to achieve their goal. Cornering large numbers of armed rebels, they drove them to the Jordan. Those who were not slaughtered on the riverside drowned while trying to swim to safety. So many bodies filled the river that it was impassable for a time, and countless bloated corpses subsequently floated down into the Sea of Galilee. According to Josephus, 15,000 Jews were killed here by Placidus and his troops, with another 2,200 taken prisoner, and large quantities of oxen, sheep, asses, and camels were captured for use by Roman army quartermasters.

Placidus and his troops then ranged through all the Perea district, securing cities and towns including Abila, Bezemoth, and Julias—the latter being a Romanized fishing village on the eastern shore of the Sea of Galilee named for the emperor Augustus's daughter Julia. Also known by the Jewish name of Bethsaida, Julias had been the birthplace of the fishermen brothers Shimon, Andreas, and Philippos, who became known as the Christian Apostles Simon-Peter, Andrew, and Philip.

All of Perea from the Sea of Galilee to the desert fortress of Machaerus was progressively cleared of rebels by Placidus and his troops. Machaerus itself remained in partisan hands for now. It would take a major siege to dislodge its rebel defenders. A number of partisan deserters came over to Placidus during this Perean operation, and he trusted them with guarding the principal towns of Perea for Rome when he and his troops withdrew to link up with General Trajan's approaching column. These turncoats remained loyal to Rome for the remainder of the war.

Vespasian, meanwhile, camped at Corea near Jericho with the remaining cohorts of the 15th Apollinaris Legion and waited for Trajan to join him. When Trajan's column approached with the 10th Fretensis and Placidus's recently returned troops, Vespasian established a large camp just outside Jericho, where Trajan's and Placidus's forces combined with his. On June 21, with his now enlarged army, Vespasian marched on Jericho.

As the Roman force approached, partisans poured out of the city. Some stood to fight in the open, others fled to the mountains. Those who fought were overwhelmed and massacred. When Vespasian marched into Jericho, he found it deserted and desolate. Placing a garrison of auxiliary and allied troops there, he sent legionaries against the nearby hilltop fortress at Cypros, site of the earlier massacre of a 3rd Gallica Legion cohort. Cypros was easily overrun and subsequently demolished. As a result, Vespasian's troops now blocked the route to Jerusalem from east of the Jordan, preventing fresh Jewish recruits from as far away as Parthia reaching the rebel capital.

Before Vespasian returned to Caesarea, he ventured south from Jericho to the Dead Sea, or Lake Asphaltitus as the Jews called it, to play tourist. Told that it was possible to float unaided in this lake, Vespasian had several bound Jewish prisoners thrown into the water to test the claim. He was highly amused when the Jews indeed floated. The Jews concerned were no doubt highly relieved. It is likely these prisoners came from the community of the Essene Jewish sect that had a monastery at Qumran, nine miles from Jericho and on the northwest fringe of the Dead Sea. The famous Dead Sea Scrolls would be found in caves nearby in 1946–47 and 1956. The Qumran monastery had been captured by Vespasian's cavalry, which established an outpost there.

On Vespasian's return to Caesarea, he gave orders for all field units to prepare to march on Jerusalem. Shortly after his return, however, official word arrived by sea from Rome that Nero was dead and Servius Galba had been hailed emperor by the Senate, even though Galba was in Spain. Vespasian immediately put all offensive operations on hold until the situation at Rome was clarified. For one thing, it was uncertain what position the troops at Rome would take in relation to Galba, especially the Praetorian Guard.

Galba was preparing to march overland from Spain with an army to take the throne, by force if necessary. His deputy was Marcus Otho, governor of Rome's third Spanish province, Lusitania, which covered much of today's Portugal. Galba's preparations included the raising of a new legion in his province of Nearer Spain—he would leave the province's resident legion, the 6th Victrix, in place to maintain order after he departed. Because the new Spanish legion was raised from Roman citizens resident in the traditional Spanish recruiting grounds of the 7th Claudia Legion, the unit was initially known as the 7th Galbiana, literally Galba's 7th Legion, later becoming the 7th Gemina after combination with another legion.

Auxiliary cavalry and auxiliary light infantry based in Spain would join Galba's march on Rome. One auxiliary infantry unit we can state with some confidence to have been in Galba's force was a cohort of British auxiliaries whose officers would include a handsome Briton named Florus—his Latin name means "beautiful." He was a favorite of Galba's, who would grant him Roman citizenship, after which he took the name Sulpicius Florus. He would shortly be listed among officers in Rome with Galba and Otho.[67]

As Galba and his troops entered Italy, Praetorian Prefect Nymphidius, son of a freedwoman, claimed that he was the illegitimate son of the late emperor Caligula and a legitimate claimant of the throne. His withdrawal of protection for Nero, which had led directly to Nero's demise, had clearly been intended by Nymphidius as a prelude to installing himself on the throne. But his Praetorian Guard didn't agree; it put an end to his lofty ambitions—with the sword.

When Galba reached Rome in October, he was met on the outskirts of the capital by the unarmed seamen who had earlier been formed into the 1st Legion of the Fleet by Nero. Blocking Galba's path, they vowed to serve him but clamored for the Roman citizenship promised by Nero. In response, the notoriously taciturn Galba, a very experienced, no nonsense general who no doubt scoffed at the idea of a legion made up of lowly freedmen, sent his cavalry against them; thousands of these men who wished to serve him were mown down and killed.

With this innocent blood on his hands and his reputation soiled, Galba entered Rome. His brief rule was to be characterized by arrogance, brutality, and chaos. Troops summoned to the city by Nero still remained there. Galba didn't send them back to their original commands, so they simply milled discontentedly around the city. Neither did Galba send orders to Vespasian for the continuance or cessation of the Judean War. This left Vespasian sitting idle and frustrated in Caesarea while Jewish rebels continued to hold Jerusalem.

By December, even though the sailing season was over and winter storms could be expected on the Mediterranean, Vespasian tired of waiting for guidance from Rome and decided to send his son Titus to the new emperor to pay Vespasian's respects to Galba and to seek orders. King Herod Agrippa II chose to accompany Titus to Rome, also to pay his respects but mainly in hopes of having his territories and powers in the Middle East confirmed by the new emperor.

Vespasian had known Galba for many years, but no one ever described them as close, and they never had a client/patron relationship. New emperors invariably put their favorites—relatives and clients—into positions of power, and Vespasian occupied the most powerful position in the Roman East, with nine legions at his command. Did Galba wish him to remain in that post and press on with the conquest of Jerusalem? Or would the new emperor send out a replacement for Vespasian, complete with new lackeys and new orders?

A squadron of fast Liburnian warships was prepared at Caesarea, and in January of AD 69, in a lull in the weather, Titus and Agrippa parted from Vespasian and set sail, planning to coast all the way rather than head directly across the Mediterranean to Italy as warships frequently did. This meant their journey would take longer than if they took the direct route, but it would be safer, allowing them to duck into port should storms brew. Their little flotilla was sailing via ports in Achaea, en route to Italy, when news was received on board that Galba had been assassinated at Rome on January 15, after a reign of just seven months.

Galba's unpopularity had spiraled after he parsimoniously refused to give his troops a "donative," or bonus, which had become the norm when new emperors ascended the throne. In the end, even his friends Marcus Otho and Florus the Briton turned their backs on him. Galba's own bodyguards deserted him as he was being carried in a litter through the Forum. A number of idle soldiers from the provinces and Evocati veterans had milled around Galba after he was dumped from the litter, calling for his blood. It was a legionary named Camurius, one of the men of the 15th Primigenia Legion sent to Rome from Dalmatia on Nero's orders, who killed Galba. As the aged emperor lay winded on the flagstones, Camurius had put his sword to Galba's throat and with his foot on the blade pressed down hard, decapitating him. Galba's head was soon being paraded around Rome on a pike.

In Galba's place, his associate Otho had been hailed emperor by the Praetorian Guard after he sagely promised its men the expected donative. Otho was not a popular choice in some quarters. Aged thirty-six, he was ambitious, slippery, overweight, and vain—he wore an expensive wig to hide his premature baldness. Of particular interest to Vespasian was the fact that Otho appointed Vespasian's brother Flavius Sabinus to be his city prefect, returning him to the powerful post as chief of Rome's police and firefighters that he'd held under Nero. On learning all this, Vespasian's son Titus decided to turn about and return to his father at Caesarea with the news. Agrippa chose to continue on to Rome, where he had a family palace, to pay respects to new emperor Otho on his behalf and on Vespasian's behalf.

On the Rhine, the eight legions in Rome's two German provinces disapproved of Otho's appointment. The four legions in the province of Lower Germany hailed their proconsul Aulus Vitellius emperor in competition with Otho, then sent delegates to the legions in Upper Germany and convinced them to also salute Vitellius emperor. The empire now had two emperors, Otho and Vitellius. As Vitellius prepared to send elements from his eight legions to Rome to take the throne from Otho, the 1st Italica Legion marched to Italy from Gaul to support Otho. Meanwhile, the legions in Moesia and Pannonia vowed allegiance to Otho and also sent troops marching to Italy to support him. Leading the troops from Moesia were the 3rd Gallica Legion's six cohorts that had recently gained fame for slaughtering the Roxolani raiders.

On March 14, as Vitellius's Rhine army marched on Italy in several columns led by his subordinates, two columns marched out of Rome to do battle with them in Otho's name. Otho's columns comprised troops of the Praetorian Guard, German Guard, survivors of the 1st Legion of the Fleet, more sailors lately pressed into service as soldiers, and the troops that had been summoned to Rome earlier by Nero. Two thousand professional gladiators were even brought into Otho's ranks. One of these columns headed for the south of France to terminate support for Vitellius in Gaul. The other aimed to head off the Vitellianist army just then entering Italy from the northwest.

Spirits in Otho's Italian column were buoyed when the force was joined by experienced troops who had marched from Pannonia to support Otho; three cohorts of the 13th Gemina Legion and three from the 14th Gemina Martia Victrix Legion, the latter a unit famous for leading the termination of the British revolt led by Boudicca eight years earlier. Morale elevated even more when the Roman general who'd defeated the rampaging Britons in AD 60–61, Gaius Suetonius Paulinus, joined the column and was given overall command by Otho, who arrived late from Rome leading another new, untried legion, the 1st Adiutrix, or 1st Supporter Legion, which had been raised in Gaul the previous year to support late emperor Galba, a unit whose men were "high-spirited and eager to gain their first victory," according to Tacitus.[68]

Early skirmishes in Gaul and northern Italy went Otho's way before, on April 15, at Bedriacum in central Italy, Otho's army and the Vitellianist army met on the main highway and did battle. Vitellius's army of battle-hardened Rhine legionaries, considered the best troops in the Roman army, overwhelmed the mostly inexperienced Othonist troops. The 14th Gemina Martia Victrix held its ground when others ran, but even it was forced to surrender.

Otho escaped, but even though more legions arrived from the Balkans overnight to support him, the following day, April 16, he committed suicide. All Otho's troops then capitulated, leaving Vitellius sole emperor of Rome. He would only enter the capital in July, disbanding the current Praetorian Guard for opposing him and filling the unit with his best legionaries, and sending far away other units that had fought bravely for Otho—the 14th Gemina Martia Victrix, for example, was ordered back to its old station in Britain, while the 1st Adiutrix was sent to Spain.

Vespasian knew Vitellius well. Both had survived under Caligula and prospered under Claudius. Grossly overweight, bisexual with a notorious boyfriend, and with a severe limp as a result of his boyhood friend Caligula driving a racing chariot into him, Vitellius had become more interested in feasting than governing. When news of Otho's death reached the East, the governor of Syria, Mucianus, wrote to Vespasian urging him to oppose the vice-ridden Vitellius and claim the throne for himself.

As Vespasian considered the idea, and after relocating his headquarters from Caesarea to Beirut, he went to Mount Carmel, home to a grotto housing a famous oracle, and sought the oracle's advice. There, too, he met with Mucianus, who told him that the king of Parthia, Vologases, had offered forty thousand horse archers to help him take the Roman throne— Mucianus had clearly already sounded out the Parthian ruler on the idea. Vespasian declined the Parthian offer, but the oracle of Mount Carmel seems to have encouraged the general's hopes, and after meeting with his officers and receiving their unanimous support, he wrote to Tiberius Alexander, prefect of Egypt, with a request, and Mucianus returned to Syria.

On July 4, Prefect Alexander convened an assembly of his two resident legions, the full 3rd Cyrenaica Legion and the four cohorts of the new 18th Legion, at which they swore allegiance to Vespasian as their emperor. Eight days later, the three legions currently based in Syria, the 4th Scythica, 6th Ferrata, and 12th Fulminata, assembled on the orders of Mucianus and likewise hailed Vespasian as emperor. The legionaries stationed in various parts of Judea, including the men of the lone remaining cohort of the 3rd Gallica as well as the 5th Macedonica, 10th Fretensis, and 15th Apollinaris Legions, immediately followed suit. Rome again had two emperors.

Soon, word reached the West that nine legions of the East had hailed Vespasian their emperor. Immediately, the six cohorts of the 3rd Gallica Legion currently on the Danube came out for Vespasian, and as their senior officers argued about what they should do, the legionaries set off to march on Rome under their chief centurion Arrius Varus, planning to gather other troops around them as they went. The 7th Galbiana Legion joined them, led by a convicted forger who had been kicked out of the Senate, Marcus Antonius Primus. An energetic fast-talker, Primus had been given command of the 7th Galbiana just months before by Galba. Primus, who significantly outranked Varus, took charge of the combined units. Making Varus his deputy, Primus led the march to Italy to depose Vitellius.

Meanwhile, in Syria, Proconsul Mucianus was also putting together a task force to place Vespasian on the throne at Rome. He called up thirteen thousand retired Evocati reservists living in the province and, adding these veterans to the complete 6th Ferrata Legion and auxiliaries, commenced preparations for an overland march to Rome. Vespasian also withdrew two thousand legionaries from his legions in Judea and sent them marching north to join Mucianus in Antioch for the Italian campaign. All up, Mucianus would take nearly thirty thousand men to Italy. At the same time, Vespasian wrote to Marcus Antonius Primus, telling him to wait for Mucianus and his troops to join him before advancing on Rome, at which time he wanted Mucianus to take charge of their combined forces.

Vespasian and son Titus now relocated to Alexandria, from where Vespasian could control the vital grain supply to Rome. He would only sail to Italy once Mucianus had dealt with Vitellius. But there was a fly in the ointment. Primus had no intention of waiting for or answering to Mucianus. Intending to push on to Rome with his own troops, he knew that in Britain, the rank and file had come out for Vespasian, but their centurions supported Vitellius, so Britain's legions were staying put. In Spain, the 1st Adiutrix Legion led the 6th Victrix and 10th Gemina Legions in swearing loyalty to Vespasian, but they were too far away to affect a fight in Italy. But on the Rhine, Vitellius's remaining tens of thousands of legionaries were still solidly behind the emperor they had created. So, Primus devised a cunning plan to prevent reinforcements reaching Vitellius from the Rhine and so protect his own back.

Primus knew that Vespasian had an old friend on the Rhine. Julius Civilis was a Batavian noble who served as a prefect commanding a Batavian auxiliary cohort attached to the legions that had invaded Britain in AD 43. Fighting alongside Vespasian's 2nd Augusta Legion back then, Civilis had befriended Vespasian. "My respect for Vespasian is longstanding," Civilis himself would write in AD 70. "While he was still a subject (of other emperors), we were called friends."[69]

Primus wrote several letters to Civilis, suggesting he foment trouble on the Rhine to tie up Vitellius's troops there, as a favor to Vespasian. Civilis would grab this suggestion and run with it. The revolt he unleashed later that year rolled along the Rhine and saw several of Vitellius's legions defect to the rebel cause. Primus's "diversion" was to prove too successful as far as Vespasian was concerned. It certainly prevented reinforcements reaching Vitellius in Italy, but it threatened to permanently destroy Roman control on the Rhine and in Gaul, and would ultimately require Vespasian to mount a major military operation to defeat Civilis and his rebel allies.

Civilis's chief ally in the Rhine uprising was Julius Classicus, a noble of the Treveri, a Belgic tribe occupying the lower Moselle River Valley. The Treveri had been conquered by Julius Caesar a century before this and ever since had provided auxiliaries to the Roman army, including highly valued cavalry. Like Civilis, Classicus had served as a prefect commanding auxiliaries for Rome. In AD 61 he'd arrived in Britain from the Rhine as prefect of the 6th Nerviorum Cohort, a light infantry unit filled by men from the Nervii, another Belgic tribe. With two other auxiliary cohorts, Classicus and his men had cleaned up London following its destruction by Boudicca's rebels and then built a new London fort on Watling Street. While the 6th Nerviorum would remain in Britain until the fifth century, Classicus was back on the Rhine by the time of Civilis's revolt. He is likely to have known Vespasian's son Titus when both had served on the Rhine.[70]

In Italy, Primus and his deputy Centurion Varus, disregarding Vespasian's order to wait for Mucianus, marched in the early autumn into Italy, gathering disgruntled former Praetorian guardsmen and entire legions such as the 7th Claudia and 8th Augusta to Vespasian's banner en route. On October 24 at Bedriacum, the very same place where Otho had been defeated just months before, Primus's troops defeated an army sent by Vitellius to intercept them. Many men from Vitellius's army fled to the nearby city of Cremona, which was bulging with visitors attending its annual fair.

Primus surrounded and assaulted Cremona that same day, soon breaking into it. While he himself then took a bath, Primus's troops and thousands of camp followers were let loose in Cremona. Being non-Italians, Primus's legionaries had no sympathy for the Italians of Cremona who had given refuge to enemy troops. Led by the sun-worshipping Syrians of the 3rd Gallica Legion, Primus's men raped and looted their way through the city, taking many civilians as their personal slaves. When Primus subsequently banned this enslavement of Roman citizens, the legionaries put their prisoners to death rather than free them. More than forty thousand civilians died at Cremona.

Primus's army then marched on the capital. Struggling through the snows covering the Apennine Mountains north of Rome, Primus and his troops were only within striking distance of the city by mid-December. In the city, the city prefect, Vespasian's brother Sabinus, prematurely declared allegiance to Vespasian and led the troops of the Night Watch in occupying the Capitoline Mount, with Vespasian's youngest son, Domitian, and Sabinus's son Clemens sheltering with him. The German Guard, the then imperial bodyguard, laid siege to the Capitoline Mount to prove its loyalty to Vitellius. In the process, they set fire to the Temple of Jupiter Best and Greatest, Rome's oldest and largest temple. The building, many treasures stored inside, and the other structures on the hill were destroyed by the fire.

From north of the city, Quintus Petilius Cerialis, a relative of Vespasian by marriage and a client of his, set off with a thousand cavalry provided by Primus with the aim of breaking into Rome, reaching the Capitol, and saving Vespasian's son, brother, and nephew. Previously watched over by Vitellius because of his connection with Vespasian, Cerialis had escaped from Rome disguised as a farmer, linking up with Primus just after his army crossed the Apennines. While Primus and his troops continued on down the Flaminian Way from the north at a pace dictated by its baggage train, Cerialis diverted to the Salarian Way with his speedy cavalry, aiming to enter Rome from the northeast and surprise Vitellianist defenders.

Cerialis was notoriously rash. Nine years earlier, while commander of the 9th Hispana Legion in Britain, he'd led his troops into an ambush by Boudicca's rebels. He had lost two thousand legionaries and only escaped death himself by galloping away. Now, anxious to save Sabinus and Domitian, he blundered into unfamiliar winding alleys and gardens in Rome's northeastern suburbs, where Vitellius's troops ambushed him. Many of Cerialis's troopers turned and fled. Some were captured. Cerialis himself made an ignominious retreat.

With Cerialis's rescue attempt a failure, the fate of Vespasian's brother was sealed. On the burning Capitoline Mount, Sabinus's Night Watch troops, former slaves, were no match for the elite German guardsmen, who overwhelmed them. Sabinus was captured and beheaded, although Domitian and Sabinus's son managed to escape disguised as adherents of the god Isis. They were subsequently hidden in the city home of one of the family's freedmen.

As soon as Primus and his army reached Rome, they attacked its walls and closed gates. After several days of heavy fighting, they forced an entry into the city. The German Guard made a last stand at the Castra Praetoria, castle-like barracks of the Praetorian Guard, fighting to the last man. More than fifty thousand soldiers on both sides died in the taking of Rome. Domitian and his cousin were safely secured by Primus, and on December 21, the quaking emperor Vitellius was discovered alone at his Palatium on the Palatine, hiding in an "unseemly" place, according to Tacitus's *Histories*—a janitor's room, with a dog tethered outside the door, according to Suetonius's *Twelve Caesars*. Dragged out by a tribune of either the City Guard or Night Watch, the emperor of eight months was put to death while begging for his life. The following day, the Senate met and proclaimed Vespasian emperor, conferring the rank of consul on Vespasian's conquering general Primus.

Mucianus and his army from the East reached Rome very shortly after. En route, Mucianus's force had fortuitously intercepted a Sarmatian invasion across the Danube in Moesia and mercilessly quashed it. Mucianus had also dispatched one of his officers, Virdius Geminus, with an Evocati detachment and a squadron of Liburnians he'd based at the city of Byzantium to deal with the Anicetus Revolt in Pontus. Anicetus, a freedman of the late King Polemon II of Pontus, had risen up with a band of supporters and slaughtered the cohort of Roman troops stationed in Pontus since AD 64. Previously serving the king, the men of this cohort had been granted Roman citizenship by Nero. Claiming to be supporting Vitellius, Anicetus had gone on to burn ships docked at Trapezus. But his revolt proved short-lived. While trying to escape Geminus, Anicetus was captured by local tribesmen at the mouth of the Cohibus River (today's Enguri) and handed over to his Roman pursuers. Geminus executed Anicetus, and stability was returned to Pontus in Vespasian's name.

Immediately upon reaching the capital, Mucianus assumed the reins of power, sidelining Primus. He would wield that power until Vespasian arrived. Mucianus also promptly took Vespasian's son Domitian under his wing, and directed seven legions to converge on the Rhine to deal with Civilis's revolt. Vespasian's relative Petilius Cerialis was sent ahead with the 21st Rapax Legion and auxiliaries, while the remaining troops marched from several provinces. Given this last chance to prove himself, Cerialis would not fail Mucianus or his emperor. It would be a grueling campaign, but in a series of AD 70 battles, Cerialis would terminate the rebellion and reclaim the Rhine for Rome. His reward from Vespasian would be a return to Britain in AD 71 as the province's new governor, a role he would perform with distinction.

Meanwhile, hearing that power had gone to the head of Antonius Primus, who had secretly proposed putting another leading senator on the throne, Mucianus quickly deprived Primus of his power base by sending his 7th Galbiana Legion back to the Balkans and sending the six cohorts of the 3rd Gallica Legion marching overland home to Syria. Primus's able deputy Varus was removed from the 3rd Gallica and made superintendent of Rome's grain supply. Primus himself was dispatched by Mucianus to Alexandria to see his emperor. There, Vespasian would treat Primus courteously, but Primus and power would no longer be bedmates; he would receive no more government appointments. A decade and a half later he would be living in quiet retirement and be mentioned by the poet Martial.

And so closed the infamous Year of the Four Emperors, with the civil war that had torn the Roman Empire asunder now at an end. As soon as word reached Vespasian in Alexandria in January of AD 70 that hostilities had been terminated in Italy and he was now officially emperor, he ordered preparations made for a crossing of the seas to Italy in the summer. He then appointed Caesennius Paetus to replace Mucianus as governor of Syria. This was the very same Paetus who'd performed so badly in Armenia years before, but he was a client of Vespasian, having married Vespasian's niece Sabina, daughter of his late brother Sabinus.

Vespasian also gave his son Titus a mission—return to Judea, this time as Roman commander in chief, and complete the task they had jointly embarked upon three years earlier: the conquest of Jerusalem.

XIII

TARGET JERUSALEM

While the Roman military campaign in Judea was on prolonged hold due to politics across the seas, Jerusalem had continued to be run by Jewish partisans as the center of their rebel state, and they had used the lull in Roman hostilities to complete the city's third wall on the northern outskirts, the wall commenced by King Herod Agrippa II's father close to thirty years earlier.

Commerce and religious practice continued much as usual in the city. The rebels even minted their own currency in Jerusalem, melting down Roman coins and bronze to produce revolutionary shekels depicting images of palm branches and citron fruits that were not offensive to Jews and showing the year of the Jewish revolution in which they were minted, with AD 66 as Year 1 and AD 70 as Year 4. One such AD 70 coin, unearthed in Jerusalem in modern times and now held by the Israeli Antiquities Authority, was produced with the inscription: "To the Redemption of Zion, Year 4."

Although business and religion had been uninterrupted, internecine leadership struggles continued among the Jews in Jerusalem through these years as ambition and ego came before cohesion and cooperation. By the time that Titus set out from Alexandria at the commencement of the spring of AD 70, planning to march overland to Caesarea, where the Roman forces allocated to the upcoming assault on Jerusalem were ordered to assemble, a Jewish tussle for power had been underway behind Jerusalem's walls for three years. That tussle had claimed the lives of thousands of Jews, including some of their most notable and capable leaders.

A farrago of factions emerged as this cancer took hold. There were the Zealots, headed by Eleazar ben Simon. A rival religious faction was led by Ananus ben Ananus, the former high priest, who was determined to overthrow all rivals and take sole power for himself. Ananus had, he thought, eliminated one rival in the person of peasant leader Simon bar Giora, the hero of Beth Horon, whom he put in charge of the toparchy of Acrabatene, removing him from Jerusalem. But when Simon began building a large personal following in Acrabatene, Ananus had sent an armed party to deal with him. As a result, Simon and a few followers had fled back to the Masada fortress, where Sicarii leader Eleazar ben Ya'ir had again admitted them. Wary of Simon this time, Eleazar had kept him and his men in what Josephus describes as the lower part of the fortress to begin with, but before long Simon gained Eleazar's confidence and his trust.[71]

From Masada, Simon and his men joined Eleazar's Sicarii in raiding nearby villages for supplies, always on foot. But when the Sicarii showed no interest in ranging farther afield, Simon and his band raided villages in the hills, forcing the inhabitants to give up their goods, and then ventured down onto the plain of Idumea. With each passing day, Simon added new recruits to his band so that, instead of just leading slaves and robbers, Simon attracted large numbers of men from the general population. According to Josephus, Simon wasn't as crafty as other Jewish leaders such as John of Gischala, but he was clearly charismatic to attract a following that soon grew into the thousands.

With this force, Simon returned to the Acrabatene toparchy, forcibly occupying it in defiance of the Jewish leadership at Jerusalem and building a fortress at the village of Nain in Lower Galilee, today's Nein, just to the south of Nazareth, which he made the headquarters of his now large band. All Simon's ill-gotten gains were secreted in "the caves of Paran," as Josephus calls them. These otherwise unidentified caves in the south of the Judean Mountains are likely to have been the Beit Guvrin caves where Niger of Perea hid from Centurion Antonius's troops. Meanwhile, at Nain, Simon continued building his army and training his men, making no secret of his ultimate ambition—taking control at Jerusalem.[72]

From Jerusalem, Eleazar and the Zealots, who were determined to eliminate the growing threat posed by Simon's faction, launched an attack on him in Galilee. But Simon was prepared and met the Zealots in pitched battle with twenty thousand well-disciplined foot soldiers. Not only did Simon inflict heavy casualties on the Zealots, they were driven all the way back to Jerusalem. As tempting as an assault on Jerusalem was, Simon decided that his army was not yet strong enough for the task. Instead, he turned toward Idumea.

The Idumeans, putting together an army of twenty-five thousand infantry to defend their territory, met Simon on his approach. After a day-long battle ended in stalemate, both sides withdrew. Now, an Idumean commander named Jacob volunteered to go to Simon to discuss a settlement, but as soon as he met Simon he offered to betray his own people. When Jacob returned to Idumean ranks, he discreetly told fellow officers that the army of Simon he'd seen was four times larger than theirs. This was partly true; in addition to his twenty thousand fully armed men, Simon had attracted a following of another forty thousand men who only wanted for arms.

When next Simon led his army into Idumea and the Idumean army confronted him, Jacob rode off, deserting his men, as did other officers he'd spoken with. The Idumean foot soldiers, left leaderless and in confusion, broke and ran, enabling Simon to roll through Idumea, taking and burning village after village and finally taking, without a fight, the grand prize of the ancient city of Hebron, which Simon's men gleefully looted.

The Zealots were fully aware of this and alarmed by it. So they sent out parties to set up ambushes in the mountain passes. One of these was able to surprise and capture Simon's wife and her attendants as they passed through en route to joining Simon. Taking their opponent's wife back to Jerusalem, the Zealots paraded her through the streets as if they had made a prisoner of Simon himself, then locked her up. Simon was known to love his wife dearly, so the Zealots waited, expecting him to offer to lay down his arms in return for her release. Instead, Simon flew into a rage and marched on Jerusalem with his men.

When Simon arrived outside the city's closed gates with his sixty thousand followers, he vowed death to all who took and kept his wife. His men surrounded Jerusalem and seized anyone who ventured out in search of vegetables and firewood—women, children, and old men. Those they didn't kill they sent back inside with their hands chopped off. This terrorism campaign worked. After the common people implored the Zealots to give Simon what he wanted, Eleazar eventually relented. Simon's wife was sent out to him.

Simon marched away, back to Idumea, only for word to reach him that a Roman force of cavalry and infantry was marching into Idumea. This force, from Emmaus, was headed by General Cerialis, commander of the 5th Macedonica Legion. This was the spring of AD 69, and Vespasian, still at Caesarea, had learned of the chaos wrought by Simon and his men and had sent Cerialis to put a stop to their rampages.

First occupying the Acrabatene toparchy and denying Simon his headquarters there, Cerialis and his detachment of several thousand men came bent on occupying Upper Idumea. Josephus rode with Cerialis as his guide and translator, having been made a free man by Vespasian—because, Josephus was to say, he had predicted Vespasian would be emperor. On Vespasian's orders, the soldier who removed Josephus's chains ceremonially cut them into pieces in front of him to demonstrate that he would never again be bound.

As Cerialis's force approached, Simon and his army drove every Idumean they could find to Jerusalem, then camped outside the city walls, demanding admittance. Behind him, Cerialis swiftly overran Upper Idumea, sweeping through cities and villages before lastly taking Hebron, which his troops devastated. Cerialis then returned to Emmaus. His swift campaign meant that the only fortified places now in rebel hands outside Jerusalem were Masada, Machaerus, and Herodium—a circular fortress built by Herod the Great atop a conical manmade hill on the edge of the Judean Desert, which contained Herod's tomb. Herodium was much closer to Jerusalem than the two other fortresses—lying just eight miles south of the city and three miles southeast of Bethlehem.

While Simon and his men encircled Jerusalem and killed anyone who attempted to leave, within the city walls John of Gischala took advantage of the chaos to attack the Zealots, forcing them to retreat to the Temple. John and his followers subsequently tyrannized the rest of the city, killing anyone they didn't like. For reasons unknown, many of John's men dressed as women and failed to observe even basic religious practices. This incensed the priestly faction, and High Priest Matthias ben Boethus invited Simon and his men to come into the city to deal with John, his heathen band, and the Zealots. It was to prove a big mistake.

As soon as Simon and his men were granted entry to Jerusalem, they set themselves up as rulers of the city, in opposition to the three other factions, and before long killed High Priest Matthias and his three sons. With John of Gischala intimidated and many of his followers deserting him, Simon launched an attack on the Zealots in the Temple. From the walls, the Zealots rained missiles down on his men, causing heavy casualties, and Simon's followers quickly tired of the attack. With Simon's Temple siege faltering, then halting, he withdrew with his men to the Upper City, which he made his fiefdom, turning the Phasael Tower, part of Herod's Palace in the southwest of Jerusalem, into his residence.

This allowed the Zealots to emerge from the Temple and threaten the rest of the city's regions—the New City, Old City, and City of David. Ananus, the former high priest, had assumed leadership of the religious faction, and he took advantage of Simon's pullback to attack the Zealots. The force that Ananus put together outnumbered the Zealots, but the Zealots were better armed and had more fighting experience through their involvement in the revolt from its beginning. Ananus's men fought the Zealots in the streets, driving them back to the Temple, where the Zealots again barricaded themselves inside the Inner Court with extensive provisions. Rather than shed blood inside the Temple's holy Inner Court, Ananus posted six thousand guards around it, hemming in the Zealots and hoping to eventually starve them out.

John of Gischala, having lost his own power base, now very visibly allied himself to Ananus, swearing an oath to support him, going everywhere about the city during the day with the former high priest as Ananus discussed the Zealot problem with other leading men of Jerusalem, and accompanying him by night as he checked the sentry posts. John was able to convince Ananus to send him into the Temple as his envoy to the Zealots, with a proposal for a truce for the following day to allow Ananus and his followers to enter the Temple, unarmed, on a fasting day, to carry out important religious observances.

Once John was admitted to the Inner Court, he vowed to Eleazar and his men that he had been their secret supporter all along. Convincingly, he assured them that Ananus was planning to send word to Vespasian, offering to open the city's gates and surrender Jerusalem. John also declared that Ananus was requesting a truce for the next day so that he and his men could enter the Inner Court with hidden arms, and then, with the Zealots off guard, fall on and destroy them before sending ambassadors to the Roman general. John went on to suggest the Zealots seek foreign assistance against Ananus and his people. The only "foreigners" in a position to offer rapid aid were the Idumeans to the south.

John withdrew to tell Ananus that the Zealots were considering his request of a truce, and Eleazar and his deputy, Zacharias bar Phalek, dispatched two fast runners who escaped the Temple, apparently via one of the tunnels beneath it, and hurried to the Idumeans, who had returned to their destroyed towns and villages following Cerialis's sweep. The Idumeans quickly appointed four commanders and again put twenty thousand men under arms. This force at once set out for Jerusalem. Learning that the Idumeans were coming along the Hill Road from Hebron, Ananus had Jerusalem's city gates closed, and he and his men took to the walls with their arms.

Jesus ben Damneus, eldest of the former high priests next to Ananus, called down to the Idumean commanders from the First Wall, urging them to lay down their arms and withdraw. Simon, one of the Idumean commanders, called back indignantly that they were going nowhere. Idumeans spread out to besiege the city from the west and the north. But, not expecting to have to camp in the open, they had come unprepared, without tents, and when a thunderstorm broke over them that night they huddled together for warmth in the open and held their shields above them as protection against the rain. Seeing this, Ananus instructed his sentries to stand down for the night and sleep under cover.

The Zealots, meanwhile, using the noise of the storm to cover their activities, employed saws that had been intended for use in planned Temple extensions and sawed through a city gate. They then sent for the Idumeans, who filed in through the open gate, entering the city under the very noses of Ananus and his unwitting men. The Zealots, coming out of the Temple into the city, welcomed their new allies. Jointly, they set about killing Ananus's sleeping sentries. But some of those sentries raised the alarm, and Ananus's men awoke and ran to defend against what they thought was a Zealot raid.

When it became apparent that Idumeans were inside the city, the older men among Ananus's followers, who had no experience as soldiers, lost the will to fight. Casting aside their weapons and dropping to their knees, they bewailed their situation and accepted their fate, leaving their younger counterparts to desperately fight a losing battle. By daybreak, 8,500 of Ananus's men lay dead and the Idumeans were rampaging through the city, slitting throats and looting. Among the further 12,000 fellow Jews killed in the Idumean onslaught were Ananus and his priestly colleague Jesus. Josephus was to lament that Ananus was an enormous loss to the Jewish cause. The fall of Jerusalem, said Josephus, began with the former high priest's murder on this day.

The Zealots now took charge in the Lower City and New City, and set up a show trial in the Temple of a much-respected priest named Zacharias, charging him with secretly being in favor of surrendering to the Romans. Zacharias scoffed at the charge, and as the trial judges began to show signs of exonerating him, two Zealots jumped up and executed the accused on the spot. The Idumean commanders, being convinced by a Zealot leader that the Zealots, having wheedled out the rotten apples from the partisan leadership, would now be able to successfully defend Jerusalem from Roman attack, packed up and went home to Idumea. Before they departed, the Idumeans freed two thousand Jewish prisoners from the city prisons. Most of these men fled straight to Simon bar Giora in the Upper City. For the moment, even as the number of his followers swelled by the addition of the former prisoners, Simon kept his head down and his mouth shut.

The Zealots subsequently led a crackdown in the sectors of Jerusalem under their control, eliminating anyone who they believed posed a threat to them. One of the victims of this purge was Niger of Perea, who had been welcomed into Jerusalem as a hero several years earlier after being the sole survivor of the bloody battles in Idumea against Centurion Antonius and his men. Others were indiscriminately cut down in the street by the Zealots, with their bodies left where they fell and their families forbidden to bury them. As the stench of death filled the streets and alleys of Jerusalem, such fear and dread gripped the general population that some of the bolder men succeeded in escaping and reaching the Mediterranean coast. There, they told of the crazy, self-defeating fight for power in their holy city.

Word of this inevitably reached Vespasian while he was still at Caesarea, and before his transfer to Alexandria. His officers urged him to take advantage of the Jews' internal strife by marching on Jerusalem at once, to catch them divided and disorganized. Apart from the fact that his troop numbers had been reduced by the allocation of men to Mucianus's Italian task force, Vespasian, whose eyes were on Rome, told his officers that it would be more advantageous to let the Jews continue to fight among themselves, weakening their resources and their resolve. And so the Roman army continued to sit in its quarters throughout Judea and Galilee.

During this period, too, Eleazar ben Ya'ir, rebel commander at Masada, had led a party of his Sicarii down from Masada to the regional capital of Ein Gedi. In a night attack, they drove resident Jewish males out of the city. Separating seven hundred women and children from the rest of the population, they slit their throats. Historians and scholars have long puzzled why these women and children were segregated and murdered. However, it is likely that these were the de facto wives and illegitimate children of the 3rd Gallica legionaries killed at Masada in AD 66. After looting the homes of these victims and helping themselves to fruit stored in the city, Eleazar and his men returned to Masada. They would continue to periodically raid villages of the area to top up their food supplies and find new recruits.

In Jerusalem, the fight for power continued, with John of Gischala and his faction making a move to topple Eleazar and his Zealots, who retreated once more into the Temple with stocks of food and wine and closed the doors. John's men mounted assaults on the Temple to dislodge the Zealots and used lumber set aside for Temple extensions to build artillery to bombard them. All the while, as the priestly workers at the Temple attempted to go about their daily religious duties, a number became casualties to missiles in this firefight.

Simon bar Giora, seeing the other factions at odds with each other, took his chance to attack John of Gischala's men from behind, leading his men from the Upper City. John was now defending himself on two fronts. In this fighting, buildings around the Temple were burned, and in some, much of the grain that had been laid up for the city's population in anticipation of a Roman siege was also burned. Repulsing Simon's attacks, John again focused on the Zealot-held Temple, commencing construction of wooden siege towers, which he would soon be forced to abandon by the movement of Roman forces.

Titus had arrived at Caesarea, having marched from Alexandria with a small force based around his cavalry bodyguard and the two thousand men of the 18th Legion that had been stranded in Egypt by the change in Nero's fortunes, plus men detached from the 3rd Cyrenaica Legion— apparently a thousand of them, in two cohorts. These six legionary cohorts from Alexandria were commanded by a tribune, Eternius Fronto, who was a friend and client of Titus. Tiberius Alexander also marched from Alexandria with Titus. Vespasian had replaced him as prefect of Egypt with another Equestrian Order member so that Alexander could serve as Titus's deputy and chief adviser for the Jerusalem assault.

In Caesarea, Titus linked up with units allocated by Vespasian to the Jerusalem campaign. The 5th Macedonica Legion was waiting at Emmaus still commanded by General Sextus Cerialis. The 10th Fretensis was in Jericho, where it had wintered and received a new young commander, the legate Aulus Larcius Lepidus, who had previously served as quaestor, or administrative assistant, to the proconsul of Crete and Cyrenaica. Marcus Trajan, who had faithfully commanded the 10th since AD 67, had been appointed governor of Cappadocia by Vespasian, who would later reward him further with a consulship and the prized governorship of Syria. The 15th Apollinaris Legion was in Caesarea, having spent the Year of the Four Emperors there. Its commander was now the legate Titus Frigius.

All three legions were still minus the two thousand men who had been sent to Italy with Mucianus. Those cohorts would eventually return to the East and reunite with their legions, but in the meantime, the three thousand men of the 18th and 3rd Cyrenaica Legions that Titus brought with him from Alexandria were intended, says Josephus, to temporarily "replenish" the three legions and partially make up for the absent troops.[73]

Titus would embark on this phase of the Judean War with more troops than his father had possessed at the campaign's outset, with the addition of a fourth legion, none other than the disgraced 12th Fulminata, the legion that had lost its eagle to the Jews in AD 66. The 12th Fulminata had marched down to Caesarea from Laodicea to join Titus. In Laodicea, it had undergone its discharge of men who'd served out their twenty-year enlistments and were going into retirement, and received its intake of new recruits. The legion's two cohorts garrisoning Sepphoris would have been withdrawn to Laodicea to rejoin the other cohorts and take part in the discharge process.

Some men of the 12th Fulminata's old enlistment signed up for second enlistments, but the majority of the men who brought the legion up to full strength at 5,225 legionaries were new recruits aged between eighteen and forty-six. Roman citizens were required to give their names to the local authorities at the cities where they lived, and when the recruitment officers working for the province's quaestor came around, they were given lists of these registered citizens from which to choose fit and able conscripts. Most recruits were draftees, not volunteers, although a few criminal types and down-and-outs were known to volunteer for legion service. A conscripted man could even officially pay for another to substitute for him, although that was rare.

The revitalized 12th Fulminata Legion's centurions and optios came from both the old enlistment and via transfer and promotion from other legions. In this process the 12th Fulminata received a new chief centurion, Gaius Velius Rufus. Relatively young for a chief centurion, probably in his forties at most, he would have a long military career after the Judean War, stretching out for another two decades. It's also likely he was promoted to the 12th Fulminata after serving as a first-rank centurion with the 15th Apollinaris Legion in Judea, for his good friend Marcus Alfius Olympiacus, who would raise a memorial to him after his death, was eagle-bearer of the 15th Apollinaris.

Chief Centurion Velius Rufus was a highly decorated soldier. We know from his later memorial in Heliopolis that he was awarded several bravery decorations by both Vespasian and Titus during the Judean War. More than once, Rufus earned gold neck torques, *phalerae*, which were round medal-like decorations worn on the chest, and *armillae*, or armbands, in Judea. These were relatively low grade and common decorations for valor in battle. More importantly, Rufus was also awarded the gold Crown of Valor in this war. Also known as the Rampant Crown, this went to the first man to cross the ramparts of an enemy camp in an assault and survive. There would be no mention of Rufus being the first man to cross the ramparts during the siege of Jerusalem. So this rare and highly valued decoration seems to have come to Rufus from Vespasian as a result of a successful assault such as that at Japha, when the centurion was with the 15th Apollinaris Legion. A torque and armillae were also later awarded to him by Titus following the fall of Jerusalem.

No legate took command of the shamed 12th Fulminata at this rebirth of the legion. After its humbling in Armenia and loss of its eagle in Judea, it seems that no senator was prepared to be associated with the unit. In this new campaign of AD 70 it would continue to be commanded by a senior tribune. It's unlikely this officer was the 12th Fulminata's tribune for the past year, Placidus. He isn't mentioned again by Josephus following the tribune's rampaging activities through Galilee in AD 67, and it's likely that in the spring of AD 68, following the AD 67–68 discharge and enlistment of his legion, he left the unit and sailed home to Rome. There, he is likely to have received another military appointment, probably with the Praetorian Guard, and he may have been the Julius Placidus, a pro-Vespasian "tribune of a cohort" at Rome in December of AD 69, who is mentioned by Tacitus.[74]

When the men of the old enlistment departed the 12th Fulminata Legion in Laodicea and went into retirement, they took their silver maniple "hand" standards with them, to be stored in temples wherever they settled post-legion and to become a focal point for their Evocati militia assemblies. Many of these 12th Fulminata retirees enjoyed little more than a year in retirement before being involved in Mucianus's AD 69 call-up of thirteen thousand Evocati veterans for the march on Rome.

As the unit had lost its old eagle to the Jewish rebels, come the annual legionaries' oath of allegiance at a mass assembly in January, AD 68, the standard bearers of the legion would have been presented with a new golden eagle along with the twenty new manipular standards customarily presented at this time, which would be blessed at an annual religious ceremony the following March.

Titus clearly added the new 12th Fulminata to his task force not only because it was now at full strength but also in expectation that its officers would drive their raw recruits to extraordinary deeds to overcome the legion's recent disgraces. Indeed, Josephus tells us that the new enlistment of the 12th Fulminata was bent on restoring their legion's reputation with this campaign.

By early May of AD 70, all preparations for the year's campaign had been made, and Titus set out from Caesarea, bound for Jerusalem via inland Samaria. The new enlistment of the 12th Fulminata Legion and the understrength 15th Apollinaris Legion marched with him. Also in the column were numerous auxiliary units plus troops provided by the same four allied kings who had contributed to Vespasian's original campaign—Josephus says that even more allied soldiers were now involved than in AD 67–68. These allied troops included mercenaries, says Josephus, men whose only allegiance was to gold. We know that bands of Scythian archers served with the Roman army during this period as mercenaries, so they may have been among the men referred to here by Josephus.[75]

Josephus describes Titus's army on the march. The allied troops of three kings marched first. King Antiochus of Commagene had sent troops for the previous campaigns, but his contribution was delayed this time. The allied units were followed by the three thousand legionary reinforcements from Egypt. Next came the legionary road maintenance and camp preparation party, inclusive of surveyors to map out and mark the site for each night's camp. The mules and carts of the commander's baggage train trundled along next, carrying Titus's tents, furniture, and dinnerware, together with the troops assigned to the train's protection, who were fully armed and ready to spring into action at a moment's notice.

After them came Titus himself. He had turned thirty the previous December 30. Accompanying him were his senior commanders and advisers, including Tiberius Alexander, King Herod Agrippa II and other Middle Eastern royals, and Josephus, who was now serving as an adviser and interpreter to Titus. All were mounted. They were followed by several hundred legionaries detached from one particular legion by lot for the honored assignment as the Commander in Chief's Guard, with their traditional twelve-foot spears of the bodyguard pointing skyward like a forest of saplings. Immediately after them came the cavalry squadron of the legion from which these bodyguard troops had been detached.

Next in the column came the artillery of all the legions, apparently not dismantled and loaded in pieces on mules as had been the case with Gallus's army in AD 66, but packed onto carts. Behind the artillery marched the tribunes and cohort-commanding centurions of the legions, with legionary escorts, followed by the trumpeters of the legions, who preceded the eagles and other legion standards, which were carried in a bunch.

The legions themselves followed, with their men in marching order, six abreast, with helmets hanging around their necks, their laden baggage poles on one shoulder and shields on the other. The servants of the legions and the baggage animals of the army came next, with the mercenaries following and the legions' cavalry squadrons bringing up the rear.

As Titus was en route through Samaria, General Cerialis and the 5th Macedonica Legion were on the march from Emmaus and General Lepidus and the 10th Fretensis Legion from Jericho, aiming to link up with their commander in chief outside Jerusalem. In Samaria, Titus camped for a night at the town of Gophna, today's Jifna. In the hands of a Roman garrison since AD 67, Gophna was where Vespasian had relocated Jewish priests and other

Jews who had fled the rebels. From Gophna, Titus advanced his force due south on the morning of May 9 to a valley near the hill village of Gibeah, two and a half miles north of Jerusalem.

As was the Roman custom, Titus's army had marched in the morning, reaching its selected campsite by the middle of the day. Impatient to spy out the lay of the land at Jerusalem, Titus had six hundred cavalrymen detached to accompany him, and then, as the legions began to dig the trenches and walls of their overnight camp and set up the tents at the Gibeah site, he rode the several miles to his ultimate objective. He went wearing only his normal tunic and cloak, having left his helmet and armored breastplate back in camp, but with his sword belt over his shoulder. In the mid afternoon, Titus and his mounted escort arrived atop Mount Scopus, site of Gallus's camp three and a half years earlier. Their arrival was no doubt heralded by a cloud of dust raised by the hooves of the six hundred horses, sending shouts of alarm running around Jerusalem from lookouts in the towers of the city's new Third Wall.

Keen to take a closer look at the city, Titus rode down off Mount Scopus, taking the Damascus Road, the usual entry route to the city from the north, followed by his escort. Unexpectedly diverting from the road and turning left, Titus rode along the northern side of the new Third Wall, studying it, but being careful to stay out of the range of missiles from wall and towers. His path took him through well-tended gardens that formed part of the Queen Helena monument on lower Mount Scopus and brought him opposite the new Psephinus Tower, which occupied the Third Wall's northwest corner. This tower, one hundred and fifteen feet high, offered views from its top as far as the Mediterranean to the west and the mountains of Arabia to the southeast.

Titus's diversion had left many of the men of his escort strung out behind him, with some still on the Damascus Road. Seeing this, partisans gathered quickly, and a gate near the wall's Women's Gate suddenly opened. Out streamed thousands of yelling Jewish rebels, running to cut off the Roman commander. Titus was taken by surprise. Finding himself hemmed in by garden trenches and tall hedges to his front, he saw only one way out.

"Follow me!" he yelled to the cavalrymen closest to him.[76]

Turning his horse around, Titus drew his sword and charged directly at the Jews. Cutting and barging his way through the mob, using his horse as a weapon, he managed at the same time to avoid a cloud of missiles that flew his way, later telling Josephus that he heard darts whistle past his ears. Miraculously, he escaped the trap he had made for himself without a scratch.

Several cavalrymen who had closed around their general to protect him took darts in the back and side but also succeeded in escaping alive, but two troopers of his escort weren't so lucky. Partisans rained darts on one man, and both he and his horse went down, never to arise. Another cavalryman had his horse killed under him. As the horse dropped, the soldier jumped to the ground, sword in hand. Rebels gleefully surrounded him and cut him to pieces. Round one to the Jews, who stripped the Roman dead and celebrated long and hard back behind their city's walls. After that narrow escape, Titus returned to the camp at Gibeah. How different would the fate of Jerusalem have been had the Roman commander in chief been killed on this reconnaissance of the city?

That night, Cerialis and the 5th Macedonica arrived at Gibeah after a forced march, making camp alongside Titus's main force. The following day, May 10, Titus advanced on Jerusalem with his now enlarged force. Halting at Mount Scopus, he ordered the 12th and 15th to fortify Gallus's old Mount Scopus camp for their use and for Titus's headquarters. He had the march-weary men of the 5th Macedonica build a new camp for themselves, a little behind and shielded by this larger camp.

That afternoon, as Roman camp construction was well underway at the two Mount Scopus sites, with auxiliaries and allied troops out foraging, General Lepidus and the 10th Fretensis arrived atop the Mount of Olives to the northeast after marching along the Jericho Road. Titus sent orders for the 10th to build their camp there on the Mount of Olives. This camp would rise not far from the Garden of Gethsemane, where Jesus Christ had been arrested some thirty-seven years earlier. The garden sat lower down the western slope of the mount, closer to the city.

Almost all the troops assigned to the Roman assault on Jerusalem had now arrived. Below them, the city stood with its gates closed, with Jewish sentries on its walls and in its towers, and with as many as 1.2 million Jewish men, women, and children behind its walls. The siege of Jerusalem had begun.[77]

XIV

TITUS TIGHTENS
THE NOOSE

On the morning after the arrival of the Roman army, with the marching camps on the northern and eastern heights overlooking Jerusalem undergoing further fortification, the leaders of the three rebel Jewish factions inside the city—Eleazar of the Zealots, John of Gischala, and Simon bar Giora—realized that the Romans meant business and it was time to put their differences to one side and put their heads together to defend their holy city.

As the Jewish leaders met, word arrived that Roman legionaries of the 10th Fretensis Legion had incautiously laid aside their weapons and were digging entrenchments below their camp on the Mount of Olives. Apparently these Romans believed that the deep valley that lay between the mount and the eastern walls of Jerusalem, the Kidron, would protect them. Seizing their opportunity, partisans donned their armor, took up their weapons, and flooded out gates on the northeastern side of the city.

Dashing across the Kidron, rebels fell on the digging Romans. Legionaries were required to wear their swords even when digging entrenchments but were permitted to stack their shields, javelins, and helmets nearby. As the Jews came running at them, some legionaries of the 10th dashed for their equipment, while others fled up the mount. Men of the guard cohort trotted from the camp to the assistance of their comrades, and a series of hand-to-hand struggles ensued on the slopes of the Mount of Olives.

When word of this reached Titus at his camp on Mount Scopus, he put together a relief force and hurried to the aid of the 10th. By the time that Titus and his reinforcements arrived on the Mount of Olives, legionaries of the 10th had succeeded in driving off Jewish attackers, only for even more partisans to be encouraged by a sentry on the city wall who waved his cloak at them. They came streaming out of the city and in turn drove the legionaries back up the slope. Titus and his men arrived just in time to drive into the left flank of this new partisan wave on the slope.

The mounted Titus, finding himself in the thick of the fighting, refused to give ground. Before long, he and a few of his friends and bodyguards were separated from the bulk of the Roman troops, who were withdrawing up the slope, and once more the young Roman general was in danger of being killed or injured. His friends begged him to disengage—he was not only their commander, he was their new emperor's son and heir. But Titus ignored them. Parrying blows with his shield, he stabbed in the face those rebels who ran at him, then pushed them back down the slope with his horse and finished them off with a slashing blow. Singlehandedly, Titus stemmed the flow of the rebel assault, driving attackers back, until the entire 10th Legion, now called to arms, came down the hill to support him, forcing the Jews to flee. Dead partisans were left lying in heaps in the Kidron as the survivors ran back into the city, closing the gates behind them. Round two to the Romans.

Days later, with the coming of Passover's Feast of the Unleavened Bread, Eleazar and the Zealots opened the Temple gates to admit all in Jerusalem who wished to carry out religious observances. Among the tens of thousands who crowded into the Temple were John of Gischala and his men, hiding their weapons and armor beneath their cloaks. On John's command, his men drew their weapons. The Zealots, lulled into thinking that all factions were now working together, were totally unprepared for this treachery. Those Zealots who weren't cut down fled to the subterranean passages of the Temple Mount, allowing John's ten thousand men to occupy the Temple, which John made his headquarters.

Eleazar and his deputy, Simon ben Arinus, decided to throw their lot in with John, and they and 2,400 Zealots came over to his side and vowed to follow John's commands. In one fell swoop, the factions in Jerusalem had been reduced to two—John's and Simon's. John, now controlling all of Jerusalem apart from the Upper City, sifted through the thousands of worshippers who had come into the Temple. Those with whom he had a grudge were separated from the rest, led out, and executed.

While Jew was killing Jew inside the city, outside on the northern and northwestern flanks of Jerusalem, Titus's troops were busy. Titus wanted to move his camps closer to the city, so, on their general's orders, legionaries demolished and filled in all the groves of trees, gardens, buildings, walls, and ditches that lay between Mount Scopus and Jerusalem's Third Wall, creating a level space northwest and west of the city between the mountain and King Herod's monuments and the Serpent's Pool. All the while, a large force of auxiliary cavalry and infantry stood guard to prevent the Jews from attacking the workers. At the same time, Titus sent Josephus riding to the Third Wall to call an offer of terms of surrender to those inside the city. Josephus genuinely wanted the Jews to accept this offer, as his wife, brother, and parents were all trapped inside Jerusalem. He failed to receive a civil answer to the offer.

While this leveling activity was taking place, the partisans came up with a cunning plan. A large group of men emerged from the Women's Gate in the northwest of the Third Wall and milled about below the wall, calling out to the Romans that they wanted peace and would open the gates to them. At the same time, other Jews on the wall called out insults to the men below and threw the occasional stone at them. The plan was to make Romans think the men outside the wall were Jewish deserters.

Although Titus was immediately suspicious of this display and sent orders for his men to all stay where they were, the order never reached some of his legionaries, who left their work, took up their arms, and hurried to the wall to collect the men of this supposed peace party. As soon as the Roman troops came within range, they were attacked from all sides and from the wall above. Only with difficulty, and with heavy casualties, were these legionaries able to extricate themselves. They were pursued by rebels all the way to Queen Helena's monument on Mount Scopus before the partisans stood, rapped their shields, and jeered the Romans before retiring through the city gate, which closed protectively behind them. Another round to the Jews.[78]

In camp, Titus went to see the survivors of the party tricked by the rebels. Their officers had already upbraided them, and Titus now also told them that although the Jews had employed a sneaky trick, the legionaries had gone forward without the orders of their officers. "Even those of you who are victorious when you go to the attack without the orders of your officers act disgracefully in my eyes," he told them.[79]

This led the troops involved to sink into despair, believing that they were going to be executed. As Titus was enlarging on this with his officers, his headquarters tent was surrounded by men of the legions, who beseeched him to spare their fellow legionaries. Titus agreed not to execute the men involved, but he put all under caution—he wouldn't be so lenient if they acted without orders a second time.

The leveling of the ground north and west of the city took four days. On the fifth day, once that work was complete, three legions built two forward camps close to the city. Protected by a line of auxiliaries, cavalry, and archers seven ranks deep which faced the city, baggage trains then relocated equipment down off Mount Scopus to the new camps. One of those camps was located two hundred and fifty yards from the Psephinus Tower, which occupied the northwest corner of the Third Wall. Here the 12th and 15th would again be encamped together, along with Titus's headquarters.

The second camp became the new home to the now rested 5th Macedonica, which leapfrogged the other two legions to sit two hundred and fifty yards from the Second Wall on the western side of the city, opposite the Hippicus Tower. This was one of the towers of Herod's Palace where doomed men of the 3rd Gallica Legion had spent their last days close to four years earlier. The 10th Fretensis meanwhile remained in its camp on the Mount of Olives.

Looking for a weak spot in the Third Wall, which had been thrown up quickly, Titus now rode around the northern and western sides of the city, accompanied by his senior officers and Josephus. He found that weak spot on the western side of the city, where recent wall construction did not match the height of the old First Wall nearby. While on this reconnaissance, Titus and his party went a little too close to the wall, and an officer in the general's entourage, Tribune Nicanor, former commander of the 3rd Gallica and friend of Josephus, was wounded in the shoulder by a Jewish dart thrown from the Third Wall, and needed attention from legion doctors. But once again, Fortune deemed that Titus would escape harm.

Titus now ordered artillery banks thrown up within range of the wall to the north, west, and east, and every tree in the city's outermost suburbs cut down and every building there demolished to permit a clear field of fire. The artillery pieces built by the 10th Fretensis Legion and employed by it against the eastern walls of Jerusalem were markedly larger than those used by the other legions. On the western side of the city, the 5th, 12th, and 15th Legions also began construction of three wooden siege towers on Titus's orders. One of those siege towers collapsed mysteriously at midnight one night while under construction, but the other two were completed and, covered by Roman artillery fire, rolled up to the Third Wall as Jewish darts and stones bounced off their iron-plate reinforced exteriors.

In the Upper City, Simon bar Giora, who commanded ten thousand peasant partisans and five thousand remaining Idumeans aided by fifty-eight deputy commanders, controlled all the rebel artillery—the weapons looted from Gallus's column in the Beth Horon Valley, plus those artillery pieces captured from the Romans with the fall of the Antonia Fortress. But even though several Roman deserters had shown his men how to use these weapons, Simon's gunners were inexpert, and their darts and stones did little to hamper Titus's troops as they went against the Third Wall with their siege towers.[80]

The Romans, on the other hand, had expert gunners. To gauge the range from their firing banks to the wall, Roman artillery officers threw lengths of string attached to lead weights from the banks, after dark. The catapult balls that were now launched against the Third Wall to both keep defenders' heads down and weaken the structure were sixty pounders, more roughly hewn than those used in the siege of Gamala, and cut from stark white stone. We know this because more than seventy of these balls were discovered alongside the foundations of the Third Wall in 2016, in today's Russian Compound. These balls had fallen to the ground after smashing into the wall.

Later, once a breach was made here, Titus had the Third Wall demolished down to the foundations, with all the surroundings leveled. The legionaries doing this work didn't even bother to salvage these seventy-plus ballista balls; they simply covered them over with rubble. Admittedly, some were cracked, but most were reusable. The Roman troops who covered them over clearly thought there were plenty more where they came from.

Once the Third Wall was breached, Jewish spotters learned to call a warning to their comrades when the stark white Roman ballista balls were coming their way: "Baby coming!" When this was reported back to

Roman gunners by front line troops, they painted balls with black pitch, which was kept by the weapons to seal their ropes and coat the stones when incendiary balls were called for. Now, the gunners used the pitch to blacken the balls and make them more difficult to spot as they whistled toward their targets.[81]

Under cover of barrages from the more than two hundred Roman artillery pieces employed by the four legions, battering rams in the two towers' bowels began to relentlessly pound the stones of the wall. It seems that the Roman siege towers and the rams inside them were not connected. The rams were attached to their own wheeled frames that could be rolled into the wheeled siege tower via its open rear end. Although all fighters retired come nightfall, each side suspected the other of getting up to tricks, and off-duty men of both sides slept in their armor. As the two rams continued their work, day in, day out, the Jewish defenders gave an ironic nickname to the larger of the rams—they called it Nico, meaning "conqueror."

On May 25, the fifteenth day of the siege, a section of the Third Wall gave way to Nico, and Roman assault troops flooded through the breach it had created and opened gates in the Third Wall to thousands of comrades. Rebels defending this wall fled back to the safety of the First and Second Walls, abandoning the New City entirely. It was now that Titus had his troops pull down the Third Wall and destroy everything that still stood in the New City—many of the buildings destroyed here by Gallus's troops in AD 66 had been rebuilt by the people of Jerusalem.

Of the million-plus Jews now trapped in the city, less than thirty thousand were armed fighters. Those fighters kept the bulk of the city's food supply for themselves, claiming that the fighting men needed the sustenance. Some Zealots who knew the way down into the subterranean passages beneath the Temple Mount had secret stores of food down there, where they would cook and consume it, as indicated by cooking utensils discovered there in modern times.

Titus now transferred his largest camp from the northwest into the New City. There was a spot in the northwest corner of the New City that had long been called the Camp of the Assyrians. It was said that here, in 701 BC, an Assyrian army had encamped during an unsuccessful siege of Jerusalem. The campsite was quite near the small rocky hill called Golgotha, or the Skull, because of its shape, location of Jesus Christ's crucifixion. Here at the Camp of the Assyrians, out of bowshot of the Second Wall, Titus had his newest siege camp built.

Once this transfer was completed, Titus set those legions now encamped to the west of the city to work with three siege towers and rams against that part of the Second Wall that stood just to the north of the Palace of Herod, midway along the western side of Jerusalem. This was in Simon's sector, but he surprised rival leader John by sending a message inviting him to send men to join his partisans defending the Second Wall. John, who had moved his headquarters to the lone remaining tower of the burned-out Antonia Fortress, whose western wall faced the now relocated Romans, didn't entirely trust Simon, but he nonetheless warily sent numbers of his men to reinforce his faction, and they were soon fighting side by side.

Carrying burning torches, these combined forces rushed out to attack the siege towers and the mantlets that protected them, trying to pull apart the mantlets and burn the Roman towers even as the rams were at work. In response, Titus quickly stationed cavalry and archers on either side of the siege towers, and these succeeded in driving off successive Jewish raids.

The Second Wall was of much more solid construction than the Third. Sixty feet high, with foundations that went down another sixty feet underground, this wall, built by Herod the Great, was as thick as a house. Although no mortar held its stones in place, they had been fitted so precisely together that this wall proved much more resistant to ramming. After several days of nonstop pounding, with numerous shift changes of the ramming crews, the ram of the 15th Apollinaris could only manage to weaken a tower on the wall's western corner. But otherwise, as Titus watched impatiently with his staff day after day, the Second Wall showed no signs of yielding to the trio of rams.

The Jews mounted yet another raid on the Roman siege works, bent on burning them. Emerging from a small gate, they attacked the siege tower that was operating against the Hippicus Tower. Killing a number of Romans at the tower, they forced others all the way back to the walls of their nearest camp. There, they were confronted by the four cohorts of the 18th Legion, which stood firm with shields fixed. Longinus the tribune, their commander, leapt from the Roman ranks with a javelin in hand. Singlehanded, he ran at a Jewish officer who, with a comrade, charged him with sword raised.

Sidestepping his two assailants, Tribune Longinus stabbed his javelin into the mouth of one opponent—with such force that the point apparently emerged from the back of his victim's head. As the man went down, Longinus pulled the javelin from his skull and gave chase to the other rebel who, in sudden terror of him, had turned to run. Quickly overtaking the fleeing man, Longinus plunged the javelin into the man's unprotected side. This double use was unusual; Roman javelins' metal shafts were designed to bend on impact, so the enemy couldn't easily throw them back.

As Longinus withdrew to the cheering men of the 18th, Titus arrived on the scene, leading cavalry reinforcements, and entered the fight. Personally killing twelve rebels, Titus, joined by his troopers, drove the raiders back to the gate from which they had come. A leader of the Idumean rebels named John was killed at this time by an arrow from an Arabian archer; he proved a great loss to the rebel cause, according to Josephus.

When Titus returned to his infantry after terminating this latest Jewish foray, he was far from happy. Instead of commending Tribune Longinus for his solo action, which Longinus would have argued was, under Roman military law, deserving of the coveted golden spear award, the general gave his men a short, sharp speech from the back of his horse, denouncing acts that exposed individuals to danger. In this sour mood, Titus ordered a Jewish rebel who had been captured in this fight to be crucified on the camp wall in full view of the occupants of the city.

When Titus subsequently relocated one ram-equipped siege tower to the north, at the Second Wall, rebels inevitably mounted a sally against it, again with the aim of setting it afire. As perspiring legionaries manning the ram in the base of the siege tower ceased operations to defend themselves, Arabian archers stationed on the upper levels of the tower drove off the partisans. When their comrades retreated, eleven rebels lay on the ground as if wounded, their torches still burning beside them. One of these Jews, a fellow named Castor, called out to Titus, who was watching proceedings, begging to be saved, as he wished to surrender. Five of his companions yelled that they had no intention of surrendering and then pretended to plunge their own swords into themselves. This was all a ploy to draw Roman troops to them.

As Castor was calling out, a Scorpio dart was unleashed at him from a Roman artillery mound. The dart hit him, lodging in his nose. Plucking out the bloodied dart, Castor held it up. "That's unfair!" he cried.[82]

Titus, turning to the gunner responsible for the shot, rebuked him for firing at the man while he was conversing with him, then called forward

Josephus, and instructed him to go the man, take his oath of surrender, and bring him back to Roman lines. Josephus refused point blank, suspecting that this was another Jewish ruse, telling Titus so. When several of the Jewish servants allocated to Josephus by Vespasian urged him to go their countryman, still Josephus refused.

"Somebody should come and take the money I have with me," Castor now called, trying another ploy to lure Romans.[83]

One of Josephus's bodyguards, a Jewish deserter named Eneas, now volunteered to go to Castor in Josephus's place, as did one of Titus's legionaries. In his enthusiasm, Eneas went without even taking a shield as protection. As the pair scuttled over the open ground toward Castor, with Eneas in the lead, Castor jumped up with a good-sized stone in his hand and threw it. Eneas was nimble enough to dodge the stone, but the soldier behind him failed to see it coming and took the stone fair in the face. As the "dead" men with Castor rose up with their weapons, Eneas helped the legionary to hurriedly withdraw, likely with the vocal encouragement of Roman troops. Titus turned to Josephus, no doubt with a wry smile in acknowledgment of the fact that Josephus had been right about Castor and his friends all along.

"Mercy in war is a ruinous thing," Titus confessed with a sigh, before ordering missile fire to be directed at Castor and his companions and bidding the rammers to commence work again.[84]

The pause in Roman operations gave Castor and his men the opportunity to run to the nearest wooden siege tower with their torches and set it alight. As fire took hold, the eleven Jews appeared to jump into the flames at the front of the tower. They had in fact spotted a vault in front of that section of the wall, and into this they dived to take refuge. For a long while, the Romans thought that these Jews had committed suicide in the flames. The ultimate fate of Castor and his tricky friends is unknown, but the siege tower fire they ignited was soon extinguished. And ramming continued.

XV

CRUCIFIXIONS AND A STRANGLEHOLD

Five days after the breach of the Third Wall, Titus's unrelenting rams finally created a slender gap in the Second Wall. This was in Simon bar Giora's Upper City sector and opened onto narrow streets where Jerusalem's wool merchants, cloth marketers, and braziers had their stores. Titus, rather than waiting for the gap to be widened, chose his bodyguards and another thousand legionaries to form an assault group that would go in through the breach with him at once. As his deputy for the assault he chose Tribune Domitius Sabinus of the 15th Apollinaris Legion. A likely client of his father or himself, Sabinus had acquired a reputation for unequalled bravery.

Before they entered the city, Titus ordered his men to take prisoner all Jews who offered to surrender. He also instructed them to not set buildings alight. This liberality was intended as a signal to the rest of Jerusalem, a signal that the Roman commander was prepared to spare the city and its residents if they gave up the fight. Once Titus and his men poured in through the narrow breach, they found the constricted streets that extended in front of them forbidding, with heavily armed partisans ready to oppose them. Slowly, Titus and his troops fought their way along the alleys, where just two men could fight side by side, forcing defenders back step-by-step, only to be attacked from houses they passed. Behind them, more partisans suddenly burst from several city gates. Running outside the city, these men came around behind the Roman assault group, sealing off their exit and isolating the siege towers before turning to face more Roman troops sent from the siege wall to deal with them.

Titus again found himself in a trap, with many of the men with him soon wounded. Retreat proved the only option. To cover that retreat, Titus sent out instructions for archers to mount the wall directly above the alleys where he and his men were boxed in. Once the archers were in position, they were able to fire down into the alleys, and with Titus and Tribune Sabinus acting as a rearguard, the legionaries, helping wounded comrades, made their escape back through the opening via which they had entered the city. Titus and Sabinus then followed, and once again Titus emerged from a tight situation unscathed.

Creating a wall of their own dead opposite the hole in the Second Wall, the partisans rejoiced that they had driven the Romans out of their city and told themselves that they would do it time and again. Titus, meanwhile, having learned the lesson of his impetuosity, had the rams much enlarge the breach in the wall. On the fourth day following the creation of the initial breach, Titus led a larger assault force in through a much broader gap. Coming over the wall of Jewish dead, they surged into this part of the city, overwhelming and driving back defenders by sheer weight of numbers. After taking the entire length of this section of the wall, the Romans demolished it, then placed garrisons in the wall's southern towers, which they'd deliberately left standing.

Titus now surprised his own troops and rebels alike by calling a halt to Roman offensive operations. He was in no hurry. He had learned from prisoners that the people trapped in the city were verging on starvation. Many sick and elderly Jews had already died. Importantly, Titus's own men were in need of a respite. Plus, he had been reminded that his troops' pay day had arrived. Legionaries of Rome during this era were paid their then salary of nine hundred sesterces a year in installments of three hundred sesterces three times a year. The centurion's base annual salary was twenty thousand sesterces. Chief centurions received one hundred thousand sesterces a year, then the value of a small farm in Italy. Auxiliaries, who were noncitizens, were paid a meager three hundred sesterces a year, although they did receive a recruitment bounty of three hundred sesterces on enlistment.[85]

So, Titus now called an official assembly of his army. In preparation, legionaries fitted crests to their helmets. These crests, only used at parades by this time, were made of horsehair. The color is disputed. Hollywood has traditionally depicted them as red, but the only examples of Roman helmet crests ever found were yellow. Now, too, the legionaries donned their bravery decorations. Auxiliary cavalrymen attached their bravery decorations to the harnesses of their horses, then led their steeds to the parade, glittering with gold. Summoned by legion trumpets, the men of one of the legions and their associated auxiliary units formed up on the leveled ground north of the city. Silently, they stood in neat ranks, cohort by cohort, behind their standards, as Titus and his officers reviewed them.

As Titus had hoped, much of the entrapped population of Jerusalem came out to witness this glittering martial spectacle, with hundreds of thousands lining the northern wall and clambering onto the roofs of houses and public buildings to be able to see it. In stony silence, the Jews watched Roman troops march forward when summoned by name by their officers, accept their pay, then march back to the ranks. The legionaries kept their money in a legion bank administered by their standard bearers, drawing on savings to send money to loved ones and for their annual furloughs, but otherwise keeping most of their cash for their retirement. Sometimes they did invest a portion of their pay in local business enterprises. We know, for example, that centurions of the 10th Fretensis Legion had invested in businesses in Cyrrhus while the unit was based there earlier that century.

The cash for this payday had been minted in Syria and delivered to Titus's camp in pay chests. Each legion had its own minting of coins. One side of each new coin bore the profile image of the emperor—Vespasian by this time. The AD 70 minting and subsequent issues were inscribed with the new emperor's now official name, Caesar Vespasianus Augustus. Prior to this, Caesar had been the name of the ruling imperial family, of whom Nero had been the last survivor. In taking Caesar as his praenomen, Vespasian had now turned it into a title, which his sons would also adopt. On the reverse of these legion coins the images varied, but it was usually each individual legion's emblem and name. The coins to pay the men of the 5th Macedonica Legion, for example, were inscribed LEGVMAC.

The day following the first pay distribution, there was another parade, and another legion received its pay. And so it went for four days, as the men of the four legions and those of the four cohorts of the 18th Legion and all the auxiliaries were paid. By the last day, the Jewish spectators had deject-edly melted away. Josephus, who witnessed all this from the Roman side, said that it was obvious that the ordinary people in Jerusalem were awed by what they saw and were depressed by it. For the first time, many Jews fully realized the size, power, and discipline of the army that Vespasian had sent against them, as well as the astonishing organization behind the legions, and realized the hopelessness of their cause.

Those ordinary people would have willingly surrendered, Josephus was to say, but the leaders of the rebellion knew that they themselves had com-mitted such heinous crimes in the eyes of Rome, from massacring legion-aries to breaking their word and using low-down trickery that went well beyond the accepted rules of war, they could only look forward to a painful death should they fall into Roman hands. So it was that, despite the inevi-tability of the fate of Jerusalem that became patently obvious on these days of the Roman pay parades, the partisan leaders ordered the slitting of the throat of any Jew who even spoke of surrender.

When, the day after the last pay parade, the Jewish leadership still failed to send him emissaries seeking surrender terms, Titus resumed the siege with vigor. While his men had enjoyed four days' rest, he had planned his next move in detail. Now, he divided his legions into two groups, assigning the 5th Macedonica and 12th Fulminata Legions to an assault against the west wall of the Antonia Fortress, while sending the other two legions, the 10th and 15th, against the northern wall close to the tomb of John Hyr-canus, second-century BC Jewish king and high priest. The legions were under orders to raise two earth assault ramps at each site for the subsequent use of siege towers.

As this work proceeded, Simon led his men out on sallies against the southern ramps, and John led his men against the more northerly ramps, as their men also bombarded the Roman work parties with darts from three hundred Scorpios they had just constructed to Roman design and forty stone-throwing ballistas. These harassment tactics were a great annoyance to the legions, so, to save further loss of life, Jewish as well as Roman, Titus sent Josephus to again attempt to negotiate a Jewish surrender and put an end to this business that had now lasted many exhausting weeks.

Josephus's family members were of course among the people trapped in the city whose lives he was desperate to save. His father and mother had in fact by this time been imprisoned by the rebel leadership, together with their servants, with all others in Jerusalem warned not to communicate with them on pain of death. As for Josephus's wife and brother, we hear nothing of them. His wife seems to have already died, while the brother was likely to be bearing arms for the rebel cause. Going to a section of the wall where he was out of range of missile throwers, but could still be heard within, Josephus called to his fellow Jews in Aramaic.

"Spare yourselves, spare your country, spare your Temple," he implored them, as he embarked on a long speech aimed at convincing his listeners to capitulate to the all-powerful Romans, even telling them that it seemed to him that God had departed Jerusalem, had now taken up residence in Italy, and was content to allow the Romans to take his holy city. In response, Jews jeered him from the walls and tried to land their missiles on him. In the end, Josephus withdrew, again without success.[86]

The food situation grew even graver inside the city. The rich gave their all for a small supply of corn or barley, sometimes eating the grain rather than turning it into bread and risking the smell of baking drawing others bent in taking it from them. The poor stole morsels from the mouths of their children. Old men with food in their mouths were choked by neighbors to force them to spit it out, after which the neighbors ate it. In this atmosphere of dog-eat-dog, some people decided to risk sneaking out of Jerusalem at night to find food.

The Romans were accustomed to seeing many corpses of Jewish dead being carried out in the night and deposited in the valleys outside the city, and made no attempt to stop this. Those Jews who chose to risk going in search of food hoped to slip out with these burial parties and go unnoticed. But Titus was expecting this. Those Jews seeking food who succeeded in evading Roman sentinels in the darkness and escaping into the countryside beyond the city ran straight into Roman cavalry patrols stationed there by Titus for this very purpose. An average of five hundred Jews of all ages and both sexes were caught in this net every night.

Titus's legionaries were hell-bent on punishing these runaways, and the general let them have their head. First they whipped their captives, and then they crucified them, tying them to crosses that soon lined the top of the wall of the forward Roman camp, where they could be seen from the city as they died slowly and painfully. Legionaries had callous fun with these victims, vying with each other for the most creative form of crucifixion. Some victims were crucified on standard T-shaped crosses, others on X-shaped crosses. Some were crucified upside down.

The rebel leaders inside the city used the sight of these crucified Jews to their advantage. Bringing relatives of the victims to the city walls, they pointed them out and declared that this was what the Romans did to anyone from the city who attempted to surrender. When the crucifixions failed to bring the city's capitulation, Titus had the hands of the next batch of captives chopped off, then sent them back into Jerusalem with the message that this would be the fate of all who failed to surrender. This only caused the rebels to line the walls. Making a great clamor, they yelled insults about Titus and Vespasian and declared that they would rather die than surrender.

Titus resolved to press on with the siege and personally went around the slowly growing siege ramps, urging the men working on them to toil harder and faster. At the same time, Roman reinforcements arrived in the form of Epiphanes, son of King Antiochus of Commagene, leading a large unit made up of Macedonian mercenaries. Epiphanes considered himself a fine soldier, and he chided Titus for the tardiness of his troops in the siege so far. Titus smiled and said he would join with Epiphanes in any attack he cared to launch with his Macedonians. But Epiphanes ignored him and promptly led a surprise attack against a city wall with his mercenaries. While the prince of Commagene indeed proved a valiant fighter, his Macedonians made no progress against the wall and its defenders, and retired with numerous casualties. Epiphanes's only wound was to his all-consuming pride.

While the Roman legionaries were busy building their ramps, rebel commander John of Gischala and his men were equally busy moving earth. Inside the Antonia Fortress, they had covertly burrowed west under the wall and under the ramp built by the 5th Macedonica Legion, shoring up the mine they dug as they went, using timber that had been kept in the Temple for planned extensions.

Seventeen days after work had begun on raising the ramps, just as four Roman siege towers were being moved into position at the base of the ramps in readiness for the completion of the earthworks, John set fire to materials coated in pitch and bitumen that had been stacked in his underground mine. These created a fire that consumed the timber shoring. With a roar and a cloud of dust and smoke, the ramp of the 5th Macedonica collapsed into the mine beneath it, and a mighty fire billowed up from the hole. As a result, the legionaries of the 5th found their siege tower sidelined from the wall offensive. This rebel success cheered the people in the city, giving them a flicker of new hope of perhaps repelling the siege.

Two days later, the siege towers of the other three legions were rolled into place, and their rams began to make the walls shudder in three different places. In response, just three rebel fighters from Simon's force in the Upper City ran out with burning torches. Like modern-day suicide bombers, they were bent on causing maximum damage while having no thought of returning alive. These men were of varying backgrounds. One, Tephtheus, came from Galilee. Another, Megassarus, was the descendant of the servants of one of Herod the Great's wives. The third, Chagiras, who hailed from Adiabene, even had a limp. All would be remembered for their suicidal bravery, and their identities would later be passed on to Josephus.

Because they were just three individuals, these men dodged every missile that came their way and avoided every sword swung at them. To the consternation of watching Romans, all three men reached their targets, and all three Roman siege towers were set alight before the trio was killed. With the alarm raised in the Roman camps, off-duty legionaries came running to extinguish the fires. They came without pausing to strap on their armor, which was a time-consuming process, one that also required the assistance of a second man. The Romans knew that every second's delay gave the flames more opportunity to take hold.

But the Jews had not finished. To capitalize on the success of their three fire-bearing comrades, thousands of exultant, fully armed rebels from both Simon's force and John's force had been waiting for the right moment, and they now came surging out of the city via several different gates in a coordinated movement to attack the firefighters. Some rebels ran up the ramps to the now burning towers. Others ran toward the Roman camp. At the camp, the duty cohort of one of the legions hurried to stand firm in several ranks before its walls, their shields locked together. Although greatly outnumbered, they held their ground, even as other unarmored legionaries came fleeing back from the burning towers, pursued by wild-eyed rebels.

At one burning tower after another, a tug-of-war was underway. Legionaries were pulling the ram from the tower on its own wheels to preserve it from the fire. Meanwhile, partisans tried to drag the rams back into the flames, some even grabbing the red-hot iron head of a ram with their bare hands. In the end, the rebels and the flames prevailed. The wooden supports of the ramps even caught alight, and soon the ramps themselves were collapsing. As the flames rose high, legionaries were forced to retire to their camps, leaving towers, rams, and ramps to burn.

When this fiery assault had commenced, Titus had been surveying the Antonia's walls, aiming to find a location for a new ramp to replace the one built by the 5th Macedonica that John had so successfully sabotaged with his mine. Titus had upbraided the Moesians of the legion for allowing the Jews to dig their mine undetected. Now, he saw the men of his other legions on the retreat, with their siege towers and rams going up in flames. Running to the attack with the select troops of his bodyguard, Titus swept into one flank of the Jews, forcing them to turn and face him. This allowed other Roman troops to press home the attack from in front of the rebels. With both sides standing their ground, after a brief stalemate, the Jews, now assaulted on two sides, wheeled and ran back into the city, and the gates were quickly opened to admit them and then closed behind them with equal speed.

The Romans held the field, but Titus, surveying the damage, with all four ramps now out of service and three ram-equipped siege towers burned to a crisp, lamented that his army's work of weeks had been destroyed in an hour. The Roman commander in chief now called a council of war of his senior officers—but excluding his royal affiliates—and put a simple question to them: Now that the ramps had been negated, what did they do?

The bolder among Titus's colleagues counseled him to use all their troops in one mass assault. The counterargument to this was that, in the confined spaces of Jerusalem, so many men would only get in each other's way. Others advised rebuilding the ramps and rams, concentrating the legions' efforts against the Antonia Fortress. The problem with this option was that there was no timber readily available for new construction work. Every tree for miles around Jerusalem had been lopped by the Romans, including, on the Mount of Olives, the now denuded Garden of Gethsemane—literally Garden of the Olive Press in Aramaic—whose olive trees had been among those cut down. (The olive trees that today stand in the garden have been dated to the more recent eleventh and twelfth centuries.) Others among Titus's subordinates counseled ceasing all offensive operations, sealing off the city to prevent supplies being brought in, and starving the Jews into submission.

In the end, Titus decided to combine options two and three. He began by ordering Jerusalem surrounded by a "wall of circumvallation," right around the city. A deep trench backed by a high earth wall, this was designed to cut off Jerusalem from the outside world. Slicing through the former New City to the north, this Roman wall was to roughly parallel the old city walls to the south and southwest of the city, and run up the rim of the Kidron to the east. Josephus stated that Titus felt his reputation was on the line with this siege, and the longer it took to complete, the less satisfied Titus would be with the result. So, Titus drove his men to dig this earth wall as quickly as possible.

Commencing at the Camp of the Assyrians base and first pushing south, work proceeded around the clock. To beg, cajole, and demand the best from his men, Titus himself constantly went around all the workers during the first watch of each night. His deputy, Tiberius Alexander, did the same during the second watch, and the commanders of the legions followed suit during the third watch. The result was a five-mile-long wall of circumvallation, completed in just three days. No longer could Jews slip from the city to gather food. The noose had been closed around the neck of Jerusalem and her people.

All the while, civilians in Jerusalem were dying in droves. One Jewish gatekeeper who escaped to the Romans informed Titus that he had counted more than one hundred thousand dead being carried out of his gate alone, to be left in the valleys to rot. Josephus was to estimate that six hundred thousand Jewish bodies had been carried from the city. Once the wall of circumvallation went up, fresh Jewish dead were piled in houses and in the streets. Even the city prisons became mortuaries. To taunt the population, some Roman troops, whose food supplies were being regularly topped up with deliveries from Syria and other nearby provinces such as Egypt, would take their daily ration of fresh-baked bread and olive oil and eat it within sight of the city walls.

While the wall of circumvallation was being dug by legionaries, some Roman auxiliaries had been ranging far and wide, going eleven to twelve miles in search of trees to cut and shape, leaving the surrounds of Jerusalem looking like a desert for miles around. This was in readiness for the building of new ramps and siege machinery, which would signal the next stage of the campaign, Titus's planned assault on the Antonia Fortress.

XVI

THE ANTONIA AND THE
TEMPLE

It was now August. Before Titus launched the next stage of the Jerusalem assault, he sent Josephus to make one last plea to the people in the city to give themselves up, offering free pardon to all who did. Once again, Josephus ventured close to a city wall and called out to those inside. This time, he went too close, and a Jewish slinger found his mark; a stone glanced off Josephus's head as he was talking, and he fell down in a heap, unconscious. Soldiers assigned to protect Josephus quickly scooped him up, and while some carried his apparently lifeless body away, others stood to fight off a rebel party that had dashed from a gate to make the traitor's corpse a trophy. With partisan fighters thinking that Josephus was dead, a cheer went up around the city walls, and it was soon reported throughout the city that he had perished. When this news reached Josephus's mother, she pretended to the rebels that she was unconcerned.

"I have always been of the opinion," she told her jailers, "that, since the siege of Jotapata, I would never enjoy the sight of my son alive anymore." To her maidservants, who were imprisoned with her, she privately lamented that she would not even be able to bury this "extraordinary" son whom she had always expected would bury her.[87]

But Josephus was not dead. He soon recovered from the blow to the head and returned to the wall where he'd been hit to show that he was indeed alive and to repeat his offer of a pardon for all who deserted the rebel city and the rebel cause. This disheartened many Jews and inspired numbers of Jewish deserters. Some escaped by pretending to go out of the city to launch sling stone attacks on the Roman lines, only to run to the Romans. Other deserters risked breaking bones, if not their necks, by jumping from walls and then running to the Roman lines. As per Josephus's promise, these Jewish deserters were not only unharmed by the Roman troops, they were given food. Many of these Jews were bloated by malnutrition, and some now unwisely ate too much and too quickly. The very food they gobbled down to save them from starvation in fact killed them.

Josephus says that there was a great deal of gold in the city during the siege in the form of coins and jewelry. When Jews participated in this wave of desertions generated by Josephus's offer of a pardon, they first swallowed as much gold as they could. Once they had been inspected by Roman sentries and were safely in the Roman camp, they would wait until they went out at night to relieve themselves beyond the camp walls and then retrieve the gold from their excrement. This went to plan for a time, until members of a cohort of Syrian auxiliary archers saw deserters retrieving their gold. To begin with, the Syrians began combing all the excrement outside the camp for gold. Before long, members of an Arab archers unit joined them. The gold craze even spread to some Syrian legionaries.

When sifting through excrement failed to prove profitable enough, these gold hunters went a ghoulish step further. As Jewish deserters went out of camp to relieve themselves, the gold seekers fell on them, killed them, and then cut them open to extract the gold from their bowels. This business of assassination and dissection soon became such an industry that close to two thousand Jewish defectors were killed in one night, and inevitably Titus came to hear of it. Furious, he contemplated surrounding the guilty men with cavalry and then giving the cavalrymen free rein to launch their darts at the guilty parties. Only when told the number of men involved, more than a thousand soldiers, did he drop this plan.

Instead, Titus summoned all his auxiliary and legion commanders to a meeting. Dressing them down for allowing such an evil practice to go on under their noses, he ordered these officers to inform their men that this barbaric act was outlawed, and anyone found guilty of it in the future would be immediately put to death. He also ordered suspects among the troops searched for ill-gotten gold, but of course they had all hidden their hoards.

Now, to get around Titus's prohibition, the next night some of the archers secreted themselves beyond the siege wall in the darkness, intercepting Jewish deserters before they reached Roman lines and murdering and dissecting them on the spot. Other deserters making their way from the city saw what was going on and, terrified, fled back the way they had come. From them, news of the gory fate of deserters spread like wildfire within Jerusalem, and, not surprisingly, the desertions ceased, literally overnight.

Work by four legions on four new earth ramps continued. All ramps were raised against the Antonia Fortress, with one being a rebuild of the ramp that John had destroyed with his mine. After twenty-one days of toil, the ramps were complete, as were four new siege towers equipped with new rams. With such a shortage of timber, Titus couldn't afford for these ramps and towers to be destroyed, so he held the towers back for now and placed a heavy guard around the ramps to foil Jewish fire parties.

Those parties emerged, sent by John, but they were uncoordinated, and they came at the fast walk, not the run as before. The lack of food within the city meant that the fighters were losing their strength. Between immovable Roman walls of shields and showers of missiles fired down from the nearby siege towers, each Jewish foray wilted as partisans were easily beaten back.

When Titus ordered the siege towers forward, they slowly came up the ramp slopes, with sweating, straining legionaries toiling in their depths and with Jewish darts and stones raining down on them from the one Antonia tower on the western side of the fortress that the Jews had left standing. The Roman progress was painfully slow, but by the afternoon the siege towers reached the wall.

Working at one siege tower under a testudo of shields, from which bounced countless Jewish stones, a group of legionaries used crowbars to remove four stones from the Antonia's west wall before retiring at nightfall. At the ramp that had been rebuilt over John's mine, a ram was in operation against the wall until sunset. In the twilight, the Romans withdrew to their camps for the night, and hostilities halted for the day.

In the night, that section of wall that stood over the old mine and had received a pounding in the afternoon suddenly collapsed of its own accord, with the ground beneath it giving way. With the dawn, Titus and his men studied the collapsed section of wall from their siege wall. Initial Roman joy at the wall's collapse gave way to frustration when they saw that John's men had built another wall inside the first. But close inspection revealed this new wall had been thrown up quickly and appeared much easier to assault than the outer one.

That morning, Titus called an assembly of his legions. Delivering a stirring speech, addressing his men as "fellow soldiers," he called on volunteers to make a surprise attack on this inner wall of the Antonia. Declaring that he would make the first man who mounted the wall envied by his peers with rich rewards, he promised immediate promotion if the man survived the climb, and everlasting glory for those who died in the attempt.

A legionary named Sabinus stepped forward. A mature, dark-skinned Syrian, he may have been serving with the one cohort of the 3rd Gallica Legion that had remained in Judea, although Titus seems to have left that to garrison Caesarea. Alternatively, Sabinus may have been with the 10th Fretensis or the 12th Fulminata, both of which were recruiting in Syria during this era. Sabinus was a diminutive, unprepossessing man, and well wrinkled to boot. In short, Sabinus looked an unlikely soldier and an even more unlikely hero.

"I readily surrender myself to you, Caesar," said Sabinus to Titus. "I will be first to climb the wall."[88]

Eleven other legionaries followed Sabinus's example, volunteering for the do-or-die mission. Not long after 11:00 a.m. that same morning, with the shields in their left hands held over their heads and with swords in their right hands, and as partisans rained darts and stones on them from above, Sabinus and those who followed him ran to the wall. Josephus doesn't describe precisely how Sabinus and his comrades climbed the wall with both hands occupied. Even mounting long scaling ladders would have been difficult. We do know that wooden ramps were often extended from the top of ancient siege towers to the top of the wall they were targeting. In all probability a short ramp or ladder led from the top of the siege tower at this part of the Antonia's wall. Sabinus used one such ladder or ramp, coming under fire from the wall directly above and from the Antonia Fortress's now lone tower, which extended well above the wall.

Deftly fending off Jewish missiles with his shield, Sabinus topped the wall, to the cheers of the watching legions. Rebel fighters, thinking a horde of legionaries must be coming over the parapet when Sabinus appeared, went to flee from the top of the wall. Sabinus gave chase, only to stumble over a large rock and fall headlong with a clatter of his segmented armor and shield. Hearing this, the fleeing rebels turned. Seeing Sabinus down, they threw javelins at him and retraced their steps with raised swords.

Sabinus was able to raise himself onto one knee. Parrying flying javelins and sword blows with his shield, he fought off Jews who surrounded him. When Jewish blades several times wounded him in the right arm and he could no longer keep up his sword, Sabinus was done for. Peppered with javelin thrusts, the hero of the wall fell down dead. Three of the men following Sabinus also topped the wall, only to be dashed to pieces by stones. The remaining eight Romans of the assault party, all severely wounded, were pulled down from the wall by comrades.

Two nights later, twelve legionaries on guard duty on the siege wall opposite the Antonia Fortress independently put into motion another attempt to cross the fortress's wall and win reward from their general. They brought several others into their covert plan. One was the eagle-bearer of the 5th Macedonica Legion, which suggests that some or all of the sentries were from the 5th. They also recruited a legion trumpeter and two legion cavalrymen.

A little before dawn, this group of sixteen legionaries crept to the wall in the darkness, then apparently climbed a siege tower and topped the wall without being seen or heard by Jewish sentries, most of whom were asleep. The assault party slit the throats of the nearest slumbering Jewish sentries, and the Roman trumpeter then sounded his instrument to signal that legionaries had gained the wall.

This caused other Jews who had been sleeping or on guard close by and in the western Antonia tower to panic. Fearing that the entire Roman army was now in the Antonia Fortress, they fled to the Temple. In the nearby Roman camp, Titus also heard the trumpet call. He and his bodyguard hastily pulled on their armor and he then led them on a dash to the wall. Via the siege tower, they joined the sixteen men who had captured the wall. The Romans then all surged down into the interior of the fortress and ran across its internal courtyard to the gate leading to the Temple.

By this time, John of Gischala had regrouped his men, and in their thousands they flooded out to stand shoulder to shoulder to defend the Temple gate. As Josephus was to say, both the Romans and the partisans knew that when the Temple fell, Jerusalem fell, and both sides fought desperately in close-packed, hand-to-hand combat with sword and spear. As reinforcements arrived from Simon in the Upper City, the Jews began to push Titus and his outnumbered legionaries back across the Antonia courtyard. Prominent in the Jewish onslaught were John's officers Alexas and Gyphtheus, two Zealot brothers named Simon and Judas, and, from Simon bar Giora's band, Malachias and Judas ben Merto, as well the commander of the Idumeans, James ben Sosas.

As the Romans gave way and retreated to the Antonia tower, a centurion from Titus's bodyguard by the name of Julian, who was standing at Titus's side at the Antonia tower, jumped back down to the courtyard to take on the Jews singlehandedly, determined to reverse Roman fortunes with his example. Centurion Julian was from Bithynia, in today's northern Anatolia in Turkey. He was powerfully built and had a reputation for outstanding bravery. Josephus had seen him several times at the head of Titus's bodyguard in the past and knew of his fame. Slaying rebels left and right, Julian terrified the Jews with his whirlwind of violence. Partisans stopped their advance and fearfully drew back, as if he were some sort of superman.

But as Centurion Julian pursued the rebels, he slipped and fell. Josephus says his caligae, his hobnailed military sandals, caught in the stone pavement. This pavement was made from marble slabs and would have been naturally slippery, but because the centurion fell backward, it's likely he slipped on blood, of which much had been spilled on the courtyard floor. With a crash of armor and shield, he went down, bringing a shout of alarm from watching Roman troops.

This change in momentum caused Jews to rush back and surround Julian. Taking many a javelin and sword on his shield, Julian struggled to regain his footing. Several times he succeeded in getting up only to be driven back down by the weight of blows. Watching from the tower, Titus wanted to immediately jump down to the centurion's aid, but his men held him back; the courtyard was a death trap for their general.

Assailants aimed their strikes at Julian's legs and arms, wounding him time and again. Yet every Jew who ran at him felt the steel of his sword. The wounds to his limbs eventually drained his strength, and finally, when he could no longer move, Centurion Julian accepted his fate and lay on the pavement to allow the Jews to deliver the coup de grâce. The slitting of his throat was messy and far from swift, according to Josephus. Julian's death affected Titus greatly. He had admired and respected the tough centurion. He was even more distressed to see the victorious rebels carry Julian's body back into the Temple, to strip and defile it.

Now that the legionaries of his bodyguard occupied the Antonia tower, Titus instructed his men to dig away the tower's western foundations and create a broad passageway through which the entire army could enter the fortress from ground level and cross the courtyard to assault the Temple. This work was to take seven days. While it was underway, Titus asked Josephus to yet again call on the besieged and offer terms.

This move was not only designed to save lives. Titus knew of the reputation of the Temple, one of the grandest religious complexes on earth, as a place of holy sanctuary for Jews. A fearer of his own gods, like most Romans, Titus respected Roman temples as places of sanctuary, and Josephus says Titus genuinely wanted to preserve the Temple for the Jews. But Titus knew that once his troops stormed it, he would not be able to prevent them destroying it. So, he gave Josephus a message to pass on to John of Gischala: "I do not force you to defile your own sanctuary." He then promised that if John and his partisans left the Temple and carried on the fight against Rome elsewhere, he would preserve the Temple as the holy place of the Jews.

Josephus duly called the message to John and his fellow rebels, and tearfully declared that God himself would use the Romans to destroy the Temple if the rebels did not leave. Some prominent Jews would heed this warning and deserted the city that night. Former high priests and the sons of high priests, these men were welcomed by Titus and sent to the town of Gophna to join other leading Jewish deserters settled there by the Romans.

The following day, John told his followers that this priestly band had indeed gone over to the Romans, only to lie and say they'd been executed by Titus. This stemmed the tide of desertions until a new deserter informed Titus of John's propaganda. To counter this, Titus had the priestly defectors briefly brought back from Gophna and displayed within view of the city to prove they were alive and well, and these men pleaded with the rebels to vacate the Temple. When the pleas fell on deaf ears, Titus sent the priests back to Gophna and ordered the assault on the Temple to proceed at once, before the Antonia passageway was completed.

Because Roman access to the Antonia was still limited, thirty legionaries in every hundred were assigned to a Temple assault group, with each thousand of these men commanded by a tribune. The force of six thousand thus assembled was placed under the overall command of General Cerialis by Titus, with the assault on the gates on the western side of the Temple Mount set down for the last hour of darkness the following morning.

As the hour approached, Titus himself put on his armor, having decided to personally lead this attack. But his friends would not let him expose himself to danger in the inevitable crush of the assault, urging him to instead watch it go forward from atop the Antonia tower, where his men could see him. Those friends assured Titus that his men, knowing he was watching them, would fight even harder, to impress him. Titus, seeing the logic of this, stationed himself on the highest point of the tower to witness and encourage the assault.

Jewish sentries weren't asleep this time. They raised the alarm as the Roman troops came skulking through the darkness, and thousands of partisans poured from the Temple courts to resist the Romans. The battle that followed outside the Temple gate lasted through dawn and until after 10:00 that morning, with Titus's bodyguards, who were in the Antonia tower with their general, cheering on their comrades as if they were watching a sporting contest. It ended in a stalemate, with neither side giving ground. Both forces withdrew as if by silent agreement, to lick their wounds and prepare for the next battle.

As soon as the passageway through the Antonia Fortress wall was completed, the legions commenced work moving earth again to create four more ramps. One was to be built inside the Antonia, against the Temple wall at the northwest corner of the Temple Mount. Another was built against a tower on the northern side of the Temple Mount. A third went up against the western wall of the Temple Mount, opposite the Temple's outer court, the Court of the Gentiles, and the fourth against the mount's northern wall. In both the latter cases, roofed colonnades ran along the tops of the walls above.

While this work was being undertaken, some Roman cavalrymen let their horses graze in the no-man's-land between the siege wall and the city wall; all the feed elsewhere had been consumed. Seeing this, rebels boldly dashed out, grabbed several horses, and led them back into Jerusalem. But as horse meat was not kosher, they were mere trophies and wouldn't end up on Jewish dinner tables. The horses would be left to starve to death. Titus was so furious with the loss of valuable horses, he had one of the cavalry-men involved executed for negligence as an example to all others.

The Jewish rebel leadership was constantly looking for tricky new ways of keeping their fighters engaged and keeping the Romans on their toes, and one such scheme involved a surprise attack to the east, against the camp of the 10th Fretensis on the Mount of Olives. The raid's objective was to break into the camp and raid the Romans' food supply. With the focus on the north and northwest of the city up to this point, this sudden eastern foray between 5:00 and 6:00 one afternoon was designed to sur-prise legionaries as they ate their evening meal.

But the Romans had been tipped off by a deserter that such a plan was in the wind, and when the partisan force burst out of an eastern gate and ran across the Kidron toward the Mount of Olives, the alarm was raised in the two other Roman camps, and a prepared force of infantry and cavalry came rushing around the city and caught the rebels as they were attacking the earth wall of the 10th Fretensis's camp, trapping them there. To escape, the Jews were forced to fight their way through the Romans behind them and then run down the slope back to the city.

A Roman cavalryman named Pedanius galloped after fleeing rebels, and bending low in the saddle as he overtook a young Jew, he grabbed him by the ankle, yanked him off his feet, and dragged him back to camp. Pedanius was so pleased with his catch that he presented his prisoner to Titus, who ordered the Jew's execution.

With the Romans focused on their new ramps, John of Gischala set fire to the overhead wooden passageway linking the Antonia to the Tem-ple, which had been rebuilt after partisans destroyed it four years earlier. Once more the passageway was destroyed, with the Romans allowing it to burn and collapse. This denied its use to both sides. Around this same time, a rebel named Jonathan—a short, ugly man—went out onto John Hyrcanus's tomb and called to the besiegers, challenging any Roman who would engage him in single combat to come forward. None did, which brought laughter and jeers from rebels lining the wall behind Jonathan, who called the Romans cowards.

This riled an auxiliary cavalryman named Pudens, who emerged from Roman ranks and came running toward Jonathan with sword raised, bringing cheers from thousands of spectators on both sides. Relishing the contest, Jonathan jumped down and ran at Pudens. At the critical moment, just as the two were about to come together, the running Pudens tripped and fell flat on his face. This enabled Jonathan to easily slit the Roman's throat. Then, with one foot on his victim's body, Jonathan brandished his bloody sword and shook the shield in his left hand as he gloated over his easy victory, to cheers from his comrades.

Up till now, watching men on both sides had refrained from becoming involved in the contest, but as Jonathan danced about, celebrating his win, a Centurion Priscus pushed aside the legionary manning a Scorpio on the Roman siege wall, took aim, and shot a dart that flew through the air and skewered Jonathan through the neck. Jonathan staggered, then fell dead on top of his victim, the trooper Pudens. Now it was the turn of Roman spectators to cheer.

As the siege continued and the four new ramps rose day by day, like a boxing match first one contestant would throw a wounding punch, only for the other to counter with a painful blow of their own. Now it was the Jews' turn to launch an uppercut that the Romans didn't see coming. Rebels occupying the colonnade topping the wall beside the Court of the Gentiles on the western side of the Temple Mount discreetly filled it with flammable materials, including bitumen, then made a show of withdrawing. Anticipating rewards from their commander in chief, a number of imprudent legionaries didn't wait for orders. Instead, quickly equipping themselves with scaling ladders, they climbed up to take possession of the colonnade.

Now the Jews set fire to the combustible materials along the colonnade and threw down firebrands that quickly had the scaling ladders on fire and collapsing. Within minutes Roman troops were trapped along the colonnade, with fire at their backs and overwhelming numbers of attacking Jews pressing in from the front. Some wounded Romans ran through the flames and jumped from the top of the western wall to rejoin Roman forces below. However, as can be seen today at the section of the Western, or Wailing, Wall that still stands, anyone jumping from the top of the wall was not going to escape injury—today, the above-ground height is some sixty feet; the wall was considerably higher in AD 70. At best, the jumpers sustained broken bones, at worst, a broken neck.

One of the legionaries trapped on top of the western wall was a tall young man by the name of Longus. As flames licked around him and threatened to soon bring down the wooden-raftered roof to the colonnade above him, Jewish fighters called to Longus, promising him clemency if he surrendered. But Legionary Longus's elder brother Cornelius was with the thousands of Roman troops now at the foot of the wall, and he called up to Longus, telling him not to tarnish his name or that of the Roman army by surrendering, and urging him to take his own life and earn himself a noble death and a worthy reputation. That is what Longus did, drawing his own sword across his throat as his brother watched.

Other Romans trapped atop the wall followed Longus's example by committing suicide, but a legionary named Artorius came up with a plan to save himself. He spotted a comrade, Lucius, a legionary from his own eight-man *contubernium*, or squad, with whom he shared a tent and ate meals. Lucius was in the throng of anxious legionaries below the wall, looking up. These men needed permission from their centurions to bring more ladders if they were to attempt to rescue legionaries who'd climbed the wall without orders and become trapped above—permission that did not come. So, they were powerless to help their comrades, other than in the way that Artorius now conceived.

"Lucius!" Artorius yelled down to his friend as the flames licked around him. "If you will come and catch me, I will make you heir to all I possess."[89]

Whether Lucius was inspired to help his comrade by this offer or purely by friendship, we don't know, but he pushed his way through the crush of Roman troops to stand at the foot of the wall directly below Artorius, telling him to jump and promising to catch him. Artorius, casting aside his shield, jumped from the top of the wall, landing on top of his friend. But Artorius was still clad in his armor. His weight drove Lucius to the stone pavement and killed him instantly. He probably died from a broken neck or crushed skull. As for Artorius, he survived the jump without a scratch because Lucius had broken his fall.

Lucius's sad story and that of Longus's suicide would run swiftly through the Roman army, eliciting much sympathy from all ranks, including Titus. Meanwhile, the roof of the colonnade collapsed, destroying the colonnade. The following day, the Romans themselves deliberately set fire to the colonnade running along the top of the wall on the northern side of the Temple, denying it to the Jews as a place of shelter or resistance.

Inside the city, starvation was driving people to unthinkable acts. The siege and the lack of food literally sent some insane. One such sad case was later related to Josephus. A young woman named Mary, a well-to-do mother of one from the village of Bethezob in Perea, had apparently been widowed by the revolt. Worse, she had sold all her belongings for food, only for her last reserves to be stolen by rebel fighters. Mary was suckling a young son. But without food, her milk dried up, and she could no longer feed him. Losing her mind, she killed her son, then roasted him. She ate half of her son's flesh and kept the remainder for later. The aroma of cooking flesh soon drew rebel fighters, who forced their way into her lodgings and ordered Mary to hand over the meat she'd cooked, or they would cut her throat.

"I have saved a very fine portion of it for you," said Mary, revealing the half-eaten remains of a child. "This is my own son," she said matter-of-factly, as the horrified rebels reeled back, "and what has been done was my own doing." Holding up the plate containing the remains, she urged, "Come, eat this food. I have eaten of it myself."[90]

The partisans staggered from Mary's house in shock. Not even they, these ruthless men who had bullied, betrayed, and butchered their own people, could stomach this resort to cannibalism or come to terms with a mother eating her own child. And so the siege continued, and the people in the city resorted to eating grass and weeds and to gnawing their leather belts and footwear. But still the rebels who held sway over the city would not contemplate surrender.

XVII

THE FINAL PHASE

Two of the four new Roman ramps, those on the western side of the
Temple Mount, were completed on the same day. They'd had the benefit of transfer of earth from the ramps built earlier at the nearby western wall of the Antonia Fortress. Titus ordered mantlets and rams rolled
up the two completed ramps, and for six days these rams pounded away
at the upper sections of the wall, with their monotonously regular thuds
resounding around the Temple area. Yet the rams made not the slightest
impression on the wall.

There was then a single gateway on the northern side of the Temple
Mount, and while work had continued on the two rams on either side of
the gate, a group of legionaries had labored with crowbars under the cover
of shields to work loose the stones forming the gateway's foundation. After
six days, these men succeeded in removing the outer layer of stones that
framed the gateway, but the inner layer in the immensely thick wall held
firm, and the gate continued to stand strong.

Frustrated by this failure to make headway, these legionaries brought
scaling ladders and climbed up to attack the rebels in the colonnade
directly above them, some going up without shields. Jews met this impet-
uous attack in large numbers, led by an Eleazar, a cousin of Simon bar
Giora. Some Romans were thrown off when they reached the top of the
wall; others were killed on it. Partisans pushed the scaling ladders away,

some laden with climbing troops. The remaining Romans finally gave up and fell back. Titus now decided that the ramps and rams were taking too long. The only way he was going to get his troops into the Temple quickly was by burning its massive gates, and he gave orders accordingly.

Despite the latest partisan successes, two of Simon bar Giora's senior lieutenants, Ananus, a native of Emmaus, and Archelaus ben Magadatus, soon after defected to the Romans. When both were brought before Titus, he was acquainted with their reputations by Josephus, who had been told by other defectors that these two were among Simon's most bloodthirsty and murderous followers. As per his earlier promise to all defectors, Titus set the pair free, but he sent them away without any of the privileges he'd granted other defectors, such as food and water.

Fires had been set at the Temple gates by Titus's troops, and now they were ignited. The gates all had a decorative coating of pure silver that had been added by Herod the Great. But silver is susceptible to intense heat, with its melting point a little less than that of gold. As the flames grew more intense and rose higher, the silver melted, exposing the wood beneath, which also caught fire. Inside the Temple, the partisans could only stand and watch the gates burn, with neither the means nor the strength to douse the flames. Those flames rose up above the gates and ignited the rafters of the cloisters above. The gates themselves were massively thick, so these fires burned for the remainder of that day and well into the next, eerily illuminating the Temple Mount in the night. On the second day, as the gates continued to burn, Titus called another conference of his senior Roman commanders to decide the fate of the Temple.

Joining their general in Titus's pavilion in the New City forward camp were his deputy, Alexander; the generals Cerialis, Lepidus, and Frigius; Tribune Fronto, commander of the 18th Legion cohorts; Tribune Sabinus of the 15th Apollinaris Legion; Tribune Nicanor, sporting a bandaged shoulder; the unidentified tribune commanding the 12th Fulminata Legion; the tribunes who were second-in-command of the 5th Macedonica and 10th Fretensis Legions; the procurator of Judea, Marcus Antonius Julianus, who had replaced the odious Florus; and the procurators of surrounding territories, who, like Julianus and the tribunes, were of Equestrian Order rank.

Some of these officers were all for totally destroying the Temple. Titus, on the other hand, was in favor of sparing the Temple as Pompey the Great had in 63 BC, which he hoped would reflect well on Rome, and favored restricting vengeance to the rebellious. When Alexander, Cerialis, and Fronto all agreed with his view, Titus ordered preparations made for a final assault on the Temple the next day, with his troops under orders not to damage the structure. Men were selected from every cohort of the legions for this final attack, and at dawn the next day they moved into position preparatory to extinguishing the burning gates and then going forward with the attack.

Between 5:00 and 6:00 that morning, before this force was fully in place, rebels came storming through what remained of the gate from the Antonia Fortress, even as it continued to burn. They ran straight into dismounted cavalry on guard in the Antonia courtyard, and as these troopers pushed forward to oppose the Jews, Titus, watching from the Antonia tower, ordered in more cavalrymen.

The tide of battle flowed this way and that in the Antonia courtyard, with the Jews driven back and then charging again. After three hours of toe-to-toe fighting, the troopers finally drove off the rebels, forcing them to retreat across the Temple's Court of the Gentiles to the Inner Court, where they closed the Inner Court gates behind them. Seeing this, Titus gave orders for the final assault on the Temple to be postponed until dawn the next day and, leaving a large guard in the Antonia courtyard, retired to his tent.

In the evening, rebels suddenly emerged from the Inner Court and again came surging into the Antonia. But the Jews were by this time weak from lack of food and the continual fighting, and they were soon driven back by Roman cavalrymen on guard. This time, the Romans pursued the Jews through the blackened gateway, where the remnants of the double gates still burned, and into the Court of the Gentiles.

As one of those cavalrymen was passing through the gateway, he stooped to pick up a burning piece of wood before entering the courtyard. In front of him, across the courtyard, were the walls of the inner Temple building. The soldier ran to its northern wall, where there was a tall, ornate window whose framework rising above him was of gold-encrusted wood. With a comrade lifting him up, the trooper set the window alight with his firebrand. Beyond the window there was a corridor, off which opened all the rooms that surrounded the innermost sanctuary of the Temple. Soon the window was burning fiercely, with the flames rising up to the rafters of the corridor. From within came the cries of alarm of rebels and civilians quartered in the

Inner Court, calling for help to extinguish the blaze. Despite Titus's best intentions, Jerusalem's famous Temple was alight.

Word of fire in the Temple was rushed to Titus as he lay in his bed. Rising up, he sent word to his officers, then ran through the growing darkness to the Antonia, and from there into the Court of the Gentiles. He was accompanied by panting bodyguards, led by a Centurion Liberalius, who came armed with clubs for riot control. Behind Titus ran his commanders, and behind them, in no organized order, came their legionaries in their thousands. Titus arrived to find that many cavalrymen had piled in through the burning window, helping each other up and in, intent on killing and pillaging. Some had been burned in the process. They were yelling, and inside, the Jews were yelling.

"Stop!" yelled Titus to the troops, raising his right hand in the universal stop sign. "Quench the fire!"[91]

In the noise and mayhem, the general was ignored. Legionaries rushed past him and clambered up through the window, intent on grabbing a share of the spoils and the blood. In their eagerness, some soldiers trampled over comrades who were trying to get in the window ahead of them. Titus sent Centurion Liberalius to also climb in and then open a gate to him from within, and this enabled Titus to gain entry to the inner Temple precinct. Inside, he found his men running riot all around him, slitting the throat of every Jew they found, whether armed on not, and yelling to each other to burn the place to the ground.

As the commander in chief's bodyguards formed around their commanders to protect them from their own out-of-control troops, Titus ordered Liberalius and one of his men to lay into the soldiers with their clubs, to stop the orgy of destruction and get the men to extinguish the flames. But they were just two men against a greedy army, and their efforts were in vain. The Temple's inner rooms were full of gold coin, clothing, and golden ornaments, the fittings of the Temple and the offerings of the faithful, and the Roman troops were intent on enriching themselves. They looted so much gold that once they sold it to the traders who followed the army and those traders flooded the market with it in Syria the following year, the price of gold in the province halved.

When Titus, accompanied by his senior commanders, reached the inner sanctum of the Temple, Jewish bodies lay heaped before the Temple's altar, with blood running down the altar ramp like a river. When Titus entered the innermost chamber, the Holy of Holies, which, under Jewish law, was barred to all but the high priest, he found, as Pompey had found when he conquered Jerusalem after a three-month siege 133 years earlier, that the room was empty. While Titus and his commanders were in the inner sanctuary, one of their rampaging soldiers set fire to the doorframe around the brass doors to the Holy of Holies, and as fire rapidly took hold and rose into the rafters, Titus and his officers and bodyguards withdrew. There was no stopping the blaze now. This August day of AD 70—according to some authorities August 6, according to others August 30—the Temple was devoured by fire.

With the Roman troops focused on looting, many Jews inside the Temple precinct were able to escape the flames. Six thousand five hundred women and children fled out to the Court of the Gentiles. They would not be sold as slaves once the siege was at an end. So many Jews had already been sold into slavery during this war that Titus decided that only fighting men taken during the final stages of the siege of Jerusalem would be sent into slavery, and even these would be sold cheaply, for there were few buyers in the now glutted Eastern slave markets. More than forty thousand Jewish noncombatants captured at Jerusalem, mostly women and children, would be released by Titus.

Meanwhile, in the chaos of Roman looting, a number of rebel fighters made it to the Upper City and joined Simon's men. John of Gischala and many of his lieutenants were among them, although Simon would remain in charge in the Upper City. As the burning inner Temple structure lit the night sky, the noise was horrific—the roar of the fire, the yelling of the Roman troops, the groans of their victims, the ritual wailing of the Jews in the Upper City as they watched their Temple burn.

Two priests of the Temple were so heartbroken they threw themselves into the flames. Other priests and servants of the Temple clambered up onto a wall of the inner Temple and clung to it, out of reach of the flames and Roman troops. All in all, Josephus would estimate that ten thousand Jews, rebel fighters, priests, and civilians died in the Temple that night, killed by sword or flame.[92]

The following day, as the collapsed Temple ruins smoked, order and sanity returned to the satiated legions, and Titus returned to the Temple Mount. The standards of the legions, for so long forbidden from Jerusalem, were raised at the Temple's eastern gate. With the legions assembled before their general, sacrifices to the Roman gods were made in honor of their victory, and then the legionaries, with one voice and led by their officers, faced Titus and bellowed two words that echoed around the otherwise silent city:

"Hail imperator!"[93]

This ancient title of imperator was bestowed, but only rarely, on victorious Roman generals by their troops. In the days of the Roman Republic, Pompey the Great was hailed imperator by his soldiers, as was Julius Caesar, and his assassin, Marcus Brutus. The word *imperator*, which literally means "commander," ultimately led to the title "emperor" and the word "imperial." This was because, during the reigns of the emperors up to this time and later, only Rome's sovereign was entitled to be hailed imperator. Titus's troops were breaking that century-old tradition.

For days, the Jewish priests and their servants who had perched on the Temple wall remained there without food or water, with Roman guards posted below the wall to prevent their escape. One cherubic youth talked his way down, seeking water and promising to return. The Roman sentries let him go, only for the boy to scamper away and disappear. Finally, after five days, almost too weak to move, the Jews on the wall came down and begged Titus for their lives. But because they had defied him, Titus ordered all put to death.

As for Simon, John, and the rebels still holding out in the Upper City, they sent messages to Titus seeking a parley. Titus and his officers were unanimous in wanting to spare the city any further destruction, says Josephus, and, hopeful of a swift rebel capitulation, Titus agreed to talks.[94] At the southern end of the Temple's Western Wall, there was a bridge running along the top of the southern colonnade of the Xystus, a large market square also used by Jewish men for physical exercise. That bridge, running over today's Robinson's Arch, led to the Upper City, and this had been the escape route used by John and his men. Titus now came to stand at the Temple Mount end of this bridge, with his legions formed up in the Court of the Gentiles behind him. John and Simon stood at the other end of the bridge with their still thousands of freedom fighters massed behind them.

Titus sent an interpreter to deliver a message to the rebel leaders, a lengthy exhortation reminding the partisans of the might of Rome and of the numerous offers he had previously made to allow their surrender. The crux of Titus's message was a proposal—of unconditional surrender.

"If you throw down your arms and deliver yourselves up to me, I grant you your lives and will be like the mild master of a family. What cannot be forgiven shall be punished. The others I will preserve to myself for my own use."[95]

The Roman general's intent was clear. Rebel leaders guilty of the betrayal and murder of Roman soldiers would receive prompt punishment. The remainder, their followers, would retain their lives, becoming imperial property. John and Simon replied with a counteroffer—if Titus let the rebels depart with their wives and children and go into the desert to the south, he could have Jerusalem without further ado. This infuriated Titus, who was indignant that the defeated should deign to offer terms to the victor. The rebel response hardened his attitude. He sent the interpreter back with a proclamation:

"No longer come to me as deserters or hope for any further leniency. Henceforth, I shall spare nobody, and will employ my entire army against you. Save yourselves as best you can, for from this moment forward I shall treat you according to the laws of war."[96]

Titus then ordered his legions to plunder and burn all that continued to stand in Jerusalem, and at dawn the next day the legions descended from the Temple Mount into the Lower City. Methodically, they set fire to and destroyed the Council House in the Xystus and the city archives close by, then moved into the narrow lanes beyond the vast courtyard, setting alight houses filled with the rotting bodies of Jewish civilians who had died from starvation or at the hands of partisans. Individual house fires linked up and swept west through the Lower City and the remains of the Acra, an ancient fortress. Reaching a raised area called the Ophlas, or Ophel, in the City of David, Jerusalem's original residential quarter, the flames consumed the Palace of Queen Helena of Adiabene and Edessa.

As fires raged, a group of prominent Jews in the Lower City who handed themselves over to Roman troops were brought before Titus. This group was headed by the sons and brothers of King Izates of Adiabene, who had been driven from the family palace in the City of David by the fires. The Adiabene royal family had contributed financially to the rebel Jewish cause, and at least one prince had fought the Romans. When they begged for their lives, Titus agreed to let the relatives of Izates live, but had them placed in chains and put under guard.

With much of the Lower City and City of David gutted by fire, partisans living there were forced into the crowded Upper City, which was protected both by the old city walls and the fact that it sat on a rise. Some 8,400 civilians who had taken refuge in Herod's Palace in the Upper City were killed by this influx of rebel fighters, who also looted the refugees' belongings. These partisans also took two legionaries captive, one a foot soldier, the other from a legion's mounted squadron. The foot soldier had his throat cut by the rebels, with his body subsequently dragged through the Upper City and jeered by partisans as it passed. As the Roman cavalry-man was about to be executed, he swore he possessed information of vital importance to rebel chief Simon.

When hauled before the rebel leader, the Roman had nothing to offer; his claim had been a desperate bid to prolong his life. So Simon handed the legionary over to his deputy Ardalas, who led him out, blindfolded and hands tied behind his back, to be decapitated in sight of Roman troops. But before Ardalas could draw his sword, the Roman bolted and ran into the arms of fellow Romans. Surviving the enemy was one thing, but, to Romans, surrendering to the enemy was more than dishonorable; it was traitorous. The legionary was brought before Titus, who contemplated ordering the man's execution. But he relented, instead having the soldier stripped of his weapons and equipment and ejected from his legion and from the Roman camp. The man would have to try to survive as an outcast and somehow reach his homeland and family.

The following day, the legions cleared the last rebels from the Lower City and burned what buildings remained, lamenting that they found no hidden treasure; partisans had looted this part of the city ahead of them. Although the surviving rebels were now bottled up in the Upper City, some hid in the ruins of the Lower City to ambush any potential deserters from above. Those they caught were killed, with their bodies thrown to the wild "pariah" dogs roaming the city outskirts.

Titus had warned the rebels he would use his entire army against them for this final phase of the siege, and to conquer the Upper City he called for earth ramps to be erected against its walls by the legions and, unusually, also by the auxiliaries and allied troops. The legions were assigned the western side of the city. Their ramps were to go up opposite Herod's Palace, near Simon's headquarters in the Phasael Tower. The auxiliary units and allied troops were combined and put to work building ramps in the Upper City's southeast corner, in the open space of the Xystus. This way, the much-depleted rebels would be forced to defend against assaults coming from two directions at once.

Seeing this activity, leaders of the Idumean rebels in Simon's force secretly met and decided to surrender to Titus, even if that meant being sold into slavery. Five emissaries bearing this proposal slipped from the Upper City in the night. Despite having previously declared that he would no longer spare any Jews who surrendered, Titus appreciated that the Idumeans represented a sizable portion of Simon's fighters, and feeling that Jewish resistance was likely to crumble if he acceded to the Idumean request, he sent the emissaries back with his agreement to the deal.

As all the Idumeans were preparing to desert the Upper City, Simon got wind of their plan and descended on their leadership with his men. The five emissaries to Titus were immediately executed, and Jacob ben Sosias and other Idumean commanders were seized and locked up. This left the Idumean rank and file in disarray, without leaders or direction. A number decided to attempt to defect to the Romans anyway. Some were caught and killed in the act after Simon doubled the guard on the walls. Others made it to the Romans, and, as fighting men, the majority of them were added to the growing number of Jews consigned to slavery. A few Idumeans identified by earlier defectors as responsible for heinous crimes were separated from the rest for later execution.

Two other prominent defectors provided Titus with rich trophies. The Temple priest Jesus ben Thebuthus received a full pardon from the Roman commander in chief when he delivered up Temple treasures that lay hidden inside the massively thick wall of the inner Temple. These included solid gold tables, bowls, and other vessels, as well as the two purple curtains of the inner sanctuary that had previously been the responsibility of Zealot leader Eleazar ben Ananias. This hoard included priestly garments and precious stones used in Temple worship. But the crowning glory of these trophies were two massive sacred golden candlesticks, the Menorah, each with seven branches, and each of which were so heavy that they required at least eight men to carry them on a platform borne on their shoulders.

When Phineas, treasurer of the Temple, was captured, he revealed the hiding places of the coats and golden girdles of the priests, with great quantities of expensive purple and scarlet coloring and vast stocks of cinnamon, cassia, and other sweet spices used in the manufacture of the incense burned daily in the Temple. All these treasures were placed under guard by Titus for eventual removal to Rome, and both Phineas and Jesus were set free to go wherever they chose outside Jerusalem.

After eighteen days, the new ramps against the Upper City walls, built for the most part from the material in earlier ramps, were completed, and siege towers and battering rams were rolled to them from their previous locations. When the rams set to work, many Jewish defenders stationed on the walls above them retreated to the Palace of Herod, which they called the Citadel, making no attempt to impede the rams' operations—probably having run out of ammunition. That very day the legion ram pounding the wall near the Phasael Tower caused a breach at a wall tower, to the cheers of legionaries, whose spirits were high after the successes of the past weeks.

With their leaders Simon and John having melted away, Jewish defenders withdrew from the site of the breach, only to pour out a gate and rush the siege wall west of the city en masse, hoping to break through and escape. But the weakened partisans' desultory attack was easily beaten off by legionaries on guard along the wall. Many of these rebels, leaderless and without the strength to carry on, simply lost the will to fight, and instead of retreating back into the city, they fell on their faces and lamented their fate.

In the city, meanwhile, defenders were in a panic. Those in Herod's Palace fled its cloisters. Those in the three great towers, the Phasael, the Hippicus, and the Mariamne, even deserted their posts and fled into the city streets as all sought refuge in caverns and water tunnels beneath the city.

As legionaries poured into the Upper City via the western wall breach, they were amazed to meet no opposition. Even more surprising, the three great towers, whose defenders they'd expected to have to starve out, were theirs for the taking, and legionaries gleefully raised the standards of their maniples in the towers to denote their conquest. Rampaging through the streets of the Upper City, other Roman troops killed every Jew they encountered and forced their way into every house looking for rebels and booty. All they found inside the houses were recently dead occupants, while the upper floors were stacked with the rotting, stinking corpses of others who had died earlier in the siege.

Driven from the houses by the overpowering stench of death, legionaries gave up attempts to search for valuables and set each dwelling alight. The fires spread, and with nightfall the Roman troops withdrew from the Upper City, leaving the flames to complete the destruction and consume tens of thousands of bodies. It was September 25, and the siege of Jerusalem had reached its gory conclusion.

Two and half centuries later, Eusebius, the Christian Bishop of Caesarea in Palestine, would write in his *Church History*, first published around AD 313, that the Jews had brought the fall of Jerusalem on themselves. "Seditions and wars and mischievous plots followed each other in quick succession, and never ceased in all of Judea until finally the siege of Vespasian overwhelmed them. Thus the divine vengeance overtook the Jews for the crimes which they dared to commit against Christ." It had of course been the siege of Titus. As for Eusebius's belief that the Jews had been responsible for the death of Jesus Christ, this would remain the view of the Catholic Church until the twenty-first century, when Benedict XVI (2005–2013), the so-called German Pope, would finally repudiate it.

XVIII

DESTRUCTION, RETRIBUTION, AND CELEBRATION

On the morning of September 26, AD 70, Titus entered what was left of Jerusalem's Upper City. With his officers and staff, he surveyed the ruins and admired the three towers of Herod's Palace, which had escaped damage and continued to stand strong and firm.

"We certainly have had Jove as our assistant in this war," Titus remarked, referring to Jupiter, Rome's principal god, as he surveyed the impressive trio of towers, "and it was none other than Jove who ejected the Jews out of these fortifications."[97]

Those Jews who had been imprisoned by the rebels in the Upper City's subterranean cells were freed on the orders of Titus, who also stipulated that his troops kill no more Jews. All survivors were to be assembled in the Women's Court on the Temple Mount, where the guilty were to be separated from the innocent. Elderly and infirm Jews among these survivors failed to make it that far; impatient legionaries who saw them as being of no service to Rome disobeyed their general's order and put them to the sword in the Upper City.

At the Women's Court, Tribune Fronto, assisted by a senior freedman of Titus's who acted as his clerk, had the task of examining every prisoner to distinguish rebel from innocent civilian—mainly on the say-so of defectors. On Fronto's orders, Jews identified as leaders of the uprising were set aside for crucifixion. Out of the remainder, Fronto chose seven hundred of the tallest, most well-built younger Jewish men and had them set aside for Titus's Triumph in Rome, after which they would be made to entertain the Roman populace by fighting to the death in the amphitheater.

Vespasian and Titus seem to have agreed before the Jerusalem siege that each would celebrate a Triumph in recognition of their Judean War victories, although Vespasian was on record saying he'd never had the ambition for one. A Triumph was traditionally a victory parade through the streets of Rome, granted by the Senate to a Roman general who killed more than ten thousand enemy fighting men in a victorious campaign. Pompey the Great and Julius Caesar had both celebrated several Triumphs each, although the majority of Caesar's were questionable because he celebrated them for civil war victories over fellow Romans. The last celebrant of a military Triumph had been the emperor Claudius for his AD 43 invasion of Britain. His generals actually won that victory for him while Claudius was back in Rome; he did go to Britain but only for sixteen days and only after the campaign was wrapped up. Nonetheless, Claudius still took the credit for the British victory and took the Triumph.

Vespasian and Titus certainly qualified for a Triumph. An accurate number of actual partisan fighting men who were killed over three years of Roman campaigning has not been established, but the total probably exceeded one hundred thousand. Encouraged by his friends, Vespasian duly petitioned the Senate for Triumphs for his son and himself, and the Senate quickly passed the necessary resolution, with dates set for AD 71, when Titus was expected back in Rome.

Fronto also separated other prisoners into groups according to their physical stature and state of health. The least healthy were consigned to the region's amphitheaters to be pitted against wild beasts, the fate of common criminals under Roman law. Healthier specimens were earmarked for the Egyptian mines, whose output included gold, copper, and beryl. There, these men would die, sooner or later, as they labored in chains. The fitter remaining prisoners were set aside to compete in local amphitheaters as gladiators, fighting each other.

Josephus successfully petitioned Titus for the lives of relatives and friends among the prisoners. He first succeeded in saving 190 women and children he was acquainted with. They were among those herded together on the Temple Mount. He learned that his wife had perished, so too his parents, but he found his brother Matthias and fifty male friends among the prisoners and also had them freed. Then, riding with Cerialis, commander of the 5th Macedonica Legion, to find a site for a military camp at a village called Thecoa six miles south of Bethlehem, he saw partisans freshly crucified along the roadside and recognized three of the victims as old friends. On his return to Jerusalem, Josephus applied in tears to Titus for the lives of the trio, and Titus ordered the men taken down. Two of the three were too far gone to survive and subsequently died.

Meanwhile, legionaries were searching every underground hiding place for the last rebels and for treasure. Any partisan they came upon who resisted was immediately killed, although most of the two thousand Jews they found underground were already dead. These Jews had perished from starvation, had been killed by fellow Jews, or had taken their own lives rather than surrender. Some legionaries couldn't take the overpowering stench of the dead in these confined spaces and quickly resurfaced for fresh air. Others had stronger stomachs and scrambled over the dead in search of booty, of which much had been secreted away underground.

Graphic evidence of the occupation of these subterranean vaults by rebels from the Upper City was discovered near the Western Wall in 2013. Three cooking pots and a small oil lamp were found in the cramped drainage channel of a small underground water cistern that originated in the Siloam Pool on the southern edge of the City of David. None of these items would have been considered valuable by the searching Romans, who would have ignored them.

The surviving rebel commanders, Eleazar, John of Gischala, and Simon bar Giora, had yet to be located, but, driven by hunger and thirst, John soon identified himself from his underground refuge and offered to surrender if Titus granted him his life. Titus agreed, and John was brought out and loaded with chains on wrists and ankles. His ultimate fate would be decided in Rome. Simon bar Giora seemed to have disappeared from the face of the earth. He was in fact beneath it. As the fate of the Upper City had become clear to him, he'd identified an underground cave system that could not be seen from above ground. Taking lieutenants, a party of men who had formerly been stonecutters, and the last of their supplies, Simon went underground just before the Romans stormed the Upper City.

Simon and his companions were down there still, quietly cutting through earth and chipping through rock as they dug an escape tunnel in an easterly direction beneath Jerusalem. They intended that this tunnel would emerge beyond the Roman siege wall east of the city, from where they would make their great escape. As for Zealot leader Eleazar, no sign of him was ever seen again. He was absent from the record of the last weeks of the siege, and as there is no account of his dying in battle, it's to be presumed he was among the many who starved to death.

According to Josephus, 1.1 million Jews died during the siege of Jerusalem and just 97,000 survived to be processed by Fronto. This processing lasted many days, during which 11,000 prisoners died from starvation—there was barely enough Roman grain to go around, but some Jews were deprived of food by Roman guards who took a dislike to them, while other prisoners stubbornly refused to accept food from Romans.

Debate has raged through the centuries about the fate of the small Christian community that continued to live in Jerusalem following the death of Jesus Christ. Some scholars believe they escaped before Titus's siege, while others postulate that they were among the victims of the siege. Certainly, all the apostles, including the thirteenth apostle, Matthias, who was chosen by lot to replace the dead betrayer Judas, had left Jerusalem prior to AD 70. Most had died by the time of the siege of Jerusalem, in most cases in distant lands. The only ones believed to have lived well past AD 70 were Matthias, who died circa AD 80, and John, the apostle said to be Jesus's cousin. According to Christian tradition, John took Mary mother of Jesus to Ephesus in Asia, from where Roman authorities sent him into exile on the island of Patmos, apparently for preaching the teachings of Jesus. He later returned to Ephesus, where he is believed to have died of old age during the reign of Vespasian's son Domitian.

According to several fourth-century Christian writers, not long before Titus began his siege of the city the Christian community at Jerusalem received a warning from an oracle, who urged them to leave as Jerusalem was going to be destroyed. The Christian community was said to have heeded the warning, even though oracles were a pagan creation and anathema to Christians, and fled to Pella in Perea, one of the cities of the Greek Decapolis, where they settled. English twentieth-century theologian S. G. F. Brandon argued that the Christians would have remained at Jerusalem and perished there during the siege because they were allied to the rebel

Zealot movement. The apostle Simon the Zealot was part of that movement, and Brandon felt that Jesus himself had Zealot leanings. There is no firm proof of whether the Christians stayed or went.[98]

With all Jewish resistance in Jerusalem at an end, Titus climbed a large, specially built tribunal in his camp and addressed his assembled troops, congratulating them on their victory. Individual soldiers cited for bravery awards during the campaign were then called forward by the announcer of each legion and presented with their awards by Titus.

Josephus was with the group of officers and foreign dignitaries who witnessed these award presentations. He saw Titus place golden crowns on the heads of several men, place golden torques around the necks of others, and hand over golden spear and silver standard awards to even more men. The decorated men were also promoted and received silver, gold, and rich garments from the Jewish treasure trove. Among these recipients was the highly decorated Chief Centurion Gaius Velius Rufus of the 12th Fulminata Legion. Before long, he would be sent on an important mission to the king of Parthia by Titus's father. In later years, unusually for a man from the ranks, Velius Rufus would be made a member of the Equestrian Order, promoted to prefect in command of large numbers of legion vexillations, then made a tribune of the City Guard at Rome. He ended his career as a procurator in three provinces under Vespasian's youngest son, Domitian, who would become emperor in AD 81 upon the death of Titus.[99]

At this Jerusalem awards ceremony, Titus announced the future postings of the legions that had taken part in the siege of Jerusalem, postings decided by Vespasian in Alexandria. The 10th Fretensis Legion would remain at Jerusalem as Judea's resident legion, accompanied by several thousand auxiliaries. Titus appointed the senator Terentius Rufus new commander of the 10th and military governor of Judea. The legion's former commander, Larcius Lepidus, seems to have died suddenly or been in poor health, because there is no record of him receiving any further appointments following his successful command of the 10th Fretensis during the Jerusalem siege.

Terentius Rufus and the 10th Fretensis were tasked by Titus with knocking down most of the now ruined, fire-blackened city of Jerusalem and covering the site with plowed earth. Titus's intent was that Jerusalem be wiped from the map. Several structures were excepted from the destruction—the Phasael, Hippicus, and Mariamne Towers, and the western wall of the Upper City, which Titus ordered to be incorporated into a new base for the 10th Fretensis in the southwest of what had been Jerusalem.

The 5th Macedonica Legion was to march to its old post at Oescus in Moesia to again guard the Danube frontier. Their commander of the past few years, Lucius Cerialis, would before long renew his relationship with these troops with his appointment as governor of Moesia by Vespasian. The 12th Fulminata Legion was ordered to a new posting, Melitine in Cappadocia, a critical road junction, where it was to build a new permanent camp for itself. The 15th Apollinaris Legion was also to march to the Danube, returning to its earlier posting of Carnuntum in Pannonia, where it would build a new base and replace the new 7th Gemina Legion, which was being posted to Spain.

The six cohorts of the 3rd Gallica Legion that had marched on Rome to help make Vespasian emperor were already on their way overland on a return march to Syria. They were to become the resident legion at Raphanaea in southern Syria, previously the posting of the 12th Fulminata. These men of the 3rd Gallica had made themselves unpopular in Rome as arrogant bullies, so they had initially been sent by Mucianus to the town of Capua, outside Rome, where they'd proceeded to loot the houses of the elite. In returning them to the East, Mucianus was getting the troublesome Syrians out of his hair. The legion's cohort currently at Caesarea would march north to rejoin their comrades at Raphanaea, where, the following decade, future noted writer Pliny the Younger would serve for six months as a junior tribune with the legion.

The 18th Legion was abolished by Vespasian—one of several legions he disbanded in Europe following the Civilis Revolt. The 18th's six cohorts in Europe would apparently be combined with the 7th Galbiana Legion, which had suffered heavy casualties in the Year of the Four Emperors, to create the new 7th Gemini Legion—the Gemini title signified the "twinning," or combination, of two legions. The four cohorts of the 18th now in Judea with Titus would apparently be folded into the 3rd Gallica to replace the three cohorts wiped out early in the Jewish Revolt and to fill the depleted ranks of its other cohorts. The cohorts of the 3rd Cyrenaica Legion currently at Jerusalem would rejoin their legion in Egypt.

Two of the departing legions accompanied Titus when he left the ruined city. They would form his escort until he sailed from Egypt for Rome the following year. But for the three days following the announcement of these new postings, Titus, his officers, and his men all enjoyed a series of victory feasts in their Jerusalem camps. A vast number of oxen sacrificed to Mars, the god of war, in thanks for the Roman success were distributed for the feasting.

Titus then left Jerusalem and proceeded down to Caesarea on the coast, with the allied troops and his two accompanying legions herding the thousands of surviving Jewish prisoners in a column that stretched for miles. Many a captive Jew would have looked back in tears at the ruins of Jerusalem as he tramped up and over Mount Scopus in chains, and many a legionary would have looked back with a smile as he took in the vision of the site of his legion's hard-fought victory. Also in the column were thousands of mules and carts carrying the spoils of that victory. Titus would temporarily leave these spoils and a number of prisoners at Caesarea.

As Titus was arriving in Caesarea at the beginning of October, his father was finally bound for Rome in a fleet of warships of the Roman navy. The new emperor's route took him to the Greek island of Rhodes, then to several port cities of Greece itself, before touching at Korkyra on the island of Corfu. He would then land in Apulia on the boot of Italy, apparently at Taranto, before proceeding up the Appian Way to the capital. He was greeted by joyous crowds everywhere he went, and as he approached Rome, the population thronged out of the city to cheer his arrival.

When, in October of AD 70, Vespasian reached Rome, his deputy, Licinius Mucianus, who'd been running Rome with an iron fist for ten months, loyally stepped aside and handed over the reins of power. Made a consul for the third time by Vespasian two years after this, Mucianus would otherwise go into quiet retirement and write several well-regarded books, including a collection of the letters and speeches of leading Romans of the Republican period as well as a natural history of the East, neither of which survive to modern day.

Vespasian came to Rome knowing that three times the annual income of the empire had been expended on the civil war that had brought him to the throne, and tight fiscal measures were required to rebalance the books of state. He had already abolished Nero's grant of immunity from taxes to Greek cities. Progressively, he would introduce a range of new fees and taxes that would apply across the empire, and would encourage his procurators to soak up as much income as they could from their provinces. Vespasian even sold pardons for citizens convicted of crimes.

One of the new charges Vespasian imposed was a fee on the use of public urinals at Rome. Titus, after his return to Rome in AD 71, complained to his father about this tax, in response to which Vespasian handed Titus a coin from the first proceeds of the urinal tax, asking him, "Does it smell bad?"

"No," Titus replied, sniffing the coin.

"Yet it comes from urine," said Vespasian.[100]

Not long after Vespasian's arrival in Rome, he was approached at one of his regular Palatium audiences by Phoebus, the former freedman of Nero who, in Greece four years earlier, had told him to go to Morbia. When Phoebus asked for Vespasian's forgiveness and an imperial appointment, Vespasian showed him the door, saying, "Go to Morbia!" Phoebus would be neither punished for his earlier rudeness to Vespasian nor offered employment by him.[101]

*   *   *

In October of AD 70, it was too late for Titus to sail back to Italy to join his father. The sailing season was closing, and while impatient by nature, Titus had no intention of risking the ships that would carry the treasure from Jerusalem, and the prisoners, to the seasonal storms that would soon sweep the eastern Mediterranean.

Still at Caesarea on October 24, he celebrated the nineteenth birthday of his younger brother, Domitian, with a show in the city's amphitheater where 2,500 Jewish prisoners were put to death in front of a packed audience. Some were burned alive; some were pitted against wild animals. Others were required to fight each other, with the winner of each contest having to fight for his life again, until just one Jew remained to fight and die another day.

From Caesarea Maritima, Titus, still accompanied by two legions, traveled inland with Agrippa to Caesarea Philippi, which had dropped the name Neronias and reverted to its original name. A number of Jewish prisoners were in Titus's column, and while spending several weeks with the king at Caesarea Philippi, Titus celebrated a series of games in the city, the most lavish being on November 17 for the birthday of his father, with the prisoners being sent into the arena to die.

While Titus was in Caesarea Philippi, he received word that the last Jewish rebel leader, Simon bar Giora, had been captured at Jerusalem in surprising circumstances. Simon and his companions had slowly dug their tunnel east, with their food supply dwindling to a paltry daily ration and then running out altogether. Their tunnel had finally broken through into one of the tunnels beneath the Temple Mount, and one fall day a thoroughly weakened Simon had emerged on the Temple Mount via this tunnel, wearing a white gown and a rich purple cloak.

Men of the 10th Fretensis Legion were working on the Temple Mount at the time, leveling the ruins of the Temple. Stopping work, the legionaries stared at Simon in amazement, with some no doubt thinking he must be a ghost. When asked who he was, he refused to identify himself, only telling the troops to fetch their commander. Legionaries ran to find the legion's new legate, Terentius Rufus, and when he appeared on the scene Simon revealed his identity and told of how he'd come to be there. Rufus had Simon and his surviving companions, who emerged from underground behind him, put in chains, then sent a messenger to Titus informing him of Simon's capture.

In the new year, Titus returned to Caesarea, and from there, with his escort and the men of the 3rd Cyrenaica Legion, set off for Egypt via Jerusalem. As Titus passed through Jerusalem he was amused to find men of the 10th Fretensis digging for Jewish treasure where once the city had stood. From Alexandria, once the sailing season opened in March, Titus sailed to Rome, taking with him representative groups of troops from his legions, his Jerusalem spoils, the seven hundred selected young Jewish prisoners, and prize captives Simon bar Giora and John of Gischala.

Later that year, Titus and his father celebrated a joint Triumph through the streets of Rome—Vespasian had combined the two Senate-approved Triumphs into one to save money. Titus and his father rode in the traditional golden chariot of the Triumphant, and Titus's younger brother, Domitian, rode behind them on a horse. The parade was led by all the senators of Rome, on foot, and included the selected seven hundred Jewish prisoners, in chains and wearing the Temple's rich priestly garments, but looking scrawny because of lack of food. They would soon be sent to the arena, but at the head of them walked the royal relatives of King Izates of Adiabene, whose fate is unrecorded. Behind the two triumphing generals marched troops detached from Vespasian's and Titus's legions, chanting bawdy ditties about their two commanders as the laws governing Triumphs permitted.

There was a long procession of painted dioramas, some four stories high, depicting the battles of the Judean War, and wagons carrying representative spoils from the Temple, including the golden table. Eight selected centurions, wearing white robes as required in Roman religious parades—which the Triumph was considered—bore a platform on which was perched one of the two golden Menorahs taken from the Temple. Last of all came Jewish rebel leader Simon bar Giora, with his hands in chains and being led by a rope around his neck.

The Triumph followed the traditional route, in through the Triumphal Gate, along the Via Sacra, or Sacred Way, around the Circus Maximus, which was packed with spectators. All of Rome and much of central Italy had come to see and cheer the Triumph, and the streets were so packed with people that the procession's path was narrow and its pace so painfully slow that Vespasian tired of it.

"What an old fool I was to demand a Triumph," he later remarked.[102]

Once the parade eventually ended, Simon bar Giora was ceremonially executed in the Forum. It was customary for an enemy commander to be dispatched at the end of a Triumph by garroting, although it was usually carried out in the Carcer, the prison of Rome. Because Titus had given John of Gischala his word that his life would be spared if he surrendered, John would spend the rest of his days in chains, apparently in the Carcer. We don't know where or when he died. Following Simon's public execution, dignitaries and Vespasian's troops enjoyed an open-air feast.

Representative items from the Judean spoils were set aside for display in a new Temple of Peace that Vespasian commissioned in the city, also known as the Flavian Forum in honor of Vespasian's family, the Flavians. Spoils from the campaign and the state's share from the sale of prisoners into slavery—after the legion's troops and commanders received their share—were used by Vespasian to build the Temple of Peace and a grand new fifty-thousand-seat amphitheater on the site of a drained lake in the center of Rome. He also restored a giant statue of Nero, called the Colossus, which had been vandalized following Nero's death. The new stadium was officially named the Flavian Amphitheater, but after later emperor Hadrian moved the Colossus to stand outside it, it became known as the Colosseum.

Vespasian would turn the first sod on the Colosseum project by AD 72. It was still under construction when he died in AD 79. Titus, who served as his father's prefect of the Praetorian Guard, succeeded him as emperor, but only lived another two years. During his reign he opened the Colosseum and directed assistance for the cities on the Bay of Naples affected by the AD 79 eruption of Mount Vesuvius. After Titus died from a fever, his brother, Domitian, succeeded him. Domitian dedicated two triumphal arches at Rome to Titus and the conquest of Jerusalem. One of these arches, at the entrance of the Flaminian Amphitheatre on the Field of Mars, no longer survives. The single Arch of Titus, built just southeast of the Forum on the summit of the Sacred Way, still stands today and has been the model for other triumphal arches since, including Paris's Arc de Triomphe and New York City's Washington Square Arch.

Josephus, the former Jewish rebel commander, journeyed to Rome with Titus, and as a client of Vespasian was permitted by the emperor to live in an apartment in Vespasian's family home on Pomegranate Street in Rome, a house which Domitian later turned into a shrine to the Flavians. A farm in Judea owned by Josephus was turned into a Roman guard post, so, in exchange, Vespasian granted him several other Judean properties. "He also honored me with the privilege of a Roman citizen and gave me an annual pension," Josephus later wrote.[103]

During Vespasian's reign, Josephus began researching and writing his *Jewish War*. Given access to Roman war diaries, he also spoke with Roman commanders and Jewish survivors, and he received thirty-four letters from King Herod Agrippa II, who, granted additional territories by Titus following the revolt and living until at least AD 93, told his side of the story. Josephus's book was read and approved by Titus before it was published in his reign with his imprimatur. A dozen years later, during the reign of Domitian, Josephus published his Jewish Antiquities, a detailed history of the Jewish peoples that began with Adam and Eve. Remaining faithful to his Jewish religion, Josephus lived well into old age, through the later years of his life fighting published accusations from other Jews that he was a despicable Jewish betrayer and turncoat.

XIX

JERUSALEM'S
ULTIMATE FATE

Following the fall of Jerusalem, Jewish rebels were still holding out at three Judean locations, Herodium, Machaerus, and Masada. Between AD 71 and 73, the 10th Fretensis Legion, led by a new commander, the senator Lucius Flavius Silva Nonius Bassus, known as Silva, took all three centers. Apparently a relative of Vespasian's, Silva had been commanding the 21st Rapax Legion, based at Vindonissa, modern Windisch in Switzerland, when the 10th Fretensis's commander, Terentius Rufus, died suddenly of natural causes while on campaign in Judea. A decade earlier, Silva had been the military tribune of the 4th Scythica Legion in Syria, so he was familiar with the region.

In the spring of AD 73, Masada was the last Jewish stronghold to fall to the 10th Fretensis. Silva had the legion build a massive earth ramp up the western side of the Masada plateau. That ramp, ruins of the Masada Fortress, and footings of the Roman legion camps below all remain to this day. According to Josephus, when the legionaries eventually burst through a breach they made in the fortress's wall from their ramp, they found that the 960 Jews who had been inside Masada, including Sicarii leader Eleazar ben Ya'ir, had taken their own lives, killing each other after drawing lots. Just five children and two women, one of them a relative of Eleazar's, were found alive. Some scholars suggest that the 10th Fretensis actually killed the defenders after storming the fortress and that Josephus used his version of events to give a noble end to the Jews' uprising. One way or another, the Jewish Revolt in Judea, which had a starting point at Masada, ended at Masada.

After the fall of Jerusalem in AD 70, Jews were forbidden by Rome to even approach the former site of the city. When the emperor Hadrian visited in AD 130 he decided to establish a colony for legion retirees outside the legion's fortress. Colonia Aelia Capitolina it was called—Aelia referring to Hadrian's family name, Aelius.

Hadrian plowed the first furrows of the new city, which was laid out on a grid pattern by military engineers. Coins issued to commemorate the event show the emperor in the act of plowing. Among the Roman public buildings that would adorn Hadrian's new city of Capitolina would be public latrines, discovered in 2002, not far from the Temple Mount, and a small, three-hundred-seat Greek-style theater abutting the Western Wall, with the theater's audience sitting with their backs to the Temple Mount. The theater was revealed by Israeli archaeologists in 2017, semi-intact, below the feature known today as Wilson's Arch, which served as a roof to the theater and also a pedestrian access to the Temple Mount.

During his visit, Hadrian also ordered two Roman temples built. One, dedicated to Jupiter Capitolina, was erected on the Temple Mount, where trees had grown up since AD 70. This temple was apparently erected where the Dome of the Rock now stands, a little to the southwest of the original inner Temple's location, for an equestrian statue of Hadrian was erected where the Jewish Temple's Holy of Holies had stood, as witnessed by a visitor in the fourth century. The second Roman temple erected at the new city was dedicated to the goddess Venus. It was erected at the Camp of the Assyrians, over Calvary, site of the crucifixion of Christ—quite deliberately, in the view of fourth-century Christian bishop Eusebius of Caesarea.[104]

Following the failed Second Jewish Revolt, or Bar Kokhba Revolt, of AD 132–135, Jews were not permitted to live in either Capitolina or any other part of Judea. This prohibition was relaxed to an extent by the fourth century, when Jewish pilgrims are recorded visiting the city to anoint a weathered piece of stone, apparently one associated with the Second Temple. This would have taken place on Tisha B'Av, by then the one day of the year when Jews were permitted by Roman authorities to enter the city, a day when Jews commemorated the Temple and mourned its loss.

Also in the fourth century, the city was visited by Helena, mother of the emperor Constantine. Then in her late seventies and an ardent Christian convert, Helena was on a three-year pilgrimage to the Holy Land. Local Christian leaders helped her locate Christ's tomb, and, according to later legend, produced what they claimed were relics from his crucifixion three hundred years before—pieces of the "True Cross," bronze nails and a piece of rope from the cross, and even the complete tunic and cloak Christ supposedly wore to his death. Quite how or where the clothing had survived over the centuries was never explained. Local church leaders in Palestine supposedly even produced a mummified human finger—the finger that St. Thomas, so-called doubting Thomas, put into the wound in Christ's side after his resurrection, they said.

Helena joyfully took these claimed relics back to Europe. Some are today displayed at Rome, while the cloak said to have belonged to Christ would find its way to Trier, supposedly taken there by Helena along with remains of the Apostle Matthias. Subsequently, the 778 Second Council of Nicaea decree that every church altar should contain a holy relic resulted in a proliferation of claimed relics that made some communities rich as destinations for pilgrims. By the sixteenth century, noted Dutch Catholic theologian Erasmus was complaining there were enough claimed pieces of the True Cross to build several houses; French church reformer John Calvin lamented there were so many he could build a ship. By the twentieth century, churches across Europe would still lay claim to Christ's garments, sandals, crown of thorns, the vinegar sponges and lance used at his crucifixion, and his childhood foreskin (claimed by two different churches).[105]

According to Medieval legend, Helena also had twenty-eight marble steps that Christ walked up to enter the Antonia Fortress's praetorium following his arrest taken to Rome and laid at the Lateran Palace. Later relocated, they remain venerated in Rome today as the Scala Sancta, the Holy Stairs. The fact the 10th Fretensis Legion leveled the Antonia during Jerusalem's demolition suggests the steps would not have survived this, or the subsequent three centuries of non-Christian rule, or been identifiable as being from the Antonia even if they had. Notably, Eusebius, Bishop of Caesarea when Helena was in Palestine, who knew Helena and her son and outlived both, and who wrote Constantine's biography and collected the emperor's writings, always painted the acts of Constantine and his family in a hagiographic Christian light, yet never once mentioned the relics of Christ that Helena purportedly took back to Europe, something he would surely have known about and trumpeted if it indeed occurred.[106]

However, in the twentieth and twenty-first centuries archaeologists did discover some of Jerusalem's original paving stones still in place near the Temple Mount, beneath up to twelve feet of rubble deposited during the AD 70–71 demolition—flagstones that Christ may well have trod. Immediately below the Western Wall, a 220-foot-long section of a Herodian street thirty feet wide was found beneath a layer of shattered masonry rained down from the Temple Mount directly above as 10th Fretensis legionaries demolished its structures. In falling, the masonry, some of it weighing several tons, cracked or broke many of the thick flagstones. Then, in 2019, a 660-foot length of Roman-style street was unearthed almost intact, linking the Pool of Siloam with the Temple Mount's southern wall. This street was dated by coins found beneath the pavers to around AD 31, when Pontius Pilate was prefect of Judea. It also lay beneath a deep layer of demolition spoil, in this instance containing arrowheads and slingshot from the AD 70 siege. Both streets had been covered by the 10th Fretensis to create the new, raised ground level.

Helena convinced son Constantine, who would not personally fully convert to Christianity until on his deathbed, to have Capitolina's Temple of Jupiter and the Temple of Venus torn down, with the Church of the Holy Sepulcher erected on the Calvary site. Constantine would involve himself in the fine details of the Holy Sepulcher's design and fit-out, sending detailed letters to Palestine containing his instructions regarding its construction.

During the AD 361–363 reign of the emperor Julian, a quarter of a century after the death of his uncle Constantine, reconstruction of the Jewish Temple on the Temple Mount was authorized. Young emperor Julian was called Julian the Apostate by Christian writers, because, after being raised a Christian for twenty years, he converted to the faith of his forefathers, worshipping the gods of the old Roman pantheon. Julian authorized and funded the Temple's reconstruction, not to appease Jews but to annoy Christians. However, the work did not proceed far. According to Christian writers, it ceased after workmen reported balls of fire emitting from the Temple foundations, with workers supposedly refusing to continue construction.

The simpler explanation for Julian's Temple reconstruction failing to proceed is that Julian was only on the throne for twenty months, before he was mysteriously killed by a lance while on military campaign against the Persians. Julian's Christian successors, following the Church line vocalized by Eusebius, blamed the Jews for the death of Christ, and simply rescinded permission for the Jewish Temple's reconstruction.

Once Capitolina was conquered by Islamic forces in the seventh century, the Dome of the Rock mosque replaced the by then leveled Temple of Jupiter on Temple Mount, and the city's name returned to Jerusalem. Under Islamic rule, Jews were eventually permitted to live in the city once again. But it would not be until the Six Day War of 1967, just short of 1,900 years since Titus's conquest of Jerusalem, that the Jewish people were again able to take control of their Holy City, long after the fall of the Roman Empire. The wheel of Fortune had come full circle, and the Jews were the new conquerors of Jerusalem, 2,977 years after King David's army had wrested the city from its Canaanite founders.

NOTES

I. MENAHEM'S SURPRISE ATTACK AT MASADA

1. The rank of the commander of Masada's Roman cohort has not come down to us. The fact that when six cohorts of the legion went from Caesarea to Moesia six months after the Masada massacre, they went commanded by their chief centurion, Arrius Varus, the legion's next most senior officer after its camp prefect, supports the belief that the 3rd Gallica's camp prefect was killed in the early days of the uprising.
2. Josephus, *Jewish War.*
3. Deuteronomy 21:10–12.
4. Deuteronomy 23:17.
5. Deuteronomy 13:16 and 7:25.
6. Zias and Gorski, "Capturing a Beautiful Woman at Masada."

II. MAYHEM IN JERUSALEM

7. Josephus, *Jewish War.*
8. *Mishna Shekalim* 5.
9. Centurion Julius is named in Acts, New Testament. The escort of ten legionaries was typical; when, fifty years later, Ignatius Theophorus, Christian bishop of Antioch, the later St. Ignatius, was similarly sent to Rome for trial, his escort consisted of a centurion and ten legionaries.
10. Josephus, *Jewish War.*

III. REVOLT ACROSS THE MIDDLE EAST

11. Why Nero gave the new legion the number 18 is puzzling. Following the Varus Disaster massacre of Roman troops in the Teutoburg Forest, Augustus abolished the 17th, 18th, and 19th Legions, whose eagle standards had been lost in the massacre, permanently removing these numbers from the legion list. Thereafter, these numbers had never been contemplated for new legions, as they were considered unlucky by superstitious Roman soldiers.

IV. THE IMPENDING STORM

12. In the first century, a proconsul, literally "as good as a consul," was the governor of any "armed" Roman province that contained at least one legion, with the exception of Egypt. A proconsul's appointment was by the Senate, not the emperor, who could only appoint propraetors, governors of "unarmed" provinces.
13. Josephus, *Jewish War.*
14. Ibid.
15. Tacitus, *Annals.*
16. In the second century the system changed so that prefects could command auxiliary cohorts before becoming a military tribune, with the post of prefect of cavalry following the tribuneship. Under the third and fourth century reforms of Diocletian and Constantine, prefects commanded legions, with the rank of legate abolished.
17. Secundus's family name is sometimes given as Emilius. It's possible that an Aemilius Rufus who'd served as a prefect of cavalry under Corbulo in Armenia several years earlier was also related to Jucundus and Secundus.
18. Josephus, in his *Life,* says the cavalry unit left at Sepphoris was "of the legions." With Legate Gallus commanding the 12th Fulminata Legion, this unit would have been his own legion's cavalry troop—every legion had a single troop of up to 124 mounted legionaries, used primarily for scouting and courier duties.

V. A ROMAN DISASTER

19. Dating by Stern, *Calendar and Community.*
20. Josephus, *Jewish War.*
21. Frontinus, *Stratagems.*
22. Josephus, *Jewish War,* gives the numbers for Roman losses in this and later phases.
23. Tacitus, *Histories.*

VI. LIKE A VOICE FROM THE GRAVE

24. Albright, "The Excavations at Ascalon."
25. Josephus, *Jewish War*.
26. Ibid.

VII. ENTER VESPASIAN AND TITUS

27. Suetonius, in *The Twelve Caesars*, "Vespasian," describes the morning massage as a part of Vespasian's daily routine. Josephus's *Jewish War* says that Vespasian left his son in Achaea with the imperial party when he was banished. The "out of the way town" Josephus says Vespasian took himself to was likely on an Aegean island, enabling him to return promptly by sea when and if summoned by Nero.
28. Tacitus, *Annals*.
29. Suetonius, "Vespasian," in *The Twelve Caesars*.
30. Dio, *Roman History VIII*, Book LXII.
31. Tacitus, *Annals*. Dio, *Roman History VIII*. Suetonius, *The Twelve Caesars*.
32. Suetonius, *The Twelve Caesars*.
33. Josephus's *Jewish War* tells us that after escaping the rebels in Jerusalem, Philip hid for months in Gamala, from where he'd smuggled letters to the king's deputy Mobius, who passed them on to Agrippa at Beirut. In response, the king had sent cavalry to Gamala who linked up with Philip after he slipped from the city and took him to the king in Beirut. Agrippa received reports from Jewish enemies of Philip that he had sided with the rebels in Jerusalem, but the king didn't believe a word of it. Giving Philip a large cavalry force, he'd sent him to bring the royal servants trapped at Gamala to Beirut and restore the families of the "Babylonian Jews" who served in his army to their home in Batanaea in Perea east of the Jordan. Philip returned to Beirut following this mission in time to lead the king's delegation to Gallus and then Nero.
34. Nero's words, and Vespasian's assessment of him, come from Josephus's *Jewish War*. Vespasian apparently communicated both to Josephus.
35. Ibid.
36. Suetonius, "Titus," in *The Twelve Caesars*.
37. Josephus's *Jewish War* states that the two legions taken from Egypt were the 5th Macedonica and 10th Fretensis, which we know to be incorrect. The 10th Fretensis was in Syria all this time. Josephus subsequently puts the 15th Apollinaris Legion in Vespasian's force. He also states that the infantry cohorts that accompanied the legions from Egypt contained six

hundred men, which shows his outdated Roman military knowledge; that had been the case a century before, in the days of the Roman Republic, but by Josephus's day most of Rome's cohorts had been reduced to 480 men, although Roman authors invariably rounded that up to 500.

38. Suetonius, "Vespasian," in *The Twelve Caesars.*
39. Tacitus, *Annals.*

VIII. FIRE AND BLOOD IN GALILEE

40. Nineteenth-century German historian Theodor Mommsen speculated that the 10th Fretensis's title originated from a battle in the Strait of Messina, despite any evidence to support that supposition. The sea battle that Mommsen referenced didn't even occur in the Strait of Messina; it took place off the north coast of Sicily. The evidence for the Strait of Otranto origin is much stronger. See Dando-Collins, *Legions of Rome,* for a detailed discussion.
41. Clemens's career is detailed on an inscription from Heliopolis; see Campbell, *The Roman Army, 31 BC–AD 337: A Sourcebook.* Clemens's death between AD 67 and 69 can be established with some certainty by the fact his memorial described his Judean War service under Vespasian but not under Titus. Others who served in this campaign under both Vespasian and Titus, such as Chief Centurion Velius Rufus, mentioned later in this work, had both commanders mentioned on their memorials.
42. Josephus's *Jewish War* tells of the Roman troops brought out of Egypt by Titus. Roman navy expert Professor Chester Starr, in *Roman Navy,* was convinced that Titus used the Alexandrian Fleet for these troop movements in Egypt.
43. Albright, "The Excavations at Ascalon."
44. Josephus, *Jewish War.*

IX. THE SIEGE OF JOTAPATA

45. Suetonius, "Vespasian," in *The Twelve Caesars.*
46. Josephus's *Jewish War* describes this assembly routine and its triple war cry.
47. Ibid.
48. Ibid.
49. Ibid.
50. Josephus, *Jewish War.* Vitruvius, *On Architecture,* gives catapult stone weights. Vegetius, *Military Institutions of the Romans,* gives the number of catapults per cohort.

51. Metcalf, "Whistling Sling Bullets Were Roman Troops' Secret Weapon."
52. Josephus, *Jewish War*.
53. Josephus, *Jewish War*, gives these precise casualty figures.
54. Ibid.
55. Ibid.
56. Ibid.

X. TAKING TIBERIAS AND TARICHEAE

57. Plutarch, "Galba," in *Lives of the Noble Greeks and Romans*.
58. Josephus's *Jewish War* gives these numbers. Some modern scholars consider these numbers inflated.

XI. GAMALA AND GISCHALA

59. Josephus, *Jewish War*.
60. Ibid.
61. Ibid.
62. Ibid.

XII. NERO'S FATE CHANGES EVERYTHING

63. Dio, *Roman History VIII*, Book LXII.
64. Ibid.
65. Suetonius, "Nero," in *The Twelve Caesars*.
66. Josephus's *Jewish War* gives Lucius Annius's name. He is otherwise unknown. Josephus possibly confused him with Lucius Alienus, a probable client of Vespasian. Alienus was married to Domitia Longina, second daughter of the late general Corbulo. At Rome, Vespasian's youngest son, Domitian, was having a secret affair with Alienus's young wife, and in AD 70 he forced Alienus to divorce Domitia so he could marry her. If Alienus was indeed a client of Vespasian, his wife would have mixed with Vespasian's family, giving Domitian easy entrée to her. And if Alienus was away on military service in Judea with Vespasian, Domitian was free to secretly have his way with Domitia in Rome.
67. Tacitus, *Histories*.
68. Ibid.
69. Ibid.
70. One of four hundred Roman tablets discovered in London in 2014 during excavations for the new Bloomberg offices on Queen Victoria Street has

Classicus and his cohort stationed in London in AD 61. This collection is called the Bloomberg Tablets.

XIII. TARGET JERUSALEM

71. Josephus, *Jewish War*.
72. Ibid.
73. Ibid.
74. Tacitus, *Annals*, says that just two Praetorian cohorts were then at Rome, with the remaining fourteen cohorts stationed in the Apennines. Placidus was probably serving with one of the cohorts at Rome. Less likely, he'd been given command of an auxiliary cohort in the Vespasianist army of Antonius Primus—the only cohorts commanded by tribunes in this era were those of the Praetorian Guard and City Guard.
75. Josephus, *Jewish War*.
76. Ibid.
77. Tacitus, *Annals*, gives 600,000 Jews in Jerusalem; Josephus, *Jewish War*, gives 1.2 million.

XIV. TITUS TIGHTENS THE NOOSE

78. Queen Helena reportedly married King Abgarus of Edessa, consequently becoming Edessa's queen as well as queen of Adiabene.
79. Josephus, *Jewish War*.
80. Roman legionary deserters were rare. Most fled punishment for infringing Roman military law. Death was the legion penalty for cowardice, disobedience of orders, and homosexual practices.
81. Josephus says ballista balls were painted black during the Third Wall assault, but the 2016 unearthing of unpainted balls at Third Wall foundations indicates this only occurred later in the siege.
82. Josephus, *Jewish War*.
83. Ibid.
84. Ibid.

XV. CRUCIFIXIONS AND A STRANGLEHOLD

85. For details of legionary pay and its buying power, see Dando-Collins, *Legions of Rome*.

86. Josephus, *Jewish Wa*r.

XVI. THE ANTONIA AND THE TEMPLE

87. Josephus, *Jewish War.*
88. Josephus's *Jewish War* relates the Legionary Sabinus episode, inclusive of the dialogue reprinted here.
89. Ibid.
90. Josephus, *Jewish War.* Pet animals were not killed and eaten by the besieged, as Jews didn't keep pets. Dogs were considered "unclean" and couldn't be eaten under Jewish law, no matter how hungry people were. Pet dogs and guard dogs were relatively common to Greeks and Romans. There was even a pet dog at Rome's Palatium at this time.

XVII. THE FINAL PHASE

91. Josephus, *Jewish War.*
92. Ibid.
93. Ibid.
94. Ibid.
95. Ibid.
96. Ibid.

XVIII. DESTRUCTION, RETRIBUTION, AND CELEBRATION

97. Josephus, *Jewish War.*
98. Brandon, *The Fall of Jerusalem and the Christian Church.*
99. In AD 72, Rufus escorted Epiphanes of Commagene and his brother to Rome from Parthia, after they fled there following an ill-judged confrontation with Roman troops in Commagene. For Rufus's career details, see Kennedy, "C. Velius Rufus."
100. Suetonius, "Vespasian," in *The Twelve Caesars.*
101. Ibid.
102. Ibid.
103. Josephus, *Life.*

XIX. JERUSALEM'S ULTIMATE FATE

104. Eusebius, *Church History.*

105. Dillenberger, *Images and Relics*.
106. Eusebius, *Church History* and *Life of Constantine*.

BIBLIOGRAPHY

Books

Brandon, S. G. F., *The Fall of Jerusalem and the Christian Church*. London: SPCK, 1957.

Campbell, J. B., *The Roman Army, 31 BC–AD 337: A Sourcebook*. London: Routledge, 1994.

Carcopino, J., *Daily Life in Ancient Rome* (E. O. Lorimer, transl.). Harmondsworth: Penguin, 1971.

Dando-Collins, S., *Cyrus the Great; Conqueror, Liberator, Anointed One*. Nashville: Turner, 2020.

Dando-Collins, S., *Legions of Rome: The Definitive History of Every Imperial Roman Legion*. London: Quercus, 2010.

Dando-Collins, S., *Mark Antony's Heroes: How the Third Gallica Legion Saved an Apostle and Created an Emperor*. Hoboken: John Wiley & Sons, 2007.

Dando-Collins, S., *The Great Fire of Rome: The Fall of the Emperor Nero and His City*. Cambridge, Mass.: Da Capo Press, 2010.

Dillenberger, J., *Images and Relics: Theological Perceptions and Visual Images in Sixteenth-Century Europe*. Oxford: Oxford University Press, 1999.

Dio, C., *Roman Histories VIII*, Books LXI-LXX (E. Cary, transl.). Cambridge, Mass.: Harvard University Press, 1995.

Eusebius, *Church History*. Washington, DC: Catholic University of America, 2005.

Eusebius, *Life of Constantine*. Oxford: Oxford University Press, 1999.

Finkelstein, L., W. Horbury, W. D. Davies, and J. Sturdy (eds), *The Cambridge History of Judaism*, "Titus's Siege of Jerusalem." Cambridge, UK: Cambridge University Press, 1999.

Frontinus, *The Stratagems* (C. E. Bennett, transl.). Cambridge, Mass.: Harvard University Press, 2003.

Furneaux, R., *The Roman Siege of Jerusalem*. London: Hart-Davis Mac-Gibbon, 1973.

Gleaves, G. S., *Did Jesus Speak Greek?* Reservoir, VIC: Pickwick, 2015.

Holy Bible (King James Version). London: Collins, 1957.

Josephus, T. F., *The New Complete Works of Josephus* (W. Whiston, transl.). Grand Rapids: Kregel, 1999.

Plutarch, *The Lives of the Noble Grecians and Romans* (the Dryden Translation). Chicago: Encyclopedia Britannica, 1989.

Rosenthal, M., & I. Mozeson, *Wars of the Jews: A Military History from Biblical to Modern Times*. New York: Hippocrene, 1990.

Rudich, V., *Religious Dissent in the Roman Empire: Violence in Judea at the Time of Nero*. London: Routledge, 2015.

Starr, C.G., *The Roman Imperial Navy, 31 BC–AD 324*. Cambridge, UK: Heffer, 1960.

Stern, S., *Calendar and Community: A History of the Jewish Calendar, 2nd Century BCE to 10th Century CE*. Oxford: Oxford University Press, 2001.

Suetonius, G., *The Twelve Caesars* (R. Graves, transl.). London: Penguin, 1989.

Tacitus, P. C., *The Annals* and *The Histories*. Chicago: Encyclopedia Britannica, 1989.

Vegetius, F., *The Military Institutions of the Romans* (J. Clark, transl.). Harrisburg: Military Service Publishing, 1944.

Vitruvius, *On Architecture*, Books VI–X (F. Granger, transl.). Cambridge, Mass.: Harvard University Press, 2004.

Yadin, Y., *Bar-Kokhba: The Rediscovery of the Legendary Hero of the Last Jewish Revolt against Imperial Rome*. London: Weidenfield & Nicolson, 1971.

JOURNAL ARTICLES

W. F. Albright, "'The Excavations at Ascalon,'" *Bulletin of the American Schools of Oriental Research*, No. 6 (May 1922), Jerusalem.

K. R. Bradley, "The Chronology of Nero's Visit to Greece, AD 66/67," *Latomus* (Jan–March 1978), Societe d'Etudes Latines de Bruxelles, Brussells.

D. Kennedy, "'C. Velius Rufus,'" *Britannia* 14, (1983), Cambridge University Press.

T. Metcalf, "'Whistling Sling Bullets Were Roman Troops' Secret Weapon,'" *Scientific American*, June 14, 2016.

J. Zias & A. Gorski, "Capturing a Beautiful Woman at Masada," *Near Eastern Archeology* 60, no. 1 (March 2006), University of Chicago Press.

INDEX

ABOUT THE AUTHOR

STEPHEN DANDO-COLLINS is an award-winning author of forty-four books, ranging from children's novels to biographies. Australian-born, he has a background in advertising, marketing, and market research. In all of his books, Dando-Collins aims to travel roads others have not, unearth new facts, and open new historical perspectives often forgotten or overlooked. The majority of his works deal with military history, ranging from Greek and Roman times to American nineteenth-century history and World War I and II. Many of his books have been translated into foreign languages, including Spanish, Italian, Portuguese, Dutch, Polish, Russian, Albanian, and Korean. Considered an authority on ancient Rome's legions, his most recent work on the subject, *Legions of Rome,* was the culmination of decades of research. In his latest books he has returned to ancient history subjects that fascinate him, with the biographies *Caligula: The Mad Emperor of Rome* (US, 2019, and Spain, 2021), and *Cyrus the Great* (US, 2020, Spain and Latin America, 2022). His next book for Turner Publishing will be *Constantine at the Bridge: How the Battle of the Milvian Bridge Created Christian Rome.*